Cyber Security in Business and Management

Cyber Security in Business and Management

Edited by **Stephen Mason**

WILLFORD PRESS

New York

Published by Willford Press,
118-35 Queens Blvd., Suite 400,
Forest Hills, NY 11375, USA
www.willfordpress.com

Cyber Security in Business and Management
Edited by Stephen Mason

International Standard Book Number: 978-1-68285-020-6 (Hardback)

Printed in the United States of America.

Contents

Preface

This book was inspired by the evolution of our times; to answer the curiosity of inquisitive minds. Many developments have occurred across the globe in the recent past which has transformed the progress in the field.

The security of digital databases has become increasingly important in the context of modern business set-ups today. There has been a lot of emphasis on innovating and improving cyber security systems for preventing theft or hacking of vital information and databases. This book includes concepts such as developing cyber security architecture and software, assessing various cyber threats, emerging trends in cyber security, etc. that tries to outline the current progress in this field. With state-of-the-art inputs by acclaimed experts of this field, this book targets students and professionals.

This book was developed from a mere concept to drafts to chapters and finally compiled together as a complete text to benefit the readers across all nations. To ensure the quality of the content we instilled two significant steps in our procedure. The first was to appoint an editorial team that would verify the data and statistics provided in the book and also select the most appropriate and valuable contributions from the plentiful contributions we received from authors worldwide. The next step was to appoint an expert of the topic as the Editor-in-Chief, who would head the project and finally make the necessary amendments and modifications to make the text reader-friendly. I was then commissioned to examine all the material to present the topics in the most comprehensible and productive format.

I would like to take this opportunity to thank all the contributing authors who were supportive enough to contribute their time and knowledge to this project. I also wish to convey my regards to my family who have been extremely supportive during the entire project.

Editor

Cybersecurity Skills Training:
An Attacker-Centric Gamified Approach

Mackenzie Adams and Maged Makramalla

> *It is said that if you know your enemies and know yourself, you will not be imperiled in a hundred battles; if you do not know your enemies but do know yourself, you will win one and lose one; if you do not know your enemies nor yourself, you will be imperiled in every single battle.*
>
> Sun Tzu (544 BC – 496 BC)
> Military general, strategist, and philosopher
> in *The Art of War*

Although cybersecurity awareness training for employees is important, it does not provide the necessary skills training required to better protect businesses against cyber-attacks. Businesses need to invest in building cybersecurity skills across all levels of the workforce and leadership. This investment can reduce the financial burden on businesses from cyber-attacks and help maintain consumer confidence in their brands. In this article, we discuss the use of gamification methods that enable all employees and organizational leaders to play the roles of various types of attackers in an effort to reduce the number of successful attacks due to human vulnerability exploits.

We combine two separate streams – gamification and entrepreneurial perspectives – for the purpose of building cybersecurity skills while emphasizing a third stream – attacker types (i.e., their resources, knowledge/skills, and motivation) – to create training scenarios. We also define the roles of attackers using various theoretical entrepreneurial perspectives. This article will be of interest to leaders who need to build cybersecurity skills into their workforce cost-effectively; researchers who wish to advance the principles and practices of gamification solutions; and suppliers of solutions to companies that wish to build cybersecurity skills in the workforce and leadership.

Introduction

Cybersecurity training is a crucial response to a growing number of intrusions and attacks (Nagarajan et al., 2012). Human vulnerabilities account for 80% of total vulnerabilities exploited by attackers (IBM, 2013) yet the focus of cybersecurity in information technology has been on systems tools and technology (Hershberger, 2014). Human vulnerabilities include, but are not limited to, employee negligence, leadership misinformation and limited cybersecurity skills training, malicious insiders, and third parties who have access to an organization's network. The need to build cybersecurity skills and increase knowledge in the workforce and leadership has become apparent to top corporate decision makers, governmental bodies, and academic researchers (Evans & Reeder, 2010). After the 2013 data breach of Target Corporation, an analysis of the attack concluded that the Target security systems detected the breach but the leadership and employees responsible for taking the steps to respond lacked the necessary skills and knowledge (Hershberger, 2014).

Limited knowledge and skills training in cybersecurity is not unique to Target and it is not an unusual occurrence. A recent study found that almost 70% of critical infrastructure providers across 13 countries suffered a data breach in 2013, and it was found that 54% of those breaches resulted from employee negligence; however, the most unexpected finding was that only 6% of these companies provided cybersecurity training for all employees (Unisys, 2014). Any employee in an organization can be a potential point of entry for attackers; therefore, knowledge and skills training in cybersecurity for all employees is essential in reducing human vulnerabilities. Companies that did not provide security training for new hires reported average annual losses in the amount of $683,000, whereas those who conducted new-hire training reported average annual losses at $162,000 (PwC, 2014).

In general, current cybersecurity skills training are limited to IT personnel while awareness campaigns and education are often offered to all employees. Cybersecurity training for all employees is inefficient in conveying the necessary knowledge and skills for employees and organization leaders to reduce the number of successful attacks. These training approaches can include: web-based classrooms, teleconferencing, instructor-led training, thematic cybersecurity events, newsletters, and awards/incentives programs (Annetta, 2010; Cone, 2007; Nagarajan et al., 2012). These approaches were found to be ineffective because the participants were not engaged in the learning process. The training sessions provided a large amount of information in a short period of time, which created a passive, overwhelming, and disconnected learning experience (Annetta, 2010; Cone, 2007). Classroom instruction and the dissemination of online advice are ineffectual ways to learn; a more immersive and interactive training is required.

In this article, we describe a gamification approach to building cybersecurity skills in all employees and leadership in an organization. Using gamified solutions in cybersecurity skills training promotes active learning and motivation while increasing retention of the learnt skills in comparison to traditional learning approaches such as instructor-led classes (Jordan et al., 2011).

The gamification approach uses entrepreneurial perspectives, which complement attacker types based on their motivation, knowledge, and resources. We use entrepreneurial perspectives, which refer to characteristics of seeking opportunities, taking risks, and having the focus to pursue an idea to fruition (Kuratko, 2013), to help view the challenge through the eyes of cyberattackers. Some of the similarities drawn between hackers and entrepreneurs include their problem-solving capabilities, willingness to take advantage of opportunities, working hard, as well as taking risks (Blanchard, 2013; Kang, 2012; Warikoo, 2014).

In the remainder of the article, we examine the use of gamification to develop employee skills and identify various entrepreneurial perspectives that are relevant to this approach. Then, we discuss what is required to create a training approach that uses gamification to deliver immersive learning in cybersecurity. In the final section, we provide conclusions.

Using Gamification to Build Skills in Employees

Gamification is a process of enhancing a specific service by implementing game design elements in a non-game context to enhance the user's overall value creation and experience (Huotari & Hamari, 2011; Deterding et al., 2011). Deterding and colleagues (2011) define gamification as "the use of design elements characteristic for games in non-game contexts". Thus, gamification reflects the use of game thinking including progress mechanics (such as points systems), player control (such as avatar use), rewards, collaborative problem solving, stories, and competition in non-game situations (Deterding et al., 2011; Kapp, 2012). Underlying gamification is an understanding of motivation as significantly correlated with and predictive of desirable human outcomes such as achievement, success, and the attainment of distinction and rewards (Kapp, 2012). When designed and applied in an appropriate manner and setting, gamification provides an alignment between motivation and desire that leads to the anticipated purpose of its use. For instance, when used to increase employee engagement, gamification can improve teamwork and transform routine, often dull, tasks by motivating employees through "play" and competition within the same team and across teams (Korolov, 2012; Zichermann & Cunningham, 2011).

Although it is usually considered an effective user involvement tool, gamification can also be used to develop skills of participants and employees. Burke (2014) highlights the effectiveness of using gamification concepts in employee training while using the "Ignite Leadership Game" created by NTT Data as a relevant example. This specific gameful design is built on first assessing the employees' knowledge to identify their strengths and weaknesses; the identification allows them to develop the required skill sets more efficiently. The main benefits of using gamification approaches to develop skills are creating an atmosphere that enables employee active involvement (Zichermann & Linder, 2013), improving the participants' motivation to achieve better results (Burke, 2014), and enhancing the overall learning process due to the established collaborative environment (Burke, 2014).

Gamification elements

When designing games for training and educational purposes, training goals must be clearly defined (Nagarajan et al., 2012). Designing effective and relevant games requires the selection of the appropriate gamification elements that would best suit the training approach needed (Kapp, 2012). Four elements of gamification are highlighted below for cybersecurity skills training:

1. *Progress mechanics:* related to player motivation through the provision of progress tools such as points, leader boards, and badges.

2. *Player control:* the use of a character (a third-person perspective) to engage in the gamified training. This character is commonly known as an "avatar". Research has shown that the use of avatars, through the use of different roles, influences behaviour.

3. *Problem solving:* a crucial element in gamification when learning and retaining new information is the goal of the training. Collaboration and identification of a shared purpose are essential in developing strong problem-solving skills that can easily translate into practical knowledge outside of the training environment.

4. *Story:* A narrative that is present to create an attachment or a bond between the learner and their avatar, as well as a bond between the avatars participating in the gamified training. Stories also motivate the learner to keep on "playing" to find out the rest of the story

Existing gamification training solutions

Currently, a handful of cybersecurity training and awareness programs started to introduce gamification techniques in their own curricula. As shown in Table 1, six main, and most evolved, gamified approaches were identified and further elaborated. These "games" were compared according to the following four aspects:

Table 1. Existing gamified training solutions for employee cybersecurity skills

	Awareness	Defensive Strategies	Offensive Strategies	Attacker Centricity	References
CounterMeasure	• Basic knowledge	• *None*	• Authentication and password bypassing	Limited	Jordan et al. (2011)
CyberCiege	• Basic knowledge • General assessment	• Penetration prevention	• *None*	*None*	Cone et al. (2007)
CyberNexs	• *None*	• System assessment • Penetration prevention	• Capture the flag	*None*	Nagarajan et al. (2012)
CyberProtect	• Basic knowledge • General assessment	• *None*	• *None*	*None*	Labuschagne et al. (2011)
NetWars	• Skill assessment	• System assessment • Penetration prevention	• System penetration scenarios	Limited	SANS (2015)
Micro Games	• Basic knowledge • General assessment	• Penetration detection • Password management	• *None*	*None*	Wombat (2015)

1. *Awareness:* requires a minimal amount of knowledge for the participants. Awareness is mainly concerned with assessing the level of vulnerabilities in an entity, while providing participants with general knowledge in detecting and avoiding successful penetration attempts.

2. *Defensive strategy:* requires the participants – in this case the defenders – to have substantial knowledge that will provide them with proper tools and strategies to fend off cyber-attacks efficiently.

3. *Offensive strategy:* focuses mainly on putting the participants in their rivals' shoes in order to properly understand their strategies and approaches.

4. *Attacker centricity:* uses known characteristics of cyber-attackers to train participants in anticipating an attacker's motivation and behaviour in carrying out certain attacks. This anticipation enhances the creation and application of both offensive and defensive strategies against cyber-attacks.

Note that only three of the six gamified training programs incorporate offensive strategies for their participants. This observation is in line with the current dominant practice in cybersecurity to react, largely, to attacks and not engage in anticipatory or offensive strategies. Moreover, two of the six games have limited attacker-centricity, mostly based on the skills of hacking a system but not specific attacker types. Once again, this reflects a current state in cybersecurity training where the characteristics of attackers are seldom incorporated in training employees to understand these attackers or anticipate their attacks.

Attacker Types and Their Characteristics

Based on an extensive search of existing literature, and to the best of our knowledge, there are no current applications of cyber-attacker characteristics being used in gamified cybersecurity skills training for employees. As a result, we reviewed literature on cyber-attackers based on a search that included the following keywords: "cyber criminals", "insiders", and "hackers". We expanded our keyword search to accommodate the terminology differences in existing literature when describing individuals or groups that commit cyber-attacks. We focused on cyber-attackers to identify attacker types and their motivations, resources, and knowledge/skills. Identifying attacker types is import-

ant in developing more accurate profiles when creating and implementing solutions intended to reduce cyber-crimes (Rogers, 2011).

Based on the literature review, the following eight types of cyber-attackers were identified:

1. *Script kiddies:* attackers who depend on existing tools (e.g., exploit programs and scripts) and are unwilling to learn how these tools function (Hald & Pedersen, 2012). They are immature attackers whose primary motivation is to create mischief and get attention (Aggarwal et al., 2014; Rogers, 2011).

2. *Cyber-punks* (including virus writers): attackers who write viruses and exploit programs for the sake of causing trouble and gaining fame (Hald & Pedersen, 2012). Motivated by admiration and recognition, these attackers disrespect authority and social norms. They are only slightly more skilled than script kiddies (Rogers, 2011) and enter systems to cause damage (Dogaru, 2012).

3. *Insiders:* attackers who are imbedded within the organization they attack who cause intentional or unintentional harm because of their authorized access (Hald & Pedersen, 2012). Because access is not a challenge they face, most insider attackers have minimal technical skills (Williams, 2008). As such, they become easy targets for criminals who persuade them to perform an action that exposes the system (Crossler et al., 2013; Parmar, 2013).

4. *Petty thieves:* attackers who commit online fraud such as identity theft and system hijackings for ransom with no other motivation than money (Hald & Pedersen, 2012). Their activities are not sophisticated and they are not dependent on the gains from their crimes. They are attracted to criminal activities that include credit card and bank fraud (Rogers, 2011).

5. *Grey hats:* attackers who are a mix of black hats (i.e., malicious or illegal hackers) and white hats (i.e., hackers intending to improve security). They may attack systems to prove their abilities or to find flaws within a system, and may alert the target to the vulnerability (Aggarwal et al., 2014; Bodhani, 2013; Hald & Pedersen, 2012). Often highly skilled, they write scripts that cyber-punks and script kiddies typically employ (Rogers, 2011).

6. *Professional criminals:* attackers who are hired to infiltrate systems. They are also known as cyber-mercenaries (Hald & Pedersen, 2012). Sometimes these cyber-attackers act on behalf of institutions and enter competitors' systems for financial gain (Dogaru, 2012). They operate in the most secretive environment and are governed by strict rules of anonymity so they cannot be identified (Kowalski & Mwakalinga, 2011; Rogers, 2011).

7. *Hactivists:* attackers who are motivated by ideology. This type can include terrorist groups. Pushed into activism by strong psychological dispositions and beliefs, some hackers may become hacktivists and perceive their motives to be completely selfless (Hald & Pedersen, 2012; Papadimitriou, 2009).

8. *Nation states:* attackers who are assumed to be working on behalf of a governmental body. Every resource is targeted towards the disruption of the enemy's systems or the protection of the nation state's own systems. This group includes paramilitary organizations and freedom fighters, and their goals are not dissimilar to those of recognized governments (Dogaru, 2012; Hald & Pedersen, 2012; Rogers, 2011).

It is important to note a common theme found in hacker communities: willingness to share information and collaborate in problem solving with peers (Biros et al., 2008; Denning, 1996; Jordan & Taylor, 1998; Mookerjee et al., 2009). Sharing information helps build stronger bonds within the community while encouraging and challenging others to learn and engage more (Arief & Besnard, 2003).

Entrepreneurial Perspectives

Entrepreneurs are described as risk takers, innovators, and problem solvers who are confident, persistent, collaborative, able to recognize opportunities, skilled at gathering information and knowledge, have a need for achievement and reward, and seek change and profit (Blanchard, 2013; Kang, 2012; Kim, 2014). Although there are many definitions of the term "entrepreneur", the following definition is most apt for this article: entrepreneurs are "those who identify a need – *any* need – and fill it. It's a primordial urge, independent of product, service, industry, or market" (Nelson, 2012). Thus, it can be inferred that this primordial urge is driven by different motivations and capabilities, which may be better understood through entrepreneurial perspectives.

Entrepreneurial perspectives are examined in this article for two reasons: i) to consider the similarities between various entrepreneurial perspectives and cyber-attacker characteristics and ii) to remove the negative connotation connected to the term "attacker" in the training. Taking the perspective of someone about whom an individual has negative perceptions and attitudes may compromise the in-depth immersion into a cyber-attacker's motivation and approach, and reduce "buy-in" to the gamification approach to training. Thus, taking an entrepreneurial perspective helps trainees empathize with cyber-attackers so that they may better learn to protect their organizations against them.

From the literature, we identified the following six entrepreneurial perspectives:

1. *Bricolage:* a perspective where an entrepreneur uses whatever diverse resources happen to be at hand to start a new venture. The concept was originally used in artistic contexts and usually starts in an environment with limited resources (Baker & Nelson, 2005). This perspective requires creativity, and the resulting innovations may need several testing stages before then come to fruition.

2. *Effectuation:* a perspective where an entrepreneur takes "a set of means as given and focus[es] on selecting between possible effects that can be created with that set of means" (Saravathy, 2001). This perspective connotes that an entrepreneur is considered as highly knowledgeable in using their own resources. That is, they may not have access to a large amount of resources, but they are considered experts in utilizing their available resources in many innovative ways.

3. *Causation:* a perspective whereby an entrepreneur focuses on a specific goal that is highly desired and uses all the available resources to reach this certain goal. In this perspective, the setting itself is usually rich in resources which requires high knowledge in how to use these resources to achieve optimal results and achieve greater outcomes (Sarasvathy, 2001).

4. *Emancipation:* a perspective where a person, who is suffering from some kind of physical or emotional oppression, decides to break free to improve their situation. It can also apply to improving the situation in their area, community, or even country. Rindova and colleagues (2009) identified three core elements of emancipation: seeking autonomy, authoring, and making declarations.

5. *Hubris:* a perspective in which an entrepreneur's belief in the success of a new venture is based on socially constructed confidence (Hayward et al., 2006). An optimistic overconfidence propels the individual to start a venture regardless of the potential failure.

6. *Social:* a perspective where an entrepreneur's main motivations are social goals (social, political, environmental) and sharing part of their gained resources with community causes (Christopoulos & Vogl, 2015).

Proposed Gamification Approach to Build Cybersecurity Skills

Cybersecurity training is mislabelled in most organizations; it should be more appropriately referred to as cybersecurity information and awareness training that is provided to all employees. Cybersecurity skills training is mostly offered to highly technical IT administration and security professionals. All employees need foundational skills training with customizations to tailor scenarios based on functional roles and potential attack vectors with an emphasis on learning how to mitigate or cope with an attack (Council on Cybersecurity, 2014).

Based on our review of the literature, we propose a gamified approach to cybersecurity skills training. Using the elements of gamification, we outline four components required to create a comprehensive cybersecurity skills training: i) story, ii) player control, iii) problem solving, and iv) progress mechanics.

Story
The stories of the training games will be based on the eight identified cyber-attacker types and they will provide realistic, virtual recreations of the work environment and simulate the types of attacks that may occur. For this gamified cybersecurity training, there are three relevant components that help keep the trainees engaged and motivated:

1. *Feedback:* such as losing lives, triggering warning screens, receiving encouraging messages, or earning rewards. This feedback is based on the trainee's progress: as long as they are engaged in the game, the game is providing feedback, assessing skill levels, and creating obstacles to evaluate the various skillsets of the trainees and comparing those results to the target level of achievement.

2. *Increased challenges:* the complexity of the story will dictate the amount of challenges the trainee will have to overcome in order to progress.

3. *Opportunities for mastery:* providing opportunities to develop and excel.

Player control
The six entrepreneurial perspectives are used to create resource- and motivation-based attacker roles for the training solution. The entrepreneurial perspectives are matched to the attacker types as shown in Table 2. This step enables avatars to be created for the game without any preconceived notions on how the avatar should act, thereby allowing for exploratory learning in the scenarios.

Problem solving
Problem solving is an important element in gamification that allows trainees to learn and retain new information. As trainees collaborate to find answers, they create a community of shared information and purpose. Such activities are particularly helpful during attacker-centric cybersecurity skills training due to the collaborative nature of the cyber-attacker community and its ability to find common goals.

Progress mechanics
For all employees and organization leaders participating in the gamified training, the progress mechanics will vary based on the avatar's characteristics and areas of learning and achievements. For example, if an employee's avatar is "the architect" as listed in Table 2, a quick review of their in-game resources would show that the avatar has many resources available for them to complete a task so the challenge in gaining more resources or points may be linked more to problem solving skills or collaboration efforts.

Gamified Training Scenario

To understand how the training would be used and what the expected learning outcomes are, consider the following scenario. A graphic designer in the marketing department must complete his cybersecurity skills training. At the beginning of the training, he is given a short knowledge-assessment questionnaire. Based on his answers, he is assessed as having "average" cybersecurity knowledge, which would then determine his entry level in the training game. He is then given the option to choose an avatar with very little descriptive information about the avatar such as its strengths, weaknesses, and resources to progress along in the game. He selects "The advocate" as his avatar and, based on his assessment, he begins at level 2 of the training. The story he will work through is based on "The hacktivist" attacker type and an attack type of en-

Table 2. Gamification element: player control (avatars and their characteristics)

Avatars (Attacker Roles)	Avatar Characteristics (Attacker Types)
Bricolage: "The rookie"	• Script kiddies • Cyber-punks • Petty thieves
Effectuation: "The adroit"	• Insiders
Causation: "The architect"	• Nation states • Professional criminals
Emancipation: "The liberator"	• Insiders • Hacktivists
Hubris: "The optimist"	• Grey hats
Social: "The advocate"	• Hactivists

tering a secure area by following an employee who entered using their own access key to plant malware in one of the computers in a certain department. As he progresses through the game, he may need to collaborate with other trainees or other avatars in the game to complete a mission or a step. As he progresses along, there is information provided such as warnings, hints, and other learning opportunities to successfully complete the level. There are different rewards and incentives provided to keep him engaged and motivated.

By the end of this training, the employee is able to plant the malware after a few failed attempts. During the training, the employee learns the desired skills, progressing from prevention to anticipation to reaction to response, as described below:

1. *Prevention:* the importance of securing access against unauthorized individuals when entering secure areas.

2. *Anticipation:* a method used by some attackers to gain access to the system.

3. *Reaction:* the importance of communication with others in the organization.

4. *Response:* the proper procedure to follow when confronted with a similar situation. The impact of a successful attack.

In comparison, instructor-led classroom training would have provided the information to the trainee without any practical, hands-on activities to show the steps involved or to visually witness the impact of the security breach. It would also be difficult for the trainee to retain the procedural information to deal with this type of issue. Most importantly, it is difficult to keep the attention of the employee on the training material without the interactive and immersive game element.

The gamified cybersecurity skills training approach promotes:

1. The prevention > anticipation > reaction > response sequence

2. Skills training for all employees in an organization, from entry-level staff to C-level executives

3. Hands-on, immersive, and interactive training that moves away from classroom-based, instructor-led training

4. A distinction between cybersecurity awareness only training and cybersecurity skills training

Conclusion

The main objective of this article was to provide an innovative approach to train all employees and organization leaders to develop cybersecurity skills and better defend against and react to data breaches. The gamified training approach was developed by reviewing the following literature streams: gamification, cyber-attackers and their characteristics, and entrepreneurial perspectives.

In this article, eight attacker types were selected using their motivation, knowledge/skills, and resources as attacker characteristics. Furthermore, six entrepreneurial perspectives were used highlighting their motivation, knowledge/skills, and resources. The attacker types and their characteristics were combined with the entrepreneurial perspectives to create avatars for the game. By creating the avatars, the type of attacker and the characteristics of the attacker are now used in creating the story used during the training. This approach allows the trainees to experience an attack through the eyes of a cyber-attacker and therefore from entrepreneurial perspectives.

Our article is limited by the lack of practical, tested evidence that the approach would produce the expected outcomes and improve employees' abilities in preventing or reacting to data breaches. Some of the research has pointed to the importance of identifying attacker characteristics to better defend against cyber-attacks (Colwill, 2009; Cremonini & Nizovtsev, 2006; Gold, 2011; Liu & Cheng, 2009), and further research linking the attacker characteristics to the attack type may advance knowledge in cybersecurity prevention and training. We would also recommend a more comprehensive project that examines the similarities and differences between entrepreneurs and attackers.

About the Authors

Mackenzie Adams is a serial entrepreneur, a Senior Technical Communicator, and a graduate student in the Technology Innovation Management (TIM) program at Carleton University in Ottawa, Canada. She is also a VP/Creative Director at SOMANDA, a consulting company. Over the past 15 years, Mackenzie has worked in a variety of fields ranging from social work to accounting and has used those experiences to develop strong strategic and analytical skills. She is interested in the fields of artificial intelligence and quantum computing, and how they relate to cyber-security.

Maged Makramalla is a current graduate student in the Technology Innovation Management (TIM) program at Carleton University in Ottawa, Canada. He holds a Bachelor of Science degree in Mechatronics Engineering from the German University in Cairo, Egypt. For three years, he has been working as Manager of the Sales and Marketing Department of TREND, a trading and engineering company based in Cairo. His primary research interest lies in the improvement of educational techniques by introducing experiential learning into the regular curriculum while promoting gamification of educational methods.

References

Aggarwal, P., Arora, P., & Ghai, R. 2014. Review on Cyber Crime and Security. *International Journal of Research in Engineering and Applied Sciences,* 2(1): 48–51.

Annetta, L. A. 2010. The "I's" Have It: A Framework for Serious Educational Game Design. *Review of General Psychology,* 14(2): 105–112.
http://dx.doi.org/10.1037/a0018985

Arief, B., & Besnard, D. 2003. *Technical and Human Issues in Computer-Based Systems Security.* Technical Report Series: University of Newcastle upon Tyne Computing Science. Newcastle, UK: Newcastle University.

Baker, T., & Nelson, R. E. 2005. Creating Something from Nothing: Resource Construction through Entrepreneurial Bricolage. *Administrative Science Quarterly,* 50(3): 329–366.
http://dx.doi.org/10.2189/asqu.2005.50.3.329

Biros, D. P., Weiser, M., Burkman, J., & Nichols, J. 2008. Information Sharing: Hackers vs Law Enforcement. In *Proceedings of the 9th Australian Information Warfare and Security Conference.* Perth, Australia: Edith Cowan University.

Blanchard, K. 2013. Entrepreneurial Characteristics in SMEs: A Rural, Remote Rural, and Urban Perspective of Lincolnshire Businesses. *Strategic Change,* 22(3/4): 191–201.
http://dx.doi.org/10.1002/jsc.1932

Bodhani, A. 2013. Bad... In a Good Way. Engineering & Technology, 8(12): 64–68.
http://dx.doi.org/10.1049/et.2012.1217

Burke, B. 2014. *Gamify: How Gamification Motivates People to Do Extraordinary Things.* Brookline, MA: Bibliomotion, Inc.

Chiang, O. 2010. Wombat Security Makes Online Games That Teach Cybersecurity Awareness, Nabs $750,000 US Airforce Contract. *Forbes Magazine.* Accessed January 10, 2015:
http://www.forbes.com/sites/oliverchiang/2010/10/08/wombat-security-makes-videogames-that-teach-cybersecurity-awareness-nabs-750000-us-airforce-contract/

Christopoulos, D., & Vogl, S. 2015. The Motivation of Social Entrepreneurs: The Roles, Agendas and Relations of Altruistic Economic Actors. *Journal of Social Entrepreneurship,* 6(1): 1–30.
http://dx.doi.org/10.1080/19420676.2014.954254

Colwill, C. 2009. Human Factors in Information Security: The Insider Threat – Who Can You Trust These Days? *Information security Technical Report,* 14(4): 186–196.
http://dx.doi.org/10.1016/j.istr.2010.04.004

Cone, B. D., Irvine, C. E., Thompson, M. F., & Nguyen, T. D. 2007. A Video Game for Cyber Security Training and Awareness. *Computers & Security,* 26(1): 63–72.
http://dx.doi.org/10.1016/j.cose.2006.10.005

Council on CyberSecurity. 2014. *The Critical Security Controls for Effective Cyber Defense.* Version 5.1. Council on CyberSecurity. Accessed January 10, 2015:
http://www.counciloncybersecurity.org/

Cremonini, M., & Nizovtsev, D. 2006. *Understanding and Influencing Attackers' Decisions: Implications for Security Investment Strategies*. Presented at The Fifth Workshop on the Economics of Information Security (WEIS), 26–28 June 2006. Cambridge, UK: The University of Cambridge. http://weis2006.econinfosec.org/docs/3.pdf

Crossler, R. E., Johnston, A. C., Lowry, P. B., Hu, Q., Warkentin, M., & Baskerville, R. 2013. Future Directions for Behavioral Information Security Research. *Computers & Security*, 32, 90–101. http://dx.doi.org/10.1016/j.cose.2012.09.010

Denning, D. E. 1996. Concerning Hackers Who Break into Computer Systems. In P. Ludlow (Ed.), *High Noon on the Electronic Frontier: Conceptual Issues in Cyberspace*: 137–164. Cambridge, MA: MIT Press

Deterding, S., Dixon, D., Khaled, R., & Nacke, L. 2011. From Game Design Elements to Gamefulness: Defining Gamification. In *Proceedings of the 15th International Academic MindTrek Conference*: 9–15. New York, NY: Association for Computing Machinery. http://dx.doi.org/10.1145/2181037.2181040

Dogaru, P. D. S. O. 2012. Criminological Characteristics of Computer Crime. *Journal of Criminal Investigation*, 5(1): 92-98.

Gold, S. 2011. Understanding the Hacker Psyche. *Network Security*, 2011(12): 15–17. http://dx.doi.org/10.1016/S1353-4858(11)70130-1

Hald, S. L., & Pedersen, J. M. 2012. An Updated Taxonomy for Characterizing Hackers According to Their Threat Properties. In *Proceedings of the 14th IEEE International Conference on Advanced Communication Technology (ICACT)*: 81–86. Pyeongchang, South Korea: IEEE.

Hershberger, P. 2014. *Security Skills Assessment and Training: The "Make or Break" Critical Security Control*. SANS Institute InfoSec Reading Room. Accessed January 10, 2015: http://www.sans.org/reading-room/whitepapers/leadership/security-skills-assessment-training-critical-security-control-break-o-35637

Huotari, K., & Hamari, J. 2012. Defining Gamification: A Service Marketing Perspective. In *Proceedings of the 16th International Academic MindTrek Conference*: 17–22. New York, NY: Association for Computing Machinery. http://dx.doi.org/10.1145/2393132.2393137

Hayward, M. L., Shepherd, D. A., & Griffin, D. 2006. A Hubris Theory of Entrepreneurship. *Management Science*, 52(2): 160–172. http://dx.doi.org/10.1287/mnsc.1050.0483

Jordan, C., Knapp, M., Mitchell, D., Claypool, M., & Fisler, K. 2011. CounterMeasures: A Game for Teaching Computer Security. In *Proceedings of the 10th Annual Workshop on Network and Systems Support for Games*: Article 7. Piscataway, NJ: IEEE Press.

Jordan, T., & Taylor, P. 1998. A Sociology of Hackers. *The Sociological Review*, 46(4): 757–780. http://dx.doi.org/10.1111/1467-954X.00139

Kang, H. 2012. The Entrepreneur as a Hacker. *Epicenter: National Center for Engineering Pathways to Innovation*. Accessed January 10, 2015. http://epicenter.stanford.edu/story/hongwen-henry-kang-carnegie-mellon-university

Kapp, K. M. 2012. *The Gamification of Learning and Instruction: Game-Based Methods and Strategies for Training and Education*. San Francisco, CA: Pfeiffer (Wiley).

Kim, P. H. 2014. Action and Process, Vision and Values. In T. Baker & F. Welter (Eds.), *The Routledge Companion to Entrepreneurship*, 59–74. New York, NY: Routledge.

Korolov, M. 2012. Gamification of the Enterprise. *Network World*. Accessed January 10, 2015: http://www.networkworld.com/article/2160336/software/gamification-of-the-enterprise.html

Kuratko, D. 2013. *Entrepreneurship: Theory, Process, and Practice*. Melbourne, Australia: Cengage Learning.

Labuschagne, W. A., Veerasamy, N., Burke, I., & Eloff, M. M. 2011. Design of Cyber Security Awareness Game Utilizing a Social Media Gramework. In *Information Security South Africa*, 1–9. Johannesburg, SA: IEEE. http://dx.doi.org/10.1109/ISSA.2011.6027538

Liu, S., & Cheng, B. 2009. Cyberattacks: Why, What, Who, and How. *IT Professional, 11*(3): 14–21. http://dx.doi.org/10.1109/MITP.2009.46

Mwakalinga, G. J., & Kowalski, S. 2011. *Modelling the Enemies of an IT Security System-A Socio-Technical System Security Model*. Presented at The 12th International Symposium on Models and Modeling Methodologies in Science and Engineering. March 27–30, 2011: Orlando, FL.

Mookerjee, V., Mookerjee, R., Bensoussan, A., & Yue, W. T. 2011. When Hackers Talk: Managing Information Security Under Variable Attack Rates and Knowledge Dissemination. *Information Systems Research*, 22(3): 606–623. http://dx.doi.org/10.1287/isre.1100.0341

Nagarajan, A., Allbeck, J. M., Sood, A., & Janssen, T. L. 2012. Exploring Game Design for Cybersecurity Training. In *Proceedings of the 2012 IEEE International Conference on Cyber Technology in Automation, Control, and Intelligent Systems (CYBER): 256–262*. May 27–31, 2012, Bangkok, Thailand. http://dx.doi.org/10.1109/CYBER.2012.6392562

Nelson, B. 2012. The Real Definition of Entrepreneur – And Why It Matters. *Forbes*. Accessed January 10, 2015: http://www.forbes.com/sites/brettnelson/2012/06/05/the-real-definition-of-entrepreneur-and-why-it-matters/

Parmar, B. 2013. Employee Negligence: The Most Overlooked Vulnerability. *Computer Fraud & Security*, 2013(3): 18–20. http://dx.doi.org/10.1016/S1361-3723(13)70030-7

PwC. 2014. *US Cybercrime: Rising Risks, Reduced Readiness – Key Findings from the 2014 US State of Cybercrime Survey*. PricewaterhouseCoopers, CERT Division of the Software Engineering Institute, CSO Magazine, & United States Secret Service.

Rindova, V., Barry, D., & Ketchen, D. J. 2009. Entrepreneuring as Emancipation. *Academy of Management Review*, 34(3): 477–491. http://dx.doi.org/10.5465/AMR.2009.40632647

Rogers, M. K. 2011. The Psyche of Cybercriminals: A Psycho-Social Perspective. In S. Ghosh & E. Turrini (Eds.), *Cybercrimes: A Multidisciplinary Analysis*: 217–235. New York, NY: Springer. http://dx.doi.org/10.1007/978-3-642-13547-7_14

SANS. 2015. NetWars. *SANS Institute*. Accessed January 10, 2015: http://sans.org/netwars

Sarasvathy, S. D. 2001. Causation and Effectuation: Toward a Theoretical Shift from Economic Inevitability to Entrepreneurial Contingency. *Academy of Management Review*, 26(2): 243–263. http://dx.doi.org/10.5465/AMR.2001.4378020

Unisys. 2014. Critical Infrastructure: Security Preparedness and Maturity. *Unisys.* Accessed January 10, 2015: http://www.unisys.com/insights/critical-infrastructure-security

Warikoo, A. 2014. Proposed Methodology for Cyber Criminal Profiling. *Information Security Journal: A Global Perspective*, 23(4-6): 172–178. http://dx.doi.org/10.1080/19393555.2014.931491

Williams, P. A. H. 2008. In a 'Trusting' Environment, Everyone Is Responsible for Information Security. *Information Security Technical Report*, 13(4): 207–215. http://dx.doi.org/10.1016/j.istr.2008.10.009

Wombat. 2015. Security Education Platform. *Wombat Security Technologies.* Accessed January 10, 2015: http://wombatsecurity.com/security-education

Zichermann, G., & Cunningham, C. 2011. *Gamification by Design: Implementing Game Mechanics in Web and Mobile Apps.* Sebastopol, CA: O'Reilly Media.

Keywords: cybersecurity, cyber attackers, gamification, entrepreneur, training

2

The Online World of the Future: Safe, Productive, and Creative

Tony Bailetti, Renaud Levesque, and D'Arcy Walsh

" A mind is like a parachute. It doesn't work if it is not open. "

Attributed to Frank Zappa (1940–1993)
Musician, composer, producer, and director

A safer online world is required to attain higher levels of productivity and creativity. We offer a view of a future state of the online world that places safety, productivity, and creativity above all else. The online world envisaged for 2030 is safe (i.e., users communicate with accuracy and enduring confidence), productive (i.e., users make timely decisions that have an ongoing global effect), and creative (i.e., users can connect seemingly unrelated information online). The proposed view differs from other views of the future online world that are anchored around technology solutions, confrontation, deception, and personal or commercial gain. The following seven conditions characterize the proposed view of the online world: i) global-scale autonomous learning systems; ii) humans co-working with machines; iii) human factors that are authentic and transferrable; iv) global scale whole-brain communities; v) foundational knowledge that is authentic and transferrable; vi) timely productive communication; and vii) continuous technological adaptation. These conditions are expected to enable new social-behavioural, socio-technical, and organizational interaction models.

Introduction

The nature of the online world of the future is best understood by explaining the properties of safety, productivity, and creativity. Understanding these properties requires more than technology debates. Although technology is indeed important, today we have a unique opportunity to shape the future of the online world for the greater good. However, we must understand the underlying causes of the complexity that is emerging as layers of cognition, computation, and connection evolve.

We illustrate our vision as a shift over time towards increased safety and situational understanding. As Figure 1 shows, we are now living in an unsafe world with limited situational understanding. The shift over time shows us reaching the future state by first moving to a safer world with increasing situational understanding (i.e., machines are connected but humans and machines are only loosely connected) and then moving to a safe world that provides more situational understanding (i.e., human-machine convergence, awareness, and autonomy). As a result of this shift, we envision a future

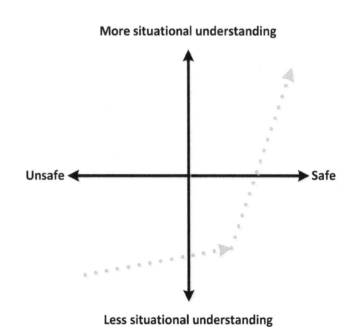

Figure 1. Progression from today's environment to our vision of the future online world in 2030

environment in which: i) productivity is uniquely enabled through instantaneously and safely connecting information elements and ii) transformational creativity is uniquely enabled through instantaneously and safely connecting together seemingly unrelated information.

In this article, we share our vision of the online world of the future by first describing safety, productivity, and creativity and then identifying the set of key conditions of a safer environment expected to enable unprecedented levels of productivity and creativity in the future. Further, we explore how the key conditions depend on one another and provide an example scenario to illustrate a domain-specific application that satisfies these conditions. Finally, we present the progression from today's environment to our vision of the future online world and position competing views of the future online world in terms of excludability and consumption rivalry using quadrant-style representations.

This article makes three contributions. First, it explicitly links safety properties to significant increases in productivity and creativity. Second, it postulates a set of research questions that should be answerable if the underlying properties of safety, productivity, and creativity are adequately understood. Third, the article identifies a set of key conditions of the online world of the future.

Online World of the Future

This section describes safety, productivity, and creativity in the context of the online world of the future.

Safety
To unleash unprecedented levels of productivity and creativity, the online world of the future must be safe (i.e., enable communication with accuracy and with enduring confidence). To be safe, the online world must be protected from: i) pernicious actors (e.g., individuals, groups, organizations, or nation-states) that strive to undermine and to unjustly benefit from the work of others, and ii) unintended disruption (e.g., user errors that have negative side effects) (Leveson, 2013). If Maslow's hierarchy of needs can be addressed with technology (Gerstein, 2014), information may be utilized as a foundational element that is authentic and is transferrable to others – in a manner that is beneficial to the world at large.

The online world of today is not engineered for safety (Leveson, 2013). We benefit from state-of-the-art knowledge of the theory and practice of safety properties in the context of cybersecurity, especially from a technical perspective. However, it is clear to us that there is no underlying theory that explains cybersecurity-related phenomena within the technical domain let alone associated safety properties that include dynamic and social characteristics, which are widely viewed to be more important than technical ones. Existing theories apply to restricted sub-domains of the overall problem space, such as cryptography, and therefore only explain phenomena within highly restricted contexts that do not have the semantic power or scope to explain other safety-related properties that concern the behaviour of the adversary and the behaviour of those who are under attack (Craigen et al., 2013).

If an underlying theory of safety existed, the following example research questions, amongst many others, would be answerable:

- Under what conditions does an attacker have an advantage over an infrastructure protector?

- Why do many infrastructure protectors and users not adopt effective mechanisms to provide safety and privacy?

- What are the resources, processes, and values to concurrently provide online safety and privacy to users?

- What are the characteristics of the individuals and organizations that are most likely to attack?

- What are the enhanced characteristics of safety through disclosure (i.e., by being open and not by being proprietary)?

Productivity
Productivity is inherently based on association or association by similarity or co-occurrence (Dubitzsky et al., 2012). We adopt the perspective that productivity is related to the efficiency and effectiveness of understanding and utilizing existing connections amongst known information elements. This view implies that information has been pre-selected to serve a purpose that is already defined and whose utility is already appreciated. Supporting technologies focus and simplify information relevant to a user's task that can accommodate discovery but within a relatively closed context. Compared to creativity gains, which are new, surprising, and of value, productivity gains, which are more conventional in nature, happen under routine conditions that are already known (Dubitzsky et al., 2012).

We foresee a future environment in which productivity is fundamentally enabled through instantaneous and safe connections among information elements. Productivity gains will remain conventional in nature but will happen in a profoundly different way. Users will be able to make timely decisions that have an ongoing global effect when information is available instantaneously, with accuracy and with enduring confidence, and senders and receivers of information are available instantaneously on a global scale. Achieving this level of productivity will require global-scale systems that interact to learn and converge on solutions autonomously when constantly assessing the meaning of connections that are known to exist amongst known information elements.

If an underlying theory of productivity existed, the following example research questions would be answerable:

• How do individuals in groups create reference frames that anchor their actions?

• How can we improve organizational performance through collective knowledge?

• How does communicating with fidelity and with enduring confidence specifically relate to productivity?

• Which communications are urgent or important?

• How are instantaneous communications and timely decisions, which can have a global effect, synchronized?

Creativity

Psychologists and neuroscientists are actively investigating the process of creativity. The work of Andreasen (2005); Csikszentmihalyi (1996); Gilovich, Griffin, and Kahneman (2002); and Kahneman (2011) are examples of well-known research within these two areas. Duxbury (2012) assesses the process of creativity and its relationship to innovation. Cognitive and computer scientists are investigating how computers can be designed to autonomously manipulate abstract concepts while Boden (1999) is concerned with computer models of creativity.

Transformational creativity constitutes the deepest form of creative processes in Boden's (1994) model of creativity. Transformational creativity leads to breakthroughs because established conceptual spaces or thinking styles, which limit types of thought, are trans-formed so that thoughts that were inconceivable within existing conceptual spaces are now possible (Dubitzsky et al., 2012). This level of creativity requires connecting seemingly unrelated information through computational creativity (Boden, 1999), bisociation (Koestler, 1964), and other approaches. These approaches lead to new, surprising, and valuable breakthroughs when normally distinct and unrelated contexts or categories of objects are mixed in one human or machine mind. Bisociation goes beyond associative styles of thinking that are based on established routines (Dubitzsky et al., 2012).

In the online world of the future, instantaneous and safe connections among seemingly unrelated information will enable transformational creativity. Humans and machines will be able to: i) communicate with accuracy and with enduring confidence and ii) make timely decisions that have an ongoing global effect. Through computational creativity and human-machine convergence, humans and machines will learn together to discover new knowledge and to assess (un)certainty.

If an underlying theory of creativity existed, the following example research questions, amongst many others, would be answerable:

• How do people working in creative domains employ creative thinking to connect seemingly unrelated information?

• What does it mean to combine elements from incompatible domains to generate creative solutions and insight?

• How do you teach humans or machines to be creative?

• How do you develop machine-based solutions that support creative thinking?

• How can machines be used to define and construct artificial conceptual spaces that generate creative insight and solutions?

Seven Conditions and Their Interdependencies

The conditions listed below characterize our view of the online world of the future. Together, they are intended to comprise the circumstances of a safer environment that will foster unprecedented levels of human-machine creativity and productivity. Within this online environment, the intellectual capacities of humans and machines converge for the betterment of humankind through unified knowledge, instantaneous communications, and continuous change, which together lead to transformational creativity. This list has been formulated based on our collective knowledge and experience.

The key conditions of the online world of the future that enables a new level of creativity, productivity, and safety for humans worldwide are:

1. *Global-scale autonomous learning systems:* Systems and networks will continuously learn at a global scale and therefore will adapt their interactions to autonomously interpret new information and to discover new knowledge, including automatically assessing the uncertainty of this new information or knowledge.

2. *Humans co-working with machines:* Humans (providing insight and understanding) and systems/networks (interpreting information at scale) will interwork to assess and to achieve joint goals to predict continuously emerging complex phenomena.

3. *Human factors are authentic and transferrable:* Cognitive characteristics, which indicate how people think, how people interact, and how societies and groups behave, will be inherent within interactions, allowing communication with fidelity and therefore with confidence.

4. *Global-scale whole-brain communities:* Societal formations, which provide human-driven informed insights, will emerge, interact, and disband in a man-

ner that is open and appropriately beneficial to community participants so that the right minds can work on the right problems at the right time.

5. *Foundational knowledge is authentic and transferrable:* Creative and productive outcomes are propagated independently of the lifetime of particular individuals or organizations; the future interpretation of these productive outcomes may happen safely.

6. *Timely productive communication:* Every contemplated interaction can happen appropriately and instantaneously with knowledge of other interactions or previous creative and productive outcomes.

7. *Continuous technological adaptation:* The online world of the future, as a safe system of systems, dynamically evolves to enable creative and productive outcomes, including the incremental transformation of the world of today to a fully digitally enabled society of the future.

We consider these conditions as a starting position. They should be continuously validated, refined, and adjusted as progress is made evolving underlying theories, as technological solutions are researched and developed, and as detailed field trials are conducted over time.

Interdependencies
Figure 2 illustrates how the seven conditions identified in the previous section relate to one another.

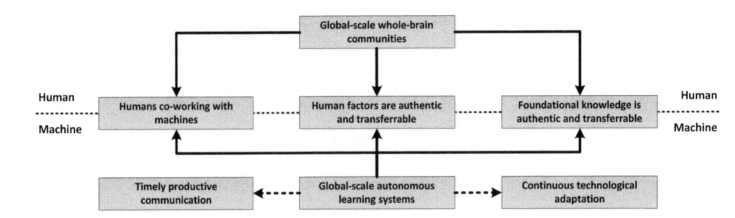

Figure 2. Dependencies among the seven conditions of the online world of the future

In our view of the online world of the future, Condition 1 (*Global-scale whole-brain communities*) is purely a human-oriented condition. Three conditions are part of the human-machine divide: Condition 2 (*Humans co-working with machines*), Condition 3 (*Human factors are authentic and transferrable*), and Condition 5 (*Foundational knowledge is authentic and transferrable*). Finally, three conditions are purely systems/network conditions: Condition 4 (*Global-scale autonomous learning systems*), Condition 6 (*Timely productive communication*), and Condition 7 (*Continuous technological adaptation*).

Figure 2 indicates that *Global-scale whole-brain communities* and *Global-scale autonomous learning systems* are two control points; the former is driven by humans and the latter is driven by systems/networks. These two conditions depend on each other through their direct dependence with *Humans co-working with machines, Human factors are authentic and transferrable*, and *Foundational knowledge is authentic and transferrable*. Within the scope of systems/networks, *Global-scale autonomous learning systems* directly depends on *Timely productive communication* and *Continuous technological adaptation*.

An Example

Here, we offer an example scenario of the online world of the future. The scenario describes the dynamic interoperation of two initially decoupled financial systems that specialize in maintaining knowledge and providing predictions about the energy sector of the economy. Consider two global-scale financial analysis systems – System A and System B – in which value is being created based on the present-value analysis of future cash flows. Each system is, in essence, implementing a future-oriented process that projects current economic performance over a time span applicable to the nature of a given business activity and its market segment. In such projections, there is often a distinction made between shorter-term and longer-term predictions and any analytic outputs may be indicator- or magnitude-based information. In this context, data-driven change that minimizes human intervention and bias must be systematically integrated with human-driven information that is the result of naturally adaptive and perceptive processes.

The clients who use System A are concerned with shorter-term predictions. The clients who use System B are concerned with longer-term predictions. Each system provides results of scenario analyses, knowledge about the energy sector and its conditions, cash flow projections, and valuation assessment for the shorter- or longer-term timeframes. For timeliness, System A projects cash flow and assesses valuations online and in real time. For greater accuracy, System B projects cash flow and assesses valuations offline and on demand.

These two systems are *global-scale autonomous learning systems* that can safely communicate with accuracy and with enduring confidence. Through known connections with known information elements in the financial domain, these two systems discover each other and establish a dynamic connection to interoperate in order to leverage each other's preferred stock predictions. System A is now able to use System B's longer-term predictions to validate its shorter-term predictions. System B is now able to use System A's shorter-term predictions to validate its longer-term predictions. This scenario provides an example of productivity gains through timely decisions that have an ongoing global effect. The predictions made by both systems have now been markedly improved. This interaction has happened autonomously because of *timely productive communication* and the dynamic reconfiguration of each system is an example of *continuous technological adaptation*.

Now consider human-driven information that is the result of naturally adaptive and perceptive processes. Because *human factors are authentic and transferrable* and *foundational knowledge is authentic and transferrable*, the human specialists of System A and System B have not only been alerted to the improved accuracy of their system's predictions but also to the human factors, the cognitive conditions, which led to how and why these new predictions were made. Because the human specialists of System A and System B are *humans co-working with machines*, they may interact with their respective systems to clarify any ambiguities or apparent contradictions and to more deeply understand the implications with respect to how they must adjust, from a human-driven information perspective, their shorter- or longer-term predictions. The new information may be utilized as *foundational elements that are authentic and are transferrable* because the two systems safely communicated with accuracy and with enduring confidence.

Finally, because they now know about each other and understand how and why each other came to the conclusions they came to, a specialist of System A and a specialist of System B, who live in very different parts of the world, start working together as a *global-scale whole-brain community* to assess any remaining ambiguities or contradictions. To resolve one contradiction, for example, one of the specialists has the sudden insight to analyze the situation from a completely different perspective by working with another specialist who is an expert in smart grids and distributed control systems for the energy sector. Acting as a *global-scale whole-brain community*, the three analysts are able to formulate a set of unique hypotheses, which they plan to test at scale through having the financial analysis systems interact in a restricted manner with the energy control systems of the companies that were associated with their financial predictions. This is an example of breakthrough thinking by connecting seemingly unrelated information.

As *humans co-working with machines*, they ensure, through *human factors are authentic and transferrable* and *foundational knowledge is authentic and transferrable* that the shorter- and longer-term predictions of their respective systems reflect this new knowledge and the thinking that was required to understand how and why this was the case.

Differentiation

In this section, we compare our view of the future of the online world and three competing visions: the Industrial Internet (Annunziata, 2013), the Internet of Things (Wikipedia, 2014), and the Internet of Everything (Cisco Systems, 2014). Figure 3 positions the four views of the future of the online world in terms of their excludability and consumption rivalry. These distinctions are import-

ant because they guide human action, and humankind can choose what to do with the Internet. For example, humankind can make Internet access similar to:

1. *air:* difficult to exclude, low rivalry

2. *public parks:* easy to exclude, low rivalry

3. *food:* easy to exclude, high rivalry

4. *fish stocks:* difficult to exclude, high rivalry

Today, depending on location, access to the Internet may follow any one of these four analogies.

Figure 3 indicates that the Industrial Internet will exclude many from benefiting from what it has to offer and will increase rivalry among the few. Our vision is represented as air; you cannot exclude people from breathing air and breathing as much air as you want does not take away the air that others breathe. There is the same technological underpinning for both cases, but very different economic models apply.

Consider further that the Internet goes beyond just access. Humankind has more choices to make, because the Internet also encompasses social and cultural issues, including intellectual property rights and ethical concerns. In general, we can think of the Internet, like other systems, as having three layers composed of the cognition, computation, and connection layers (Tibbs, 2013). Today, for Western society, most elements of the connection layer are like food (easy to exclude, high rivalry), most of the elements of the cognition layer are like parks (easy to exclude, low rivalry), and most elements of the computation layer are like fish stocks (difficult to exclude, high rivalry).

Conclusion

The safety of the online world of the future is an important precondition for a profound enhancement of human productivity and creativity by 2030. Safety properties of the online world of the future must ensure information elements are authentic and transferable to others at a global scale of interaction. We believe that, through association, enhanced productivity will be achieved by safely and instantaneously connecting known information elements, including by autonomous learning systems that operate at a global scale. We believe that, through bisociation, enhanced creativity will be achieved by safely and instantaneously connecting information elements that were previously viewed

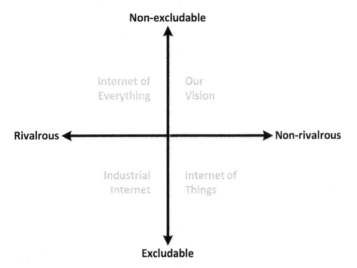

Figure 3. Positioning competing views of the future online world

to be disparate in nature, including through computational creativity and human-machine convergence.

When making progress towards understanding the scientific underpinnings of the online world of the future, we have presented a set of example research questions that we believe should be addressed or further refined. We have also presented the progression from today's environment to our vision of the future online world and positioned competing views of the future online world in terms of excludability and consumption rivalry using a quadrant-style representation.

Finally, if machines and humans are to interact and collaborate more systematically, we need to start thinking about the ethical values – and not only the creative and productive skills – that will be assigned to these machines when the outcomes of their decisions will apply to human populations, in the sense that solutions that are productive from a collective perspective can erode individual freedoms.

About the Authors

Tony Bailetti is an Associate Professor in the Sprott School of Business and the Department of Systems and Computer Engineering at Carleton University, Ottawa, Canada. Professor Bailetti is the Director of Carleton University's Technology Innovation Management (TIM) program. His research, teaching, and community contributions support technology entrepreneurship, regional economic development, and international co-innovation.

Renaud Levesque is the Director General of Core Systems at the Communications Security Establishment (CSE) in Ottawa, Canada, where he is responsible for R&D and systems development. He has significant experience in the delivery of capability and organizational change in highly technical environments. His career began at CSE in 1986 as a Systems Engineer, responsible for the development and deployment of numerous systems, including the CSE IP corporate network in 1991. In 2000 Renaud went to work in the private sector as Head of Speech Technologies at Locus Dialogue, and later at Infospace Inc., where he became Director of Speech Solutions Engineering. He rejoined CSE in 2003, where he assumed the lead role in the IT R&D section. Subsequently, as a Director General, he focused efforts towards the emergence of CSE's Joint Research Office and The Tutte Institute for Mathematics and Computing. Renaud holds a Bachelor of Engineering from l'École Polytechnique, Université de Montréal, Canada.

D'Arcy Walsh is a Science Advisor at the Communications Security Establishment (CSE) in Ottawa, Canada. His research interests include software-engineering methods and techniques that support the development and deployment of dynamic systems, including dynamic languages, dynamic configuration, context-aware systems, and autonomic and autonomous systems. He received his BAH from Queen's University in Kingston, Canada, and he received his BCS, his MCS, and his PhD in Computer Science from Carleton University in Ottawa, Canada.

References

Andreasen, N. 2005. *The Creating Brain: The Neuroscience of Genius.* New York: Dana Press.

Annunziata, M. 2013. Welcome to the Age of the Industrial Internet. *TED Talks.* October 1, 2014: http://www.ted.com/talks/marco_annunziata_welcome_to_the_age_of_the_industrial_internet/

Boden, M. A. 1994. Précis of *The Creative Mind: Myths and Mechanisms. Behavioral and Brain Sciences,* 17(3): 519-570. http://dx.doi.org/10.1017/S0140525X0003569X

Boden, M. A. 1999. Computer Models of Creativity. In R. J. Sternberg (Ed.), *Handbook of Creativity:* 351-372. Cambridge: Cambridge University Press.

Cisco Systems. 2014. Internet of Everything. *Cisco Systems.* October 1, 2014: http://www.cisco.com/web/about/ac79/innov/IoE.html

Craigen, D., Walsh, D., & Whyte, D. 2013. Securing Canada's Information-Technology Infrastructure: Context, Principles, and Focus Areas of Cybersecurity Research. *Technology Innovation Management Review,* 3(7): 12-19. http://timreview.ca/article/704

Csikszentmihalyi, M. 1996. *Creativity: Flow and the Psychology of Discovery and Invention.* New York: Harper Collins.

Dubitzsky, W., Tobias K., Schmidt, O., & Berthold, M.R. 2012. Towards Creative Information Exploration Based on Koestler's Concept of Bisociation. In M. R. Berthold (Ed.), *Bisociative Knowledge Discovery:* 11-32. Berlin: Springer.

Duxbury, T. 2012. Creativity: Linking Theory and Practice for Entrepreneurs. *Technology Innovation Management Review,* 2(8): 10-15. http://timreview.ca/article/594

Gerstein, J. 2014. Addressing Maslow's Hierarchy of Needs with Technology. *User Generated Education.* October 1, 2014: http://usergeneratededucation.wordpress.com/2014/03/12/addressing-maslows-hierachy-of-needs-with-technology

Gilovich, T., Griffin, D., & Kahneman, D. 2002. *The Psychology of Intuitive Judgment.* Cambridge: Cambridge University Press.

Kahneman, D. 2011. *Thinking Fast and Slow.* Toronto: Doubleday Canada.

Koestler, A. 1964. *The Act of Creation.* New York: Penguin Books.

Leveson, N. 2013. *Engineering a Safer World.* Cambridge, MA: MIT Press.

Tibbs, H. 2013. *The Global Cyber Game: The Defence Academy Cyber Inquiry Report.* Swindon, UK: Defence Academy of the United Kingdom.

Wikipedia. 2014. The Internet of Things. *Wikipedia.* October 1, 2014: http://en.wikipedia.org/wiki/Internet_of_Things

Keywords: future vision, online, Internet, Internet of Things, Industrial Internet, Internet of Everything, safety, security, cybersecurity, productivity, excludability, rivalry, bisociation

3

Safety in the Online World of the Future

Nadeem Douba, Björn Rütten, David Scheidl,

Paul Soble, and D'Arcy Walsh

“ *The errors of a theory are rarely found in what it* ” *asserts explicitly; they hide in what it ignores or tacitly assumes.*

Daniel Kahneman
Nobel Laureate in Economic Sciences (2002)

In this article, we address what it means to be safe in the online world of the future by advocating the perspective whereby improving safety will improve resilience in cyberspace. We adopt a specific approach towards transdisciplinarity; present a weakly transdisciplinary model of the safety context and an initial position about what existing disciplines are most relevant; and link prospect theory to risk-based decision making as one example that could lead to a new paradigm for safety. By treating safety as a transdisciplinary challenge, there is an opportunity to enable the participants of the online world to become more productive and creative than ever before. The beneficiary of this increased productivity and creativity will ultimately be the public. The perspective of this article is of interest to senior decision makers, policy makers, managers, educators, strategists, futurists, scientists, technologists, and others interested in shaping the online world of the future.

Introduction

This article focuses on the nature of safety in the future online world to enable humanity to reach profoundly new levels of productivity and creativity. Bailetti, Levesque, and Walsh (2014) envision an online world for 2030 that is safe (i.e., users communicate with accuracy and enduring confidence), productive (i.e., users make timely decisions that have an ongoing global effect), and creative (i.e., users can connect seemingly unrelated information online). Their proposed view is characterized by seven conditions of the future online world: i) global-scale autonomous learning systems; ii) humans co-working with machines; iii) human factors that are authentic and transferrable; iv) global scale whole-brain communities; v) foundational knowledge that is authentic and transferrable; vi) timely productive communication; and vii) continuous technological adaptation.

Key research questions pertaining to the safety characteristics of this future world include:

- Under what conditions does an attacker have an advantage over an infrastructure protector?

- Why do many infrastructure protectors and users not adopt effective mechanisms that provide safety and privacy?

- What are the resources, processes, and values to concurrently provide online safety and privacy to users?

- What are the characteristics of the individuals and organizations that are most likely to attack?

- What are the enhanced characteristics of safety through disclosure (i.e., by being open and not by being proprietary)?

If progress is made understanding the underlying properties of safety that are required to address these questions, then a foundation will be provided that promotes scientific progress and the arts within a society that is ever more connected on a global scale.

The Internet was not created to be safe but is being increasingly used in a way that requires that it be so. The increasing pervasiveness of cyber-based systems and infrastructure, and society's growing reliance on them, shifts the perspective concerning their proper operation from security to safety. Although defending networks and other information assets is necessary, it is part of the larger intent of securing these systems' ability to produce services and functions upon which society depends. Safety is often associated with unintended disruption, and security is often associated with intended disruption; both concepts affect the proper operation of cyber-based systems and infrastructure. Safety properties include security properties (Burns et al., 1992; Leveson, 2013; Young & Leveson, 2013). Safety is the foundation that promotes scientific progress and the arts within a society that is ever more connected on a global scale; it enables the global knowledge commons that is an engine of human progress.

This view of safety is sympathetic and compatible with the ultimate intent of copyright and patent laws. Article I of the American Constitution makes clear that the beneficiary of publications and inventions is the public – copyrights are granted and patents are issued in order "to promote the Progress of Science and useful Arts" (Menard, 2014). The thinking behind Article I is that prohibiting people from copying and selling someone else's original work should be time bound to strike an appropriate balance so that individuals and organizations have the means to further create original work but in a manner that the public can also benefit from this work in a timely fashion (Menard, 2014).

In this spirit, the concept of safety (including security) is not restricted to the protection and control of property, because ownership is a concept that can vary across social contexts. Instead, improving the safety of cyber-based systems and services focuses on the intended use of these systems. Further, safety must have enduring resilience where "cyber- [or online] resilience is about digital literacy at every level of the organization/society, distributed leadership, and a capacity to adapt in a networked and fast-changing digital ecosystem" (Rütten, 2010). Thus, there is a responsibility for safety that transcends the technological disciplines.

Based upon our knowledge and experience, current approaches toward safety and security do not make an explicit connection to productivity and creativity when contemplating the transdisciplinary aspects of the problem domain. These approaches emphasize preventing failure instead of enabling success. A new online paradigm that implies an environment that is safe regardless of how much you interact within it is necessary "to promote the Progress of Science and useful Arts" (Menard, 2014) in the future.

This article makes three contributions. First, it provides insight about a particular approach for addressing the global and transdisciplinary aspects that we believe characterize safety concerns of the online world of the future. Second, the article presents a weak transdisciplinary representation of the safety context and an initial position about what existing disciplines are most relevant. Third, by linking prospect theory to risk-based decision making within the domain of cyber-resilience, it provides an example to advance the idea of safety through online interactivity that could lead to a new paradigm for safety for the future online world.

The Safety Context is Global and Transdisciplinary

A safe online world must be created and maintained by stakeholders at multiple levels of society, which suggests that a more holistic view is required to define goals and engage participants rather than following separate approaches to the problem from distinct disciplines, which individually tend to address a subset of stakeholders. The concerns of these stakeholders are accommodated by treating relevant disciplines in a unified way. The concept of transdisciplinarity (Nicolescu, 2005), creating a unity of intellectual frameworks beyond the disciplinary perspectives (Jensenius, 2012), offers an approach for constructing a view of safety as a composition of collaborating disciplines that address the concerns of these stakeholders.

A distinction may be made between strong and weak transdisciplinarity. Strong transdisciplinarity envisions a total system of knowledge without stable boundaries between the disciplines. However, in the case of weak transdisciplinarity, traditional methods and logic can be applied. Here, we focus on weak transdisciplinarity, where a transdiscipline extends its action through coordination among disciplines at several levels of organization: the first, lowest level refers to "what exists now" (i.e., the world as it is; the empirical level), the second level refers to "what we are capable of doing" (i.e., it is composed mainly of technology disciplines; the capacity level), the third level refers to "what we want to do" (i.e., the normative level), and the fourth level refers to "what we should do" (i.e., the value level) (Max-Neef, 2005).

Thus, we do not treat safety as strictly disciplinary (specialization in isolation), multidisciplinary (no cooperation), pluridisciplinary (cooperation without coordination), or interdisciplinary (coordination from a higher-level concept), but instead we treat it as a coordination amongst all hierarchical levels.

In an effort to practice weak transdisciplinarity in a systematic manner as advocated by Max-Neef (2005), we have adopted a four-level organization model at the core of the safety context, and a set of high-level categories of knowledge that should be coordinated to achieve a safe online environment (Figure 1):

1. *Online world of the future:* speculates about the safe, productive, creative aspects that will drive the evolution of the online world, including the key conditions that will be met by the future world (see Bailetti et al., 2014).

2. S*trategy for making scientific progress and transfer of knowledge:* includes research questions, research methods and techniques, new disciplines, assessment of progress, and the transfer of knowledge through education and other means.

3. *Legal/ethical concerns:* includes issues related to privacy, security, intellectual property, regulation, disclosure, and human-machine interaction for the individual and collective good.

4. *Human sciences:* includes human behaviour, cognition, and social dynamics; how people think, how people interact, and how societies and groups be-

have; what people think, their beliefs and ideologies; cultural factors; and value systems.

5. *Technical understanding of the communication environment:* includes issues related to scientific understanding and technical aspects, including real-time, manifestation of phenomena within the online environment and the deployment of interconnected systems of systems.

6. *Related domain models:* concern the promotion of specific theories or concepts relevant to the domain, for example: the Cyber Game (information versus power); safety (unintended and intended disruption); economic models (public, private, club, common pooled resource); political science models; human behavior (decision making under risk, deception, intent); technical methods and techniques related to attack, attribution, forensics, and impact of compromise; and specific business models.

7. *Important topics:* include specific perspectives or "game changers" that represent current informed thinking about the domain (e.g., supply/value chain; duality of risk – opportunities, threats; adoption; disclosure, disruption).

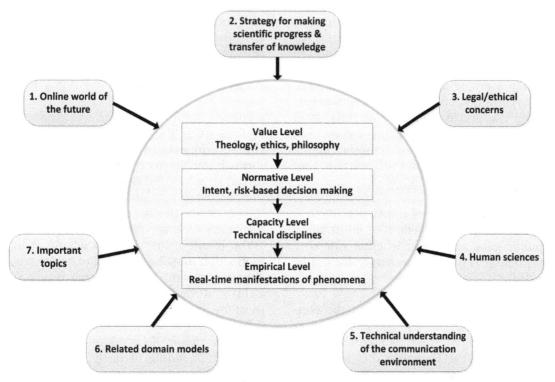

Figure 1. Four levels of concerns that need to be addressed to produce a safe online environment and seven categories of knowledge that influences the work done on these concerns.

Specific to the domain, we believe that the "Cyber Game" from the Global Cyber Game report (Tibbs, 2013) presents a useful domain analysis of the online world. The report was produced by the United Kingdom's Defence Academy, which provides education and training in a broad range of subjects – including command and staff, leadership, defence management, languages, acquisition and technology – for members of the UK Armed Forces and Defence Civil Servants. In delivering education and training, it is the Defence Academy's responsibility to prepare senior decision makers for the uncertainties and complexities of the challenges ahead. The report is a good example of this preparation as it pertains to the nature of cyberspace in the future, including cybersafety and cybersecurity.

The overall objective when producing the report was first to consider the broad question, "How should the cyber-domain be conceptualized?", and in the light of that question, to examine the implications for security strategy generally, the issues raised for state actors in the Internet age, new power relationships, possible sources and modes of future conflict, and the steps that need to be taken to prepare for a range of plausible possibilities (Tibbs, 2013).

The report examines these issues, in part, by proposing the idea of the Global Cyber Game as a framework that can be used for practical thinking about cyber strategy. Cyberpower and cybersecurity are conceptualized using a "Cyber Gameboard", which consists of a nine-cell grid. The horizontal direction on the grid is divided into three columns representing aspects of cyber-information: connection, computation, and cognition. The vertical direction on the grid is divided into three rows representing types of power: coercion, co-option, and cooperation. The nine cells of the grid represent all the possible combinations of power and information, that is, forms of cyberpower (Tibbs, 2013).

The central ideological decision of the Cyber Game is whether to play the game as if freedom of information content is a public good in itself or whether extensive control of information content is necessary for public safety (Tibbs, 2013).

Thus, the Cyber Game gives precedence to the concepts of information and power and the interrelationships that can arise when these two concepts are applied together. The Cyber Gameboard is a concise but powerful representation that permits reasoning about many of the aspects and complex interactions of cyberspace to achieve an outcome that can be successful despite, for example, known ideological conflicts, politics, and human nature whose complexity requires coordinated action.

The power dimension of the Cyber Game privileges the sub-concepts of cooperation (integrative social power), co-option (economic exchange power), and coercion (destructive hard power) as means to exercise power. On this dimension, cyberspace is a tool similar to new technologies such as airpower or net-centric warfare used to achieve effects on geopolitical actors with its own characteristics of power transition versus power diffusion.

The information dimension of the Cyber Game privileges the sub-concepts of connection (the physical data-handling domain), computation (the virtual interactivity domain), and cognition (the knowledge and meaning domain). On this dimension, an example bridging the gap from cyberspace to physical space is the Stuxnet case study of a cyber attack strategy to bridge connection, computation and cognition spaces (Kushner, 2013).

A Weak Transdisciplinary Representation of the Safety Context

This section introduces a weak transdisciplinary representation of the safety context of cyberspace and an initial position about what existing disciplines are most relevant. Because we lack a methodology for applying weak transdisciplinarity, our approach is based on our subjective confidence.

Figure 2 presents Cyber Game concepts and related disciplines using the four-level organizational model, including connections that cascade from the Value Level, through the Normative and Capacity Levels, to the Empirical level to indicate the coordination that must happen across levels amongst those concepts that are linked. Although the structure does not directly answer questions such as "What does it mean to be safe?" or "Who is safe from whom or what?", it unifies the elements that must be adjusted to evolve from the present situation toward the preferable future (Bailetti et al., 2014) in a way that addresses the multi-level complexity of the problem.

What we should do is addressed at the Value Level of Figure 2, including theology, values, security and privacy, intellectual property, regulation, disclosure, and the individual and collective good as they relate to human–machine interaction. Practical solutions must in-

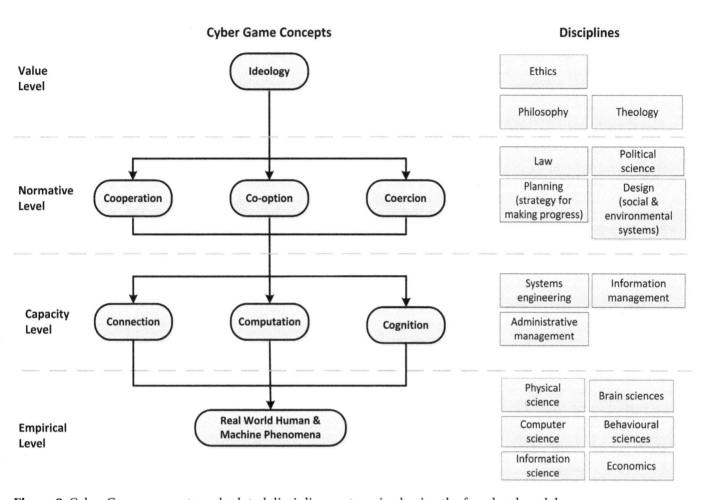

Figure 2. Cyber Game concepts and related disciplines categorized using the four-level model

volve this level to account for online participants who do not share the same views of such things as values, religion, and ethics.

What we want to do is addressed at the Normative Level of the figure, including risk-based decision making, management and planning, the strategy for making scientific progress and knowledge sharing, legal, and political concerns. We have also positioned the power dimension of the Cyber Game sub-concepts of cooperation (integrative social power), co-option (economic exchange power), and coercion (destructive hard power) at this level.

What we are capable of doing (composed mainly of technology disciplines) is addressed at the Capacity Level of the figure, including the information dimension of the Cyber Game sub-concepts of connection (physical data handling domain), computation (virtual

interactivity domain), and cognition (knowledge and meaning domain).

What exists now (the world as it is) is addressed at the Empirical Level of the figure, including physical sciences, computer science, information science, brain sciences, and behavioural and social sciences.

The weak transdisciplinary model is a representation of the safety context of cyberspace. Relevant disciplines are identified at every level and these disciplines must be coordinated to achieve the safety goal in the face of the real-world complexities and conflicts.

Safety through Online Interactivity

This section provides an example of relevant disciplines that are coordinated to achieve safety by linking prospect theory to risk-based decision making in the context of cyber-resilience. An important consequence of the example is the notion of safety through online interactivity.

The concept of cyber-resilience (Rütten, 2010) is addressed by Collier and colleagues (2014), who focus on the ability to prepare for and recover quickly from both known and unknown threats. They recommend linking technical data with decision analysis in an adaptable framework to move toward systems that are more resilient to dynamic threats by incorporating decision analysis methods and techniques "to accommodate value-centric perspectives inherent in multiple stakeholder views when addressing the challenge of establishing risk-based standards that will protect the cyber domain" (Collier et al., 2014). This approach is an example of weak transdisciplinarity.

Now consider prospect theory, which is the foundation of the field of behavioural economics. As an evolution of concepts that originate from statistics, economics, and psychology, it is another example that transcends a particular discipline. Using the concept of a reference point to indicate that the human response to losses is stronger than the response to corresponding gains (loss aversion) together with the concept of diminishing sensitivity, it is a coherent theory that can describe decision under risk: prospect theory provides a plausible way to describe different attitudes to risk for gains (as favourable prospects) and losses (as unfavourable prospects) (Kahneman, 2011).

Prospect theory should be investigated as at least a partial theoretical grounding of risk-based decision making within the domain of cyber-resilience. It would contribute to descriptions of the behavioural aspects when humans are confronted with decisions "to prepare for and recover quickly from both known and unknown threats". Based on prospect theory, risk-based standards could be enhanced to better align with the decisions humans actually make under such circumstances.

Further, because prospect theory accommodates favourable as well as unfavourable prospects, we believe it applies beyond "risk-based standards that will protect the cyber domain" (Kahneman, 2011). By accommodating both kinds of prospects, prospect theory in effect could also be considered a theory of decision making pertaining to the duality of risk, which treats each risk situation not just as a threat (an unfavourable propect) but also as an opportunity (a favourable prospect).

As an example from the medical domain (Kahneman, 2011), consider anesthesiologists, who benefit from feedback because their actions are quickly evident, and radiologists, who obtain less immediate information about the accuracy of their diagnoses. In both cases, risk can be considered as the difference between life and death. Saving a patient is an example of a favourable prospect and not saving a patient is an example of an unfavourable prospect. Anesthesiologists and radiologists become better at their profession as they save or do not save patients by continually making decisions under risk and learning and adapting (by modifying their protocol of intervention). Under very different circumstances, both kinds of medical experts must overcome their subjective confidence and must continually know the limits of their expertise as they become more experienced and knowledgeable.

In the context of cyber-resilience, viewing risk as an opportunity is a way to facilitate productive and creative outcomes within a society that is ever more connected on a global scale. When risk as an opportunity is applied within an adaptive learning framework such as the one promoted by Collier and colleagues (2014), online safety becomes a function of user online interactivity. Humans (providing insight and understanding) and systems/networks (interpreting information at scale) will interwork to assess and to achieve joint goals to predict continuously emerging complex phenomena (Bailetti et al., 2014). If such an environment existed, it would make a profound contribution in promoting the future "Progress of Science and useful Arts" (Menard, 2014): cyber-resilience in this sense is not just recovering from individual loss events, but more akin to reduction of brittleness in the protective measures (through an adaptive learning approach).

Conclusion

We presented an approach for addressing safety concerns in the online world of the future using a weak transdisciplinary model, including an initial position about what existing disciplines are most relevant. Although the model does not directly answer key research questions pertaining to underlying safety properties, it does provide a unified structure that accommodates the participation of stakeholders at multiple levels of society and a holistic view.

Instead of restricting the concept of safety (including security) to the protection and control of property, we emphasize improving the safety of cyber-based systems and focus on the intended use of these systems that could lead to profoundly new levels of productivity and creativity for the benefit of society as a whole.

In order to make progress in understanding the underlying properties of safety, and to evolve from the present situation toward the preferable future (Bailetti et al., 2014), attention should be given to applying a methodology of transdisciplinarity that exclusively concentrates on joint problem solving of key research questions pertaining to the science–technology–society triad implied by the weakly transdisciplinary model that was presented. The investigation of prospect theory as a theoretical grounding of risk-based decision making within the domain of cyber-resilience is an example.

We foresee the possibility of a new online environment that becomes progressively safer for participants the more that online interactions occur within the environment. The idea is that a participant's fingerprint is enriched the more that the participant interacts online. The more enriched a participant's fingerprint becomes, the greater the potential for ensuring the safety of the participant. At the same time, the more a participant interacts online, the more opportunity there will be for the participant to be productive and creative.

With this perspective in mind, we believe that future work should contemplate both the productivity and creativity domains in depth to better understand how their respective underlying properties relate to safety when safety is a function of interactivity.

About the Authors

Nadeem Douba is the founding principal of Red Canari, an information security consulting firm that specializes in the areas of information technology and cybersecurity. With over 15 years experience, Nadeem provides consulting and training services for organizations within the public and private sector. He has also presented at some of the world's largest security conferences and is the author of many well-known open source security tools, including one used by the Internet Archive project. His primary research interests include open source intelligence, application and operating system security, and big data. He received his BEng in Systems and Computer Engineering from Carleton University in Ottawa, Canada.

Björn Rütten is the Senior Research Associate for National Security and Public Safety with The Conference Board of Canada. Bjorn leads the Conference Board's research projects in the area of national security and public safety and is responsible for the development and execution of the research plan of the Centre for National Security. He also contributes to other security-related network and research initiatives, such as those of the Centre for the North.

David Scheidl is a recent graduate from the Global Politics program at Carleton University in Ottawa, Canada. During his studies, he focused on security intelligence and geopolitics, with special emphasis on Western security agencies in both the cybersecurity and real-world intelligence fields. He has extensive background in military communications, having served in the Army Signals Reserve since 2009.

Paul Soble is a Science Advisor at the Communications Security Establishment (CSE) in Ottawa, Canada. Over the past three decades, he has held a variety of positions at CSE in the areas of enterprise architecture, visualization and data mining, speech and text natural language processing, adaptive antenna arrays, and systems development. He received his BSc and MSc degrees in Electrical Engineering from University of Manitoba in Winnipeg, Canada, and he is a licensed professional engineer in the province of Ontario.

D'Arcy Walsh is a Science Advisor at the Communications Security Establishment (CSE) in Ottawa, Canada. His research interests include software-engineering methods and techniques that support the development and deployment of dynamic systems, including dynamic languages, dynamic configuration, context-aware systems, and autonomic and autonomous systems. He received his BAH from Queen's University in Kingston, Canada, and he received his BCS, his MCS, and his PhD in Computer Science from Carleton University in Ottawa, Canada.

References

Bailetti, T., Levesque, R., & Walsh, D. 2014. The Online World of the Future: Safe, Productive, and Creative. *Technology Innovation Management Review*, 4(10): 5–12. http://timreview.ca/article/834.

Burns, A., McDermid, J., & Dobson, J. 1992. On the Meaning of Safety and Security. *The Computer Journal*, 35(1): 3-15. http://dx.doi.org/10.1093/comjnl/35.1.3

Collier, Z. A., DiMase, D., Walters, S., Tehranipoor, M. M., Lambert, J. H., & Linkov, I. 2014. Cybersecurity Standards: Managing Risk and Creating Resilience. *IEEE Computer*, 47(9): 70-76. http://dx.doi.org/10.1109/MC.2013.448

Jensenius, A. 2012. Disciplinarities: Intra, Cross, Multi, Inter, Trans. ARJ.no. Accessed November 15, 2014. http://www.arj.no/2012/03/

Kahneman, D. 2011. *Thinking, Fast and Slow*. Toronto: DoubleDay Canada.

Kushner, D. 2013. The Real Story of Stuxnet. *IEEE Spectrum*, February 26. http://spectrum.ieee.org/telecom/security/the-real-story-of-stuxnet

Leveson, N. 2013. *Engineering a Safer World*. Cambridge, MA: MIT Press.

Menand, L. 2014. Crooner in Rights Spat: Are Copyright Laws Too Strict? *The New Yorker*, October 20, 2014. http://www.newyorker.com/magazine/2014/10/20/crooner-rights-spat

Max-Neef, M. A. 2005. Foundations of Transdisciplinarity. *Ecological Economics*, 53(1): 5-16. http://dx.doi.org/10.1016/j.ecolecon.2005.01.014

Nicolescu, B. 2005. Transdisciplinarity – Past, Present, and Future. Il Congresso Mundial de Transdisciplinaridade, 6-12 September, 2005, Brazil. http://cetrans.com.br/textos/transdisciplinarity-past-present-and-future.pdf

Rütten, B. 2010. *Digital Ecosystem Resilience*. Ottawa: The Conference Board of Canada.

Tibbs, H. 2013. *The Global Cyber Game: The Defence Academy Cyber Inquiry Report*. Swindon, UK: Defence Academy of the United Kingdom.

Young, W., & Leveson, N. 2013. System Thinking for Safety and Security. *Proceedings of the 2013 Annual Computer Security Applications Conference (ACSAC 2013)*.

Keywords: safety, security, cybersecurity, weak transdisciplinary, prospect theory, risk-based decision making

4

Securing the Car: How Intrusive Manufacturer-Supplier Approaches Can Reduce Cybersecurity Vulnerabilities

Mohamed Amin and Zaid Tariq

" *To know is to control.* **"**

Ishmael Scott Reed
Poet, essayist, and novelist

Today's vehicles depend on numerous complex software systems, some of which have been developed by suppliers and must be integrated using "glue code" so that they may function together. However, this method of integration often introduces cybersecurity vulnerabilities at the interfaces between electronic systems. In this article we address the "glue code problem" by drawing insights from research on supplier-manufacturer outsourcing relationships in the automotive industry. The glue code problem can be framed as a knowledge coordination problem between manufactures and suppliers. Car manufacturers often employ different levels of intrusiveness in the design of car subsystems by their suppliers: the more control over the supplier the manufacturer exerts in the design of the subsystem, the more intrusive the manufacturer is. We argue that high intrusiveness by car manufacturers in defining module interfaces and subcomponents for suppliers would lead to more secure cars.

Introduction

The modern car is increasingly dependent on electrical and software systems. A modern vehicle has anywhere from 30 to 70 electronic control units that monitor and control its different subsystems (Studnia et al., 2013a), which are integrated using "glue code" (Checkoway et al., 2011). The glue code enables car manufacturers to outsource the development of particular systems and subsystems, which are then integrated when the car is assembled.

However, within and between these modules, several cybersecurity vulnerabilities in the modern car have been identified and documented by researchers. Examples include vulnerabilities in sound systems, Bluetooth modules, onboard diagnostics systems, cellular communications, and the bus connecting electronic control units, (Checkoway et al., 2011; Eichler, 2007; Hoppe et al., 2009; Koscher et al., 2010; Raya & Hubaux, 2007; Wolf et al., 2004). Practitioners have also stressed how vulnerable the modern car is to cyber-attacks (Miller & Valasek, 2013; Venturebeat, 2013; Yadron, 2014). Both local and remote attacks have been documented (Studnia et al., 2013a). Theft, electronic

tuning, sabotage, and surveillance are among the goals of those who cyber-attack cars (Studnia et al., 2013a). Most vulnerabilities in the modern car arise from incorrect assumptions made by the glue code that calls functions on different electronic control units (Checkoway et al., 2011). These incorrect assumptions may occur at the subcomponent level as well as the interface level.

Checkoway and colleagues (2011) argue that the true source of the glue code problem can be traced back to the setup of the ecosystems used to manufacture cars. Auto manufacturers build ecosystems to outsource digital systems in the same way that they outsource mechanical parts. Although every supplier tests their modules, security vulnerabilities usually arise when those modules are subsequently integrated by the car manufacturers. Outsourcing module design may introduce security vulnerabilities at the interface between modules and the car (i.e., in the glue code), as well as between distinct modules designed by external suppliers. The latter source of vulnerabilities is caused by feature interaction problems between different modules and this source of vulnerabilities is outside the scope of this article.

By analyzing various security solutions that have been proposed to improve the overall security of the modern car (Bouard et al., 2013; Herrewege, et al., 2011; Studnia et al., 2013a; Stumpf et al., 2009; Wolf & Gendrullis, 2012; Wolf & Weimerskirch, 2004), we observe that the proposed solutions: i) only focus on providing technical architectures of security solutions, ii) would typically require substantial changes to existing implementation processes in the automobile industry, and iii) do not directly address the glue code problem identified by Checkoway and colleagues (2011). To address these shortcomings, we examined literature on manufacturer-supplier relationships. As will be described below, we identified that the manufacturer's level of intrusiveness in supplier design could aid in solving the interface boundary, or glue code, problem. In particular, we argue that, for manufacturers to avoid security vulnerabilities at the boundaries between electronic control units, they should be highly intrusive in the supplier design of the module interfaces and subcomponents that call other electronic control units in the car.

In the following section, we describe the proposed cybersecurity solutions for cars and existing manufacturer-supplier relationships. Next, we examine an existing analytical framework and propose our solution. We close by outlining our contribution and offering conclusions.

Proposed Solutions

Three broad categories of solutions have been proposed by various researchers: i) encryption of communications, ii) anomaly detection, and iii) improved integrity of the embedded software (Studnia et al., 2013a). Table 1 summarizes representative solutions and their salient features.

Car manufacturers have been increasingly outsourcing module design (Calabrese & Erbetta, 2005). Suppliers organize themselves around manufacturers' facilities geographically to form supplier parks (Collins et al., 1997; Larsson, 2002; Volpato, 2004). In addition to geo-

Table 1. Representative cybersecurity solutions for the modern car

Security Solution	Salient Features
Proxy-Based Security Architecture for CE Device Integration (Bouard et al., 2013)	• Proxy-based IP security solution to secure consumer electronic devices able to access a car's onboard network. • Enforces communication decoupling between internal and external networks by using a security proxy. • Approach requires partial redesign of electronic control units to support in-band signaling between the control units and the security proxy.
Multipurpose Electronic control Units and Hardware Security Module (Stumpf et al., 2009; Wolf & Gendrullis, 2012)	• A dedicated hardware security module governs all traffic between electronic control units and authenticates individual frames. • Hardware security module is then implemented in a system that uses the concept of virtualization to centralize all electronic control units in a car onto a single virtual machine • Integrates inherent features of virtual machines: integrity, trustworthiness, and authenticity.
Security in Automotive Bus Systems (Wolf et al., 2004)	• Secure the existing in-car network using controller authentication, encrypted communication and gateway firewalls. • Inter Bus communication happens through a central authentication and encryption gateway on each bus.
CANAuth (Herrewege et al., 2011)	• Backward-compatible controller area network (CAN) authentication protocol designed using hashed message authentication code (HMAC). • This protocol uses the existing CAN bus and forms an additional layer on top of the existing protocol.
Intrusion Detection System (Studnia et al., 2013b)	• Automotive security using an intrusion detection system for the CAN bus.

graphic allocation, smaller suppliers usually form a hierarchy behind large first-tier suppliers forming around car manufacturers (Volpato, 2004). Knowledge and task partitioning differ depending on the relationships between supplier and manufacturer (Cabigiosu et al., 2013; Zirpoli & Camuffo, 2009) as well as the nature of the product being co-developed (Takeishi, 2002). Manufacturers and suppliers co-develop modules with varying levels of intrusion by the manufacturer in the supplier design (Cabigiosu et al., 2013).

The Manufacturer-Supplier Co-Development Approach

Cabigiosu and colleagues (2013) compared two similar vehicle component co-development projects carried out by the same first-tier supplier with two different automakers. They used an analytical framework to analyze the manufacturer's approach to supplier integration in product development. The results showed that the two manufacturers employed different levels of "intrusiveness" in supplier design. Manufacturer intrusiveness represents the level of detail and the amount of coordination the manufacturer employed in defining the design of the respective artifact. An intrusive approach to the co-development is an approach where the manufacturer exerts high level of control over the supplier's design decisions. The level of intrusiveness influences the knowledge the manufacturer has about the interface and the subcomponents of the module. Analyzing the two different approaches reported by Cabigiosu and colleagues (2013), and the corresponding degrees of intrusiveness with each approach, leads

to insights on how the glue code problem may arise and what car manufacturers can do to prevent it.

According to Cabigiosu and colleagues (2013), manufacturers engage with suppliers at different levels of intrusiveness in:

1. *Module-to-car system-level design:* includes functional and performance parameters that the module has to adhere to in order for it to comply with overall functional and performance parameters of the car as a whole.

2. *Module-to-module interface design:* includes protocol-level functionality that the module has to adhere to in order for it to interoperate with various other modules in the car.

3. *Individual-subcomponent-to-module system-level design:* includes functional and performance parameters that various subcomponents in the module have to adhere to for the module to work as a whole.

4. *Individual subcomponents design:* functional- and protocol-level parameters that subcomponents have to adhere to.

Table 2 compares the approaches taken by two manufacturers in co-developing an air conditioning system with the same supplier (Cabigiosu et al., 2013). Manufacturer A's approach can be characterized as intrusive whereas manufacturer B's approach can be characterized as non-intrusive.

Table 2. Comparison between intrusive and non-intrusive approaches to manufacturer-supplier co-development (Cabigiosu et al., 2013)

	Manufacturer A's Approach (Intrusive)	Manufacturer B's Approach (Non-Intrusive)
Interface definition	• Stable and detailed • Definitions frozen before design starts • Specifics are clear, easy to follow, and do not change	• Fluid and changing • Set the main concept and architecture but allow supplier to suggest design
Co-development approach	• Formal information-sharing sessions monthly and bi-weekly • Daily communications, sometimes face to face • Mainly to sort out component interdependencies	• Heavily outsourced engineering tasks to supplier. • Used a standard codified co-development practice • Used rigid systems and procedures
Knowledge partitioning	• Owned component-specific knowledge	• Did not own component-specific knowledge

The glue code problem can be seen as a knowledge co-ordination problem. Suppliers design components based on performance and functional specifications provided by the manufacturer. Design decisions can sometimes be left to the discretion of the supplier, who may assume that particular components in the car work in certain ways. This was the case with the Airbiquity software component analyzed by Checkoway and colleagues (2011), where they found that the code calling this component and binding it to other telematics functions made the wrong assumptions about the component supported packet size and resulted in a buffer overflow vulnerability. Packet sizes are usually defined as part of the interfaces; given that the car manufacturer did not know the right packet size used by the software component shows that the manufacturer was non-intrusive in defining this interface. An intrusive strategy would avoid such a problem because the manufacturer would know the right packet size because it was the one defining it. Only the manufacturer is in a position that would allow a holistic view of all the different electronic control units and their inner workings. Thus, the glue code problem can be reduced if the manufacturer employs the right level of intrusiveness with different suppliers. We argue that the right level of intrusiveness by a manufacturer for avoiding the glue code problem is being highly intrusive in defining the module interfaces and the inner subcomponents of the electronic control unit module that call other modules in the car. This degree of intrusiveness in the manufacturer-supplier relationship is similar to a hybrid-control governance model of open source platforms (Noori & Weiss, 2013), where increased control yields higher quality but does require greater effort in the form of overseeing all the parties involved. Where increased quality equates to increased security, this added effort will be worthwhile.

Conclusion

As described earlier, security solutions can by broadly divided into three main categories: i) encryption of communications, ii) anomaly detection, and iii) integrity of the embedded software, where the final category refers to approaches that ensure the car's critical software is not affected by a cyber-attack (Studnia et al., 2013). Our contribution adds to this third category by identifying the manufacturer-supplier relationship that reduces the risk of vulnerabilities at the boundaries

between electronic control units and thus protects the integrity of the car's critical software modules.

Our contribution allows car manufacturers to employ the right level of intrusiveness in their supplier design to increase the level of cybersecurity in their cars. It allows individuals responsible for leading engineering efforts at both manufacturer and supplier organizations and individuals controlling manufacturer-supplier inter-firm relations to pick the right working model for building secure cars. We encourage the research community to further explore manufacturer-supplier relationship theory and other managerial theories in their search for a solution to securing the car.

Manufacturers can choose the optimal degree of intrusiveness when co-developing new products with their suppliers. We argue that an intrusive strategy can be employed by manufacturers when developing electronic control units to reduce the risk of cybersecurity vulnerabilities at the boundaries between systems. We invite further research into this domain to tackle the cybersecurity problems of the modern car. Future work could empirically test our claim that increased manufacturer intrusiveness in supplier design leads to more secure cars.

About the Authors

Mohamed Amin is an MASc student in the Technology Innovation Management program at Carleton University in Ottawa, Canada. His research interests include cybersecurity, API strategy, and industry architecture. He works as a Solution Architect for Alcatel-Lucent Canada, where he designs and delivers network solutions for various internet service providers around the world.

Zaid Tariq is completing his MEng in Technology Innovation Management at Carleton University in Ottawa, Canada. He also holds a BEng degree in Computer Engineering from McGill University in Montreal, Canada. He is a Senior Network Engineer at Cisco Systems and has 9 years experience working in the network design, architecture, and test domains.

References

Bouard, A., Schanda, J., Herrscher, D., & Eckert, C. 2013. Automotive Proxy-Based Security Architecture for CE Device Integration. In P. Bellavista, C. Borcea, C. Giannelli, T. Magedanz, & F. Schreiner (Eds.), *Mobile Wireless Middleware, Operating Systems, and Applications:* 62–76. Berlin: Springer Berlin Heidelberg.

Cabigiosu, A., Zirpoli, F., & Camuffo, A. 2013. Modularity, Interfaces Definition and the Integration of External Sources of Innovation in the Automotive Industry. *Research Policy,* 42(3): 662–675. http://dx.doi.org/10.1016/j.respol.2012.09.002

Calabrese, G., & Erbetta, F. 2005. *Outsourcing and Firm Performance: Evidence from Italian Automotive Suppliers.* Paper presented at the 13th Annual IPSERA Conference. Catania: Universita di Catania.

Checkoway, S., McCoy, D., Kantor, B., Anderson, D., Shacham, H., Savage, S., Koscher, K., Patel, S., Roesner, F., Czeskis, A., & Kohno, T. 2011. *Comprehensive Experimental Analyses of Automotive Attack Surfaces.* Paper presented at the USENIX Security Symposium. San Francisco: USENIX Association.

Collins, R., Kimberly, B., & Pires, S. 1997. Outsourcing in the Automotive Industry: From JIT to Modular Consortia. *European Management Journal, 15(5):* 498–508. http://dx.doi.org/10.1016/S0263-2373(97)00030-3

Eichler, S. 2007. A Security Architecture Concept for Vehicular Network Nodes. In *Proceedings of the 6th International IEEE Conference on Information, Communications & Signal Processing:* 1–5. Washington, DC: IEEE. http://dx.doi.org/10.1109/ICICS.2007.4449730

Herrewege, A., Singelee, D., & Verbauwhede, I. 2011. *CANAuth: A Simple, Backward Compatible Broadcast Authentication Protocol for CAN Bus.* Paper presented at the ECRYPT Workshop on Lightweight Cryptography. Louvain-la-Neuve, Belgium: ECRYPT.

Hoppe, T., Kiltz, S., & Dittmann, J. 2009. Automotive IT Security as a Challenge: Basic Attacks from the Black Box Perspective on the Example of Privacy Threats. In *Computer Safety, Reliability, and Security – Lecture Notes in Computer Science, 5575:* 145–158. Berlin: Springer Berlin Heidelberg. http://dx.doi.org/10.1007/978-3-642-04468-7_13

Koscher, K., Czeskis, A., Roesner, F., Patel, S., Kohno, T., Checkoway, S., McCoy, D., Kantor, B., Anderson, D., Shacham, H., & Savage, S. 2010. Experimental Security Analysis of a Modern Automobile. In *Proceedings of the 2010 IEEE Symposium on Security and Privacy:* 447–462. Oakland, CA: IEEE.

Larsson, A. 2002. The Development and Regional Significance of the Automotive Industry: Supplier Parks in Western Europe. *International Journal of Urban and Regional Research,* 26(4): 767–84. http://dx.doi.org/10.1111/1468-2427.00417

Miller, C., & Valasek, C. 2013. *Adventures in Automotive Networks and Control Units.* Paper presented at DEF CON 21 Hacking Conference. Las Vegas, NV: DEF CON.

Noori, N., & Weiss, M. 2013. Going Open: Does it Mean Giving Away Control? *Technology Innovation Management Review,* 3(1): 27-31. http://timreview.ca/article/647

Raya, M., & Hubaux, J. P. 2007. Securing Vehicular Ad Hoc Networks. *Journal of Computer Security,* 15(1): 39–68.

Studnia, I., Nicomette, V., Alata, E., Deswarte, Y., Kaâniche, M., & Laarouchi, Y. 2013a. A Survey of Security Threats and Protection Mechanisms in Embedded Automotive Networks. In *Proceedings of the 2nd Workshop on Open Resilient Human-Aware Cyber-Physical Systems (WORCS-2013).* Budapest, Hungary: IEEE. http://dx.doi.org/10.1109/DSNW.2013.6615528

Studnia, I., Nicomette, V., Alata, E., Deswarte, Y., Kaâniche, M., & Laarouchi, Y. 2013b. Security of Embedded Automotive Networks: State of the Art and a Research Proposal. In *Proceedings of 2nd Workshop on Critical Automotive Applications: Robustness & Safety of the 32nd International Conference on Computer Safety, Reliability and Security.* Toulouse, France: SAFECOMP.

Stumpf, F., Meves, C., Weyl, B., & Wolf, M. 2011. *A Security Architecture for Multipurpose ECUs in Vehicles.* Paper presented at the 25th Joint VDI/VW Automotive Security Conference. Ingolstadt, Germany.

Takeishi, A. 2002. Knowledge Partitioning in the Interfirm Division of Labor: The Case of Automotive Product Development. *Organization Science,* 13(3): 321–338. http://dx.doi.org/10.1287/orsc.13.3.321.2779

VentureBeat. 2013. Ford Wants You to Join It in Hacking Car Software and Hardware. *VentureBeat.* Accessed January 10, 2015: http://venturebeat.com/2013/11/06/ford-wants-you-to-join-it-in-hacking-car-software-and-hardware-video/

Volpato, G. 2004. The OEM-FTS Relationship in Automotive Industry. *International Journal of Automotive Technology and Management,* 4(2/3): 166–197. http://dx.doi.org/10.1504/IJATM.2004.005325

Weimerskirch, A. 2012. *Automotive and Industrial Data Security.* Paper presented at the Cybersecurity for Cyber-Physical Systems Workshop. Ann Arbor, MI: National Institute of Standards and Technology.

Wolf, M., & Gendrullis, T. 2012. Design, Implementation, and Evaluation of a Vehicular Hardware Security Module. In H. Kim (Ed.), *Information Security and Cryptology-ICISC:* 302–318. Berlin: Springer Berlin Heidelberg.

Wolf, M., Weimerskirch, A., & Paar, C. 2004. *Security in Automotive Bus Systems.* Paper presented at Workshop on Embedded Security in Cars (ESCAR 2004). Bochum, Germany: ESCAR.

Yadron, D. 2014. Tesla Invites Hackers for a Spin. *The Wall Street Journal Blog.* Accessed January 10, 2015: http://blogs.wsj.com/digits/2014/08/08/telsa-invites-hackers-for-a-spin/

Zirpoli, F., & Camuffo, A. 2009. Product Architecture, Inter-Firm Vertical Coordination and Knowledge Partitioning in the Auto Industry. *European Management Review,* 6(4): 250–264. http://dx.doi.org/10.1057/emr.2009.25

Keywords: cybersecurity, vulnerabilities, automobile manufacturing, car design, supplier, outsourcing, control, governance, supplier-manufacturer relationships, glue code, intrusiveness

5

Overcoming Barriers to Collaboration in an Open Source Ecosystem

Derek Smith, Asrar Alshaikh, Rawan Bojan, Anish Kak, and Mohammad Mehdi Gharaei Manesh

"Yes, we are all different. Different customs, different foods, different mannerisms, different languages, but not so different that we cannot get along with one another. If we will disagree without being disagreeable."

J. Martin Kohe
Author and Psychologist

Leveraging open source practices provides value to businesses when entrepreneurs and managers understand how to collaborate effectively in an open source ecosystem. However, the complex mix of different actors and varying barriers to effective collaboration in the ecosystem pose a substantial challenge. How can a business create and capture value if it depends on effective collaboration among these different groups? In this article, we review the published research on open source collaboration and reveal insights that will be beneficial to entrepreneurs and managers. We organize the published research into four streams based upon the following actor groups: i) governance actors, ii) competitors, iii) complementors, and iv) the core community. Then, through induction and synthesis, we identify barriers to collaboration, first by ecosystem and then by actor group. Finally, we offer six recommendations for identifying and overcoming barriers to collaboration in an open source ecosystem.

Introduction

Collaboration is the act of working with another individual or grouping to create something. It involves working jointly and openly with others. When collaborators bring their own diverse skills and experience – and new perspectives – the potential for innovation is great. However, collaboration is far from easy, and the diversity that brings benefits to the experience can also present barriers to collaboration. In an open source ecosystem, where collaboration is essential and the diversity of contributors is often high, these barriers can be substantial.

Open source collaboration is the act of working with different group of actors on a project to produce and create open source software (Nan and Kumar, 2013; tinyurl.com/k5a8yt3). For companies that wish to leverage open source software as part of their business models,

effective collaboration is essential. However, the open environment introduces business- and people-related issues that can restrict or prevent open collaboration among the different groups of actors. Entrepreneurs and managers are faced with questions such as: How open should an actor be with sensitive or confidential business information, and with whom can it safely be shared? How can we collaborate openly with a competitor? How do we collaborate with actors from around the world, where cultural differences may affect our interactions? These business- and people- related issues inherent in an open source ecosystem create barriers to effective collaboration if entrepreneurs and managers fail to understand and overcome the barriers.

In this article, we examine the barriers to effective collaboration in an open source ecosystem, and we ask whether the different groups of actors in such an ecosystem face the same or different barriers. To successfully collaborate in an open source ecosystem, entrepreneurs and managers must understand: i) the degree of similarity or dissimilarity between barriers to collaboration in such an ecosystem and ii) how the barriers relate to the different groups of actors.

In the existing literature, previous research has focused on specific actors in open source ecosystems, such as: foundations, communities, governments, complementors, competitors, leaders, developers, adapters, users, and expert users. However, there is a lack of research from the broader perspective of the collaboration barriers that may arise within and between these various groups of actors. To achieve business success through leveraging an open source ecosystem, entrepreneurs and managers need to:

1. Identify and understand barriers to collaboration common to all groups of actors in an open source ecosystem

2. Identify and understand barriers to collaboration unique to specific groups of actors in an open source ecosystem

3. Overcome all these barriers for overall effective collaboration in an open source ecosystem

In this article, we make five contributions. First, we identify barriers to collaboration common to all groups of actors in an open source ecosystem. Second, we categorize actors in an open source ecosystem into four different groups. Third, we identify open source collaboration barriers unique to the different groups. Fourth, we assemble the research articles relevant to the topic of collaboration in open source ecosystems into four streams based upon our four different groups of actors. Finally, we provide recommendations to entrepreneurs and managers to identify and overcome barriers to collaboration from a different group of actor perspective.

The article is organized into four sections. The first section summarizes the results of our literature review concerning open source collaboration. The second section provides a definition of open source collaboration as it relates to open source business and an open source ecosystem. This section also identifies open source collaboration barriers common in the ecosystem and unique to the four different groups of actors. The third section provides recommendations for entrepreneurs and managers to overcome collaboration barriers in an open source ecosystem. A final section concludes the article.

Literature Review

Table 1 summarizes the 15 papers we reviewed following a search of literature relating to open source collaboration. Based on patterns we observed, we organized the literature into four streams based on the relevance to four groups of actors in an open source ecosystem: i) governance actors, ii) competitors, iii) complementors, and iv) the core community. Organizing the literature in this way revealed insights into the common barriers in an open source ecosystem and the barriers that are unique to each group of actor.

1. Governance actors

Five of the articles we reviewed in Table 1 relate collaboration with governance actors. Lack of governance can be an overall barrier (Muegge, 2011; timreview.ca/article/495), but one of the main barriers is the disparate interests or divergent interests between actors in the ecosystem (O'Mahony and Bechky, 2008; tinyurl.com/lothrqs). Other relevant barriers include the lack of vision and standards relating to the joint efforts in the ecosystem (Kshetri and Schiopu, 2007; tinyurl.com/n74oeem; Skerrett, 2009; timreview.ca/article/219). A lack of openness and transparency (Smith and Milinkovich, 2007; timreview.ca/article/94) can also be a barrier that restricts collaboration in an open source ecosystem. Governance actors manage different interests, solidify and converge interests, and overall reduce business differences between actors in an open source ecosystem (O'Mahony and Bechky, 2008; tinyurl.com/lothrqs). Openness and transparency (Skerrett, 2009; timreview.ca/article/219) are also required for access to shared resources and gaining commitment from the actors (Smith and Milinkovich, 2007; timreview.ca/article/94). Collaboration with governance actors is a process of compromise to establish an ecosystem structure that enables business activities (O'Mahony and Bechky, 2008; tinyurl.com/lothrqs). A vision and standards are required for international collaboration (Kshetri and Schiopu, 2008; tinyurl.com/n74oeem); they enable the actors in an open source ecosystem to create value and collaborate.

2. Competitors

Three articles summarized in Table 1 relate to open source collaboration with competitors. Barriers to overcome when collaborating with competitors include a lack of trust, the need to identify shared objectives, and the need to share access to resources in contrast to a closed approach where a company looks to assimilate key resources into its business (Shamsuzzoha et al., 2013; tinyurl.com/nnvmcr2). Other barriers include concerns related to releasing confidential information

Table 1. A summary of open source collaboration literature relevant to open source ecosystems

Stream	Author (Year)	Source	Open Source Actor(s)	Focus
Governance Actors	Muegge (2011) timreview.ca/article/495	*Technology Innovation Management Review (TIM Review)*	Community members, developer, foundation, users, and adopters	A systems perspective on communities, institutions, companies, and individuals
	Smith & Milinkovich (2007) timreview.ca/article/94	*TIM Review*	Foundation	Openness, transparency, and meritocracy with resources and commitment; ability of the ecosystem to create value
	O'Mahony & Bechky (2008) tinyurl.com/lothrqs	*Administrative Science Quarterly*	Foundation (boundary organizations)	Managing the boundaries of collaboration where disparate and convergent interests of different actors are present. Recommendations include the need to identify critical differences and establish a governance structure, membership, ownership, and control over the project for enabling collaboration.
	Kshetri & Schiopu (2007) tinyurl.com/n74oeem	*Journal of Asia-Pacific Business*	Foundation (government)	Effective international collaborations requirements, including a vision and influence on a technology trajectory, setting standards, and promotion
	Skerrett (2009) timreview.ca/article/219	*TIM Review*	Foundation	Collaborative software development with competitors in a foundation governed open source community
Competitors	Lindman & Rajala (2012) timreview.ca/article/510	*TIM Review*	Competitor	Focus interactions with the user to gain user involvement. Ensure access to important external resources rather than assimilate or build new internal resources. Take advantage of open innovation process but think about the purpose of external contributions. Make the goal of collaboration clear so that it becomes easier to collaborate and reveal confidential information where it makes business sense.
	Schreuders et al. (2011) timreview.ca/article/413	*TIM Review*	Competitor	Hybrid business model based upon an open source licensing model, which allows different users different access and collaboration based upon the selected open source licensing model. The hybrid business model removes restrictions and attracts actors to the open source community, building a resource to test and validate products.
	Shamsuzzoha et al. (2013) tinyurl.com/nnvmcr2	*International Journal of Computer Integrated Manufacturing*	Competitor	Building trust and overcoming fears relating to confidentiality and the exchange of information between competitors. This requires common objectives and rules/procedures for exchanging information and foundations for cooperation. Individual objectives must be clear and aligned to the shared objectives
	Muegge (2013) timreview.ca/article/655	*TIM Review*	Complementors, suppliers, customers, competitors, developers, and users	Identifies the actors in the open source ecosystem such as customers, suppliers, competitors, and many other stakeholders.

Continued...

Table 1 *(continued)*. A summary of open source collaboration literature relevant to open source ecosystems

Stream	Author (Year)	Source	Open Source Actor(s)	Focus
Complementors	Skerrett (2011) timreview.ca/article/409	*TIM Review*	Multi-vendor, complementors, users, adopters, and contributors	License strategy is important to engage a larger portion of community. A copyleft license will generate a wider collaboration. License strategy can also earn trust and gain access to a larger portion of community. Use a vendor-neutral governance structure.
	Muegge (2013) timreview.ca/article/655	*TIM Review*	Complementors, suppliers, customers, competitors, developers, and users	Identifies the actors in the open source ecosystem such as customers, suppliers, competitors, and many other stakeholders.
Core Community	Muegge (2011) timreview.ca/article/495	*TIM Review*	Community members, developer, foundation, users, and adopters	A systems perspective on the community, institutions, companies, and individuals. Shared governance and participation are important to collaboration in an open source community.
	Evans & Wolf (2005) tinyurl.com/l9dgpea	*Harvard Business Review*	Community members, leaders, and competitors	Members belong to different organizations with no defined role or responsibility; a mix of amateurs and professionals with different skills. Competitors collaborate: must think about options and adaptability not integration and static efficiency. Build trust in the community and collaborate freely and productively. Leaders are valuable; they instruct community members, articulate clear goals, and connect people. Trust is currency and reputation is power.
	Skerrett (2011) timreview.ca/article/409	*TIM Review*	Multi-vendor, complementors, users, adopters, and contributors	License strategy is important to engage a larger portion of community. A copyleft license will generate a wider collaboration. License strategy can also earn trust and gain access to larger portion of community. Use a vendor-neutral governance structure.
	Sarker et al. (2009) tinyurl.com/l32zjuf	*IEEE Transactions on Professional Communication*	Leaders	Leadership in the community. Leaders are not reassigned; rather, they emerge from the project and are required for effective collaboration. Information systems development ability, greater contributions are identified with leadership.
	Nan & Kumar (2013) tinyurl.com/k5a8yt3	*IEEE Transactions on Engineering Management*	Developers	Size and format of a team of developers in association with the level of structural interdependency are key for effective collaboration. Positive impact on a project with a high level of structural interdependency may be achieved with centralized teams of developers and larger teams. Smaller teams required for positive impact on projects with a low level of structural interdependency; centralized teams can impact project performance on such projects.
	Colazo (2010) tinyurl.com/mwuovbm	*International Journal of Innovation Management*	Developers	Developer density is negatively associated with quality and positively associated with productivity. Centralization is positively associated with both quality and productivity. Collaborating beyond boundaries is positively associated with quality but negatively associated with productivity.
	Hemetsberger & Reinhardt (2009) tinyurl.com/qz3mszp	*Organization Studies*	Expert Users	Coat tailing is the pursuit of individual and collective needs; it requires achieving the best balance between individual and collective needs.
	Muegge (2013) timreview.ca/article/655	*TIM Review*	Complementors, suppliers, customers, competitors, developers, and users	Identifies the actors in the open source ecosystem such as customers, suppliers, competitors, and many other stakeholders.

(Lindman and Rajala, 2012; timreview.ca/article/510); removing restrictions that prevent open collaboration with competitors (Schreaders et al., 2011; timreview.ca/article/413); and the need to attract and build a larger community of competitors that may be leveraged (Schreuders et al., 2011; timreview.ca/article/413).

3. Complementors
Two articles summarized in Table 1 relate to collaboration with complementors. Barriers include intellectual property in the form of a right that prevents use and collaboration as well as an inability to share confidential information, lack of trust, moving from closed to open, vendor dominance, and trust (Skerrett, 2011; timreview.ca/article/409) and lack of transparency (Muegge, 2013; timreview.ca/article/655).

4. Core Community
Eight articles summarized in Table 1 relate to collaboration with the core community (i.e., users, adopters, contributors, leaders, developers and expert users). Barriers to overcome when collaborating with the core community include:

• *a lack of leadership*; leaders are not appointed but evolve out of the community, and there may be cultural differences in leadership (Sarker et al., 2009; tinyurl.com/l32zjuf). Collaboration with the core community requires identification of a leader or leaders of the project to ensure productivity and balance the needs of the actors in the core community

• *the size and format of the community*, which affects collaboration as well as the degree of centralization or decentralization (Nan and Kumar, 2013; tinyurl.com/k5a8yt3). Going beyond boundaries can be a barrier to productivity (Colazo, 2010; tinyurl.com/mwuovbm)

• *the individual needs of expert users*, which may not align with the needs of the community (Hemetsberger and Reinhardt, 2009; tinyurl.com/qz3mszp)

• *the mix of developer attributes*, such as the amount of skill or a lack of skill. In addition, a developer's role and responsibilities, which tend to be undefined in an open source ecosystem, (Evans and Wolf, 2005; tinyurl.com/l9dgpea) also create barriers to effective collaboration.

Open Source Barriers to Collaboration

Open source business shifts "the focus from the production value to the use value of the software artifact and emphasizes services and meta-services surrounding the artifact" (Feller et al., 2006; tinyurl.com/34eppr5). The open source ecosystem includes a number of different actors involved in the artifact and the services to provide a complete solution to customers. The ecosystem has little organization and order. The ecosystem may further include a platform where actors interact to create products or offer services. The platform offers value to the actors in the ecosystem but the platform also brings together many different technology, people and business relates issues (Kilamo et al., 2012; tinyurl.com/n5gnrgu). The actors are motivated by common interests or business models (Manikas and Hansen, 2013; tinyurl.com/lsrljj5). Common interests include a motivation to join the ecosystem where there is overlap in business and the actors work collectively towards a common task, asset, or resource. A business model is also a motivation where the business model in part relies on a non-differentiating common task, asset, or resource.

As we identified earlier, the collection of actors includes four main groups: i) governance actors, ii) competitors, iii) complementors, and iv) the core community. Governance actors are important and manage the boundaries of collaboration (O'Mahony and Bechky, 2008; tinyurl.com/lothrqs), which are essential to the operation of an open source ecosystem. The type of governance actor varies with the open source ecosystem and may include a foundation (O'Mahony and Bechky, 2008; tinyurl.com/lothrqs; Skerrett, 2009; timreview.ca/article/219; Smith and Milinkovich, 2007; timreview.ca/article/94), a federal government (Kshetri and Schiopu, 2007; tinyurl.com/nnvmcr2), or the community (O'Mahony and Bechky, 2008; tinyurl.com/lothrqs). The core community comprises the actors in the open source ecosystem that work on the open source project to develop and test the product (Kilamo et al., 2012; tinyurl.com/n5gnrgu). Actors in the core community include: leaders (Sarker et al., 2009; tinyurl.com/l32zjuf), developers (Nan and Kumar, 2013; tinyurl.com/k5a8yt3; Colazo, 2010; tinyurl.com/mwuovbm), users (Muegge, 2013; timreview.ca/article/655), adopters (Skerrett, 2011; timreview.ca/article/409; Muegge, 2011; timreview.ca/article/495) and expert users (Hemetsberger and Reinhardt, 2009; tinyurl.com/qz3mszp). Leaders provide overall leadership to the development portion of the community. Developers work on the open source project creating and testing the software. Users are important for providing requirements. Adopters are key to using the open source project. Expert users provide insight into the project for both present and future needs.

Governance actors resolve differences in the community to ensure the health of the ecosystem (Smith and Milinkovich, 2007; timreview.ca/article/94). Resolving differences involves collaboration with all other groups. Competitors create and share value while collaborating with the core community, complementors, and other competitors. Complementors help build a larger community that can be leveraged to create and share value (Skerrett, 2011; timreview.ca/article/409); they collaborate with the core community as well as competitors and other complementors. The core community includes actors such as leaders, developers, and expert users and the associated collaboration barriers are different within the core community.

Table 2 is a summary of collaboration barriers from the literature pertaining to these four main groups, including the different types of actors within each group. The barriers in this table were identified through a close reading of the articles in the literature review. For example, the barrier relating to lack of project representation, which applies to governance actors, is derived from O'Mahony and Bechky (2008; tinyurl.com/lothrqs): "Though project members were not eager to impose a 'command and control structure onto the community', this desire for 'republics' led the projects to adapt a governance structure that established project representation and preserved pluralistic control." Similarly, the governance-actor barrier relating to challenges in defining the scope of collaboration is derived from Skerrett (2009; timreview.ca/article/219): "Determining the scope of collaboration is often the most challenging aspect of starting an open source project. The key challenge is to understand which areas of technology are core and which are non-core to the business value of that organization." Another example is the inequality barrier faced by complementors, which was derived from (Skerrett, 2011; timreview.ca/article/409): "For single-vendor-dominated communities, copyright assignment was required to allow the receiving vendor the ability to create revenue streams by implementing a dual license for the project code. MySQL is the most common example of this strategy. Unfortunately, this approach creates a revenue stream that is unique to one company. In turn, this inequality creates a barrier to involvement by other companies."

These examples show how the collaboration barriers listed in Table 2 were identified from the literature. Table 3 is a synthesis of the barriers from Table 2 to reveal which barriers are common across the groups and which barriers are unique to each group.

There are four barriers to collaboration that are common to all groups in an open source ecosystem: i) intellectual property, ii) moving from closed to open, iii) openness, and iv) a lack of transparency. The literature shows that trust is important to most groups in the ecosystem with the exception of the governance actors. A particular challenge for competitors and the core community is the diverse mix of people, and the potential for undefined roles and responsibilities. A particular challenge for complementors and the core community is inequality in the ecosystem. The governance actors and the core community tend to have a broad range of different barriers to collaboration.

Recommendations for Entrepreneurs and Managers

We offer six recommendations for entrepreneurs and managers seeking to overcome collaboration barriers for successful collaboration in an open source ecosystem.

1. Identify the common and unique barriers to collaboration in your open source ecosystem
The barriers to collaboration in an open source ecosystem include barriers common to all groups of actors in the ecosystem and barriers unique to specific groups of actors. Entrepreneurs and managers need to seek out, understand, and pay attention to these very different barriers for successful collaboration in an open source ecosystem. The specific nature of a given barrier will depend on the unique circumstances of your ecosystem, but Table 3 can help you systematically identify the types of common and unique barriers to collaboration.

2. Strike a balance between open and closed
Intellectual property that is not differentiating to a business should be released into the open. This requires early and ongoing identification of assets and information that may be open to the ecosystem and other assets and information that should be kept confidential. This includes patents, copyrights, designs and potential inventions. Trademarks and know-how become more valuable and strategic to open source business.

Move quickly and make informed business decisions in the open environment of the ecosystem and be open and transparent with competitors based upon your business decisions when collaborating with any group of actors in an open source ecosystem.

3. Seek representation and effective governance
Understand the collaboration barriers that relate to representation, pluralistic control, economic balance, disparate and divergent interests, ability to cooperate, vision, and standards. Then, ensure your business has a fair share of representation and become proactive with pluralistic control. Identify different interests early and compromise when collaborating with other groups of actors. Setting a clear vision and standards will assist you with effective collaboration with the governance group of actors.

4. Collaborate effectively with the core community
Understand the barriers with the core community that relate to equality, leadership, team structures, cultural differences, and new member integration. Be fair and equitable with the core community. Attempt to identify the leader, or assist developing a leader in the community. Ensure you have an appropriate team structures to assist collaboration with the core community and pay attention to cultural differences associated with a global community, and assist with integrating new members into the community.

5. Compete and collaborate with competitors
Understand the collaboration barriers with competitors that relate to objectives, roles, responsibilities, and shared values. In advance of engaging competitors in the open source ecosystem, ensure you have clear objectives and defined roles, responsibilities, and values. Make a point of understanding your competitor's objectives, roles, responsibilities, and values. Ensure or negotiate an appropriate understanding of joint roles, responsibilities, and values for collaborating in the open source ecosystem.

6. Recognize the challenges of diversity
Be aware of the diversity in the competitor and core community groups; it can be beneficial, but it also introduces collaboration challenges. Diversity includes different levels of knowledge or education and different levels of skills. There may be actors from many different parts of the world, which creates the potential for cultural barriers to collaboration.

Conclusion

There are many barriers to collaboration in an open source ecosystem. Some of these barriers are common to all actors in the ecosystem, but others are unique to specific groups of actors in the ecosystem. Barriers common to all groups are: intellectual property, business- and people-related issues when moving from a closed system to an open system, understanding where and how to be open in business with other actors in the ecosystem including competitors, and a potential lack of transparency that can impact success. Effective collaboration requires an open approach to all groups in the ecosystem based upon informed business decisions and an understanding of the barriers in an open source ecosystem. Effective collaboration requires that entrepreneurs and managers identify and understand the collaboration barriers both common and unique to each of the four groups of actors in the ecosystem and then overcome these barriers.

Table 2. Open source ecosystem actors, sub-groups, and collaboration barriers

Category	Collaboration Barriers*	Specific Actors
Governance	Lack or type of governance (Muegge, 2011; O'Mahony & Bechky, 2008)	Foundation, community
	Lack of transparency (Smith & Milinkovich, 2007; Skerrett, 2009)	Foundation
	Intellectual property concerns (Muegge, 2011; Skerrett, 2009)	Foundation
	Moving from closed to open (Smith & Milinkovich, 2007)	Foundation
	Disparate interests; divergent interests (O'Mahony & Bechky, 2008)	Foundation, community
	Lack of project representation (O'Mahony & Bechky, 2008)	Foundation, community
	Pluralistic control (O'Mahony & Bechky, 2008)	Foundation, community
	Differences preventing collaboration (O'Mahony & Bechky, 2008)	Foundation, community
	Challenges in defining the scope of collaboration (Skerrett, 2009)	Foundation
	Reluctance to be openness (Skerrett, 2009; Muegge, 2013)	Foundation
	Economic imbalance (Kshetri & Schiopu, 2007)	Foundation, government
Complementors	Lack of transparency (Muegge, 2013)	
	Initial lack of trust (Skerrett, 2011)	
	Inequality (Skerrett, 2011)	
	Moving from closed to open and developing in the open (Skerrett, 2011)	
	Selecting the best open license strategy for wider collaboration that does not introduce a high business risk (Skerrett, 2011)	
Competitors	Reluctance to reveal confidential information (Lindman & Rajala, 2012)	
	Lack of clear goals and objectives of collaboration (Lindman & Rajala, 2012)	
	Restrictive licensing model (Schreuders et al., 2011)	
	Initial lack of trust (Evans & Wolf, 2005; Shamsuzzoha et al., 2013)	
	Inability to cooperate (Shamsuzzoha et al., 2013)	
	Lack of clearly aligned and shared objectives (Shamsuzzoha et al., 2013)	
	Lack of clear, well-defined formalized roles (Shamsuzzoha et al., 2013)	
	Unwillingness to share knowledge and competencies (Shamsuzzoha et al., 2013)	
	Lack of shared values (Shamsuzzoha et al., 2013)	
	Mix of amateurs and professionals (Evans & Wolf, 2005)	
	Mix of skills and levels of skills (Evans & Wolf, 2005)	
	Members with no defined role or responsibilities (Evans & Wolf, 2005)	
Core Community	Difficulties in relationship building (Nan & Kumar, 2013)	Developer
	Lack of a formal team structure (Nan & Kumar, 2013)	Developer
	Degree of centralization (Nan & Kumar, 2013; Colazo, 2010)	Developer
	Dealing with volunteer members (Colazo, 2010)	Developer
	Lack of transparency (Muegge, 2013)	Developer, user, adopter
	Intellectual property concerns (Muegge, 2011)	User, adopter
	Initial lack of trust (Skerrett, 2011; Evans & Wolf, 2005)	User, adopter, leader
	Inequality (Skerrett, 2011)	User, adopter
	Moving from closed to open and developing in the open (Skerrett, 2011)	User, adopter
	Selecting the best open licensing strategy for wider collaboration that does not introduce a high business risk (Skerrett, 2011)	User, adopter
	Negative selfish interest of users (Muegge, 2013)	User
	Dispersed work (Hemetsberger & Reinhardt, 2009)	Expert user
	Mix of different skills expertise (professional and amateur) (Hemetsberger & Reinhardt, 2009; Evans & Wolf, 2005)	Expert user, leader
	Challenges in integrating new members (Hemetsberger & Reinhardt, 2009)	Expert user
	Members without defined roles or responsibilities (Evans & Wolf, 2005)	Leader
	Leadership in a virtual environment (Sarker et al., 2009)	Leader
	Perception of leadership (Sarker et al., 2009)	Leader

*See Table 1 for links to cited articles.

Table 3. Barriers to collaboration in an open source ecosystem, by actor group

Potential Barriers to Collaboration	Actor Group			
	Governance	Complementors	Competitors	Core Community
Intellectual property concerns	✓	✓	✓	✓
Moving from closed to open and sharing information and knowledge with everyone in the ecosystem	✓	✓	✓	✓
Reluctance to be open	✓	✓	✓	✓
Lack of transparency	✓	✓	✓	✓
Lack of trust		✓	✓	✓
Challenges of interacting with a diversity of people with different knowledge and experience			✓	✓
Lack of clearly defined roles/responsibilities			✓	✓
Inequality		✓		✓
The business' lack of representation in the ecosystem	✓			
Pluralistic control	✓			
Economic imbalance between actors of different size	✓			
Disparate/divergent interests	✓			
Inability to cooperate	✓			
Lack of vision/standards	✓			
Lack of clear objectives			✓	
Lack of shared values			✓	
Lack of leadership				✓
Lack of a format team structure to achieve a project objectives (size/format/degree of centralization or decentralization)				✓
Cultural differences				✓
Challenges with integrating new members into the ecosystem, team, or project				✓

About the Authors

Derek Smith is the founder and principal of Magneto Innovention Management, an intellectual property consulting firm that assists entrepreneurs and small businesses with difficult intellectual property issues. He has over 20 years of experience working as an intellectual property management consultant and patent agent for IBM Canada, Bell Canada and, most recently, Husky Injection Molding Systems where he was Director, Global Intellectual Property. Prior to entering the field of intellectual property, he was an advisory engineer at IBM Canada where he was involved in a variety of leading-edge software development projects. Derek is currently a graduate student in the Technology Innovation Management (TIM) program at Carleton University in Ottawa, Canada. He also holds a BEng degree in Systems and Computer Engineering from Carleton University and is a registered patent agent in both Canada and the United States.

Asrar Abdulqader Alshaikh is a graduate student in the Technology Innovation Management (TIM) program at Carleton University in Ottawa, Canada. She holds a Bachelor of Accounting degree from King Abdulaziz University in Jeddah, Saudi Arabia. Her work experience includes customer service in a sale for distribution and communication company as well as working for the Alahli Bank (NCB) in Jeddah, Saudi Arabia. Her main area of research interest is collaborative consumption.

Rawan Mohammad Bojan is a graduate student in the Technology Innovation Management (TIM) program at Carleton University in Ottawa, Canada. She has professional experience in the banking industry and holds a Bachelor of Science in Accounting from King Abdulaziz University in Jeddah, Saudi Arabia.

Anish Kak is a graduate student in the Technology Innovation Management (TIM) program at Carleton University in Ottawa, Canada. He holds a BEng degree in Computer Science Engineering, from Birla Institute of Technology in India. Anish has two years of experience in the information technology services sector, which he gained while working for Hewlett-Packard in India. His research interests include the electronic sports ecosystem.

Mohammad Mehdi Gharaei Manesh is a graduate student in the Technology Innovation Management (TIM) program at Carleton University in Ottawa, Canada. He holds an MBA degree from Carleton University's Sprott School of Business and also has a degree in Biomedical Engineering from Tehran Polytechnic University in Iran. He has 5 years of working experience in a medical equipment company and his main area of interest relates to crowdsourcing and international business.

Keywords: business ecosystem, open source, communities, governance, core community, competitors, complementors, collaboration, collaboration barriers

6

Cybersecurity Capability Maturity Models for Providers of Critical Infrastructure

Walter Miron and Kevin Muita

" The truth is rarely pure and never simple. "

Oscar Wilde (1854–1900)
Writer, poet, and playwright

Critical infrastructure such as power generation and distribution systems, telecommunications networks, pipelines and pipeline control networks, transportation control networks, financial networks, and government information and communications technology (ICT) have increasingly become the target of cyber-attacks. The impact and cost of these threats, as well as regulatory pressure to mitigate them, have created an impetus to secure these critical infrastructures. Managers have many controls and models at their disposal to help them secure infrastructure technology, including cybersecurity capability maturity models to enable measurement and communication of cybersecurity readiness to top management teams, regulators, and customers, thereby facilitating regulatory compliance, corporate responsibility, and improved brand quality. However, information and awareness is lacking about which models are most appropriate for a given situation and how they should be deployed.

This article examines relevant cybersecurity capability maturity models to identify the standards and controls available to providers of critical infrastructure in an effort to improve their level of security preparedness. These capability models are described and categorized by their relevance to different infrastructure domains, and then recommendations are provided on employing capability maturity models to measure and communicate readiness. This article will be relevant to regulators, critical infrastructure providers, and researchers.

Introduction

The critical infrastructures that make our way of life possible are increasingly vulnerable to cyber-attack. These critical infrastructures are defined as assets or systems required for the security and well being of citizens, including systems to produce and distribute water, electricity, and fuel, and communication networks (Public Safety Canada, 2009; Yusta et al., 2011; European Commission, 2013; U.S. Department of Homeland Security, 2013). Accordingly, disruption to one or more of these critical infrastructures usually incurs substantial human and financial cost, which is often the point of a cyber-attack and the reason such infrastructures are targeted by actors who may be motivated by profit or sociopolitical causes, among other motivations (Grau & Kennedy, 2014).

As the types of connectivity and volumes of data flow increase, the potential for cyber-attacks increases (Dupont, 2013) and brings greater focus on the security of critical infrastructures. In preparing their systems to withstand cyber-attacks, operators of critical infrastructure are faced with myriad controls and standards, and many of their implementations are incomplete or inconsistent, which further exacerbates the threat environment and provides a false sense of security (Chaplin & Akridge, 2005). To properly secure critical infrastructure and accurately report on its readiness to withstand cyber-threats, operators need a common measurement apparatus in addition to standard controls.

Providers of critical infrastructure have turned to cybersecurity capability maturity models to provide a framework for assessing and reporting cybersecurity readiness. A capability maturity model improves the maturity and efficacy of controls employed to secure critical infrastructures. Such models delineate a sequence of maturity levels for a class of objects and represent an anticipated, desired, or typical evolution path of these objects shaped as discrete stages (Becker et al., 2009). This evolution should be sequential in nature and should have defined criteria for measurement (Wendler, 2012). A cybersecurity capability maturity model should be interpreted by subsector organizations of various types, structures, and sizes for the purpose of augmenting existing enterprise cybersecurity plans (U.S. Department of Energy, 2014). Cybersecurity capability maturity models have been developed for specific industry subsectors, but government implementation methods vary globally: public-private collaborations are the most common form of implementation in the United States and Canada, whereas regulatory schemas are more common in Europe and elsewhere (Yusta et al., 2011). And, as we will show in this article, the existing models tend to be descriptive, not prescriptive, in nature.

Given that cybersecurity is a global priority and a shared responsibility, there should be adequate motivation to develop more comprehensive critical infrastructure definitions and cybersecurity capability maturity models (Agresti, 2010). But, unfortunately, as we argue in this article, our toolkit of cybersecurity capability maturity models is itself insufficiently mature to address the full extent and magnitude of cyber-threats facing critical infrastructure today.

The purpose of this article is to examine current cybersecurity maturity models and evaluate their applicability to providers of interdependent critical infrastructures such as municipal governments. It contributes to practice by identifying a new category for assessing cybersecurity issues resulting from the interdependency of critical infrastructure. The article also highlights a gap in the existing cybersecurity literature relative to the adoption of capability maturity models by operators of interdependent critical infrastructures such as municipalities, which are often responsible for power, water, and emergency services, for example. By understanding this new category, researchers and practitioners alike will be better equipped to influence adoption of capability maturity models in securing and reporting on critical infrastructure cybersecurity readiness.

The article is organized as follows. First, we examine definitions of critical infrastructure and related regulat-

ory frameworks in the European Union, the United States, and Canada. Next, we outline common threats to critical infrastructure. Then, we review and categorize the characteristics of current cybersecurity capability maturity models and their applicability to critical infrastructure operators, particularly those who have interdependent systems, such as municipalities. Finally, we offer managerial recommendations for employing cybersecurity capability models, identify gaps in the literature, and highlight areas for further study.

What is Critical Infrastructure?

Critical infrastructure includes any element of a system that is required to maintain societal function, maintain health and physical security, and ensure social and economic welfare (Yusta et al., 2011). Widely accepted examples of critical infrastructure are energy and utilities, financial systems, food, transportation, government, information and communications technology, health, and water purification and distribution. However, these elements do not operate in isolation today. Increasingly, connectivity and interdependencies between such systems increase the complexity of managing critical infrastructure and modelling the risks of cybersecurity threats (Rahman et al., 2011; Xioa-Juan & Li-Zhen, 2010). Indeed, Xiao-Juan and Li-Zhen (2010) state that "the computerization and automation of critical infrastructures have led to pervasive cyber interdependencies". And, Rahman, Martí, and Srivastava (2011) discuss the difficulty in assessing the effects that failures in communications networks may have on municipal infrastructures such as hospitals and emergency services. They further state that cyber-interdependencies comprise a fundamental class of interdependency in critical infrastructure networks.

To help cope with the security risks associated with the complexity and interdependencies within various critical infrastructure systems, standards bodies and federal agencies in at least twelve countries or regions have defined criteria for security standards as well as implementation methods (Yusta et al., 2011). For example, the European Union (EU) has moved towards a legislated critical infrastructure regimen through the European Programme for Critical Infrastructure Protection (EPCIP), and the United States has adopted a cooperative model between the Department of Homeland Security and industry with the National Infrastructure and Protection Plans of 2009 and 2013. In Canada and the United Kingdom, cooperative frameworks are also in place through the National Strategy for Critical Infrastructure and the Centre for the Protection of National

Infrastructure, respectively (Table 1). As a EU member, the United Kingdom has authored its own framework as recommended in the EPCIP.

In these four examples of federal government regulatory frameworks, only the EPCIP legislates a response from government and industry operators of critical infrastructure. In the EPCIP, obligations on EU nations are specified and supports are made available for EPCIP adoption by member states. In each of the remaining three examples – Canada, the United Kingdom, and the United States – a cooperative framework between government and operators is employed to foster communication of best practices for critical infrastructure and threats against it. These frameworks rely on adoption by operators rather than mandating compliance.

The literature on critical infrastructure emphasizes the importance and difficulty of assessing the cybersecurity readiness of interdependent networks. Each of the four frameworks in Table 1 recognizes interdependencies of critical infrastructure based on geographic considerations and specifies that collaboration is required to ensure an adequate response to critical infrastructure failures. However, when defined critical infrastructure such as water and power distribution, traffic control, emergency services, and the like are considered, the linkage between interdependent critical infrastructure and municipal governments as operators of multi-faceted critical infrastructure becomes apparent. Municipal governments require a framework suitable for evaluating and reporting the readiness of their interdependent critical infrastructures.

Threats to Critical Infrastructure

As the complexity and interdependencies of critical infrastructure increase, providers of critical infrastructure must cope with increasing vulnerability of their management systems to cyber-threats. As outlined in the *US National Strategy for the Physical Protection of Critical Infrastructures and Key Assets* (Office of the US President, 2003), three effects may constitute vulnerability on a system:

1. *Direct infrastructure effect:* Cascading disruption or arrest of the functions of critical infrastructures or key assets through direct attacks on a critical node, system, or function.

2. *Indirect infrastructure effect:* Cascading disruption and financial consequences for government, society, and economy through public and private sector reactions to an attack.

3. *Exploitation of infrastructure:* Exploitation of elements of a particular infrastructure to disrupt or destroy another target.

The increasing complexity of such system vulnerabilities, and the complexity of the threats themselves, necessitates cooperation between the industry and the government. These existing and emerging trends lead to a requirement for the consistent implementation of cybersecurity by industry stakeholders, key infrastructure providers, and government in order to protect critical infrastructure vital to financial, commercial, and social well being.

Table 1. Examples of cybersecurity regulations and frameworks

Region	Regulation	Model
European Union	European Programme for Critical Infrastructure Protection (EPCIP) tinyurl.com/nwgajk2	Regulation
Canada	National Strategy for Critical Infrastructure (NSCI) tinyurl.com/qcvryqv	Cooperative Framework
United Kingdom	Centre for the Protection of National Infrastructure (CPNI) tinyurl.com/kuplrq5	Cooperative Framework
United States	National Infrastructure and Protection Plan (NIPP 2013) tinyurl.com/n5ppvhs	Cooperative Framework

Cybersecurity Capability Maturity Models

Increased awareness of threats to constituents, and compliance frameworks at the federal government and industry levels, have created a need to assess and report on the readiness of the critical infrastructure provider using cybersecurity capability maturity models. With their roots in the software industry, capability maturity models originally represented a path of improvements recommended for organizations that want to increase their software process capability (Wendler, 2012). Typically, a capability maturity model has two components: i) a means of measuring and describing the development of an object in a sequential manner showing hierarchical progression, and ii) criteria for measuring the capabilities of the objects such as conditions, processes, or application targets. Together, these components provide a sequence of maturity levels for a class of objects. In other words, a capability maturity model represents an anticipated, desired, or typical evolution path of these objects shaped as discrete stages (Becker et al., 2009). They allow an organization to examine its capabilities sequentially in multiple dimensions and show hierarchical progression, thereby generating yardsticks representing defined maturity levels.

The concept of capability maturity models has been extended to the domain of cybersecurity and can be applied to the protection of critical infrastructure. In lieu of simple checklists, managers now have well-defined criteria against which to measure the maturity of their preparedness against cyber-threats (Debreceny, 2006; Lahrmann et al., 2011; Siponen, 2002), with models shifting from early examples such as the International Organization for Standardization's Systems Security Engineering Capability Maturity Model (SSE-CMM), Citigroup's Information Security Evaluation Model (CITI-ISEM) and Computer Emergency Response Team / CSO Online at Carnegie Mellon University (CERT/CSO) around the turn of the century to modern initiatives such as the current International Organization for Standardization (ISO/IEC) standards, the National Institute of Standards and Technology (NIST) Cybersecurity framework, the U.S. Department of Energy's Cybersecurity Capability Maturity Model (C2M2), and the U.S. Department of Homeland Security's NICE-CMM released in 2014. These modern cybersecurity capability maturity models provide the stages for an evolutionary path to developing policies and processes for the security and reporting of cybersecurity readiness of critical infrastructure.

The U.S. Department of Energy's C2M2, as well as the companion capability maturity models ES-C2M2 and ONG-C2M2, provides a maturity model and evaluation tool to facilitate cybersecurity readiness for operators of energy production and distribution networks. However, this tool is specific to the energy sector, which limits its applicability.

The U.S. Department of Homeland Security's NICE-CMM and the Software Engineering Institute at Carnegie Mellon University focus on workforce development, process maturity, and operational resilience practices to aid organizations in cybersecurity readiness. They do not offer specific cybersecurity best practices, however. Additional frameworks must be employed in conjunction with these models.

The ISO standards provide guidance covering the range of device certification (ISO/IEC 15408), information security management systems (ISO/IEC 27001), and software security engineering processes (ISO/IEC 21827 or SSE-CMM). Used together, these standards provide a complementary regimen for an organization's cybersecurity readiness; however, navigating the many standards is complicated and has time and cost implications.

The NIST cybersecurity framework provides a set of activities to aid organizations in developing individual readiness profiles. Although this framework is robust, it relies on operators to voluntarily develop individual profiles for their organizations.

The models described here – and summarized in Table 2 – provide guidance for organizations to prepare cybersecurity readiness plans, but aside from the ISO standards, they offer only high-level advice, and many apply only to specific industry verticals. The ISO standards, while offering more specific advice, are complicated to implement and do not specifically address our operators of interdependent critical infrastructure such as municipal governments. Thus, a model specific to this category of operator is required to adequately prepare for the possible cyber-attacks on municipal critical infrastructure.

Adoption of Cybersecurity Capability Maturity Models

Our review of the available cybersecurity capability maturity models shows that they are complicated to implement, have time and cost implications, and an

Table 2. Cybersecurity capability maturity models for critical infrastructure

Model	Publisher	Purpose
C2M2 (tinyurl.com/kvtuacm)	US Dept. of Energy	Assessment of cybersecurity capabilities for any organization comprised of a maturity model and evaluation tool
ES-C2M2 (tinyurl.com/pe62edg)	US Dept. of Energy	C2M2 tailored to energy subsector
ONG-C2M2 (tinyurl.com/mx3qzyk)	US Dept. of Energy	C2M2 tailored to the oil and natural gas subsector
NICE-CMM (tinyurl.com/m3224qv)	US Dept. of Homeland Security	Defines three areas: process and analytics, integrated governance, skilled practitioners and technology for workforce development
CERT-RMM (tinyurl.com/mp85m7y)	CERT/SEI	Defines organizational practices for operational resilience, security, and business continuity
ISO/IEC 15408 (tinyurl.com/mvw3dxl)	ISO	Criteria for computer security certification
ISO/IEC 27001 (tinyurl.com/kh2t2uo)	ISO	Information Security Management System (ISMS) specification
ISO/IEC 21827 SSE-CMM (tinyurl.com/obfeup3)	ISO	Evaluation of software security engineering processes
NIST Cybersecurity Framework (tinyurl.com/kugdfug)	NIST	Framework for improving federal critical infrastructure through a set of activities designed to develop individual profiles for operators

organization's processes may need to be refined during implementation. However, three of the regulatory frameworks in Table 1 rely on their voluntary adoption by operators of critical infrastructure, leading us to ponder how adoption of these models can be fostered effectively in an unlegislated environment.

Rogers (1983) explains that large organizations such as municipalities can be seen as laggards in his diffusion of innovation adopter categories. Diffusion of innovation theory also identifies five factors that impact adoption: relative advantage (i.e., the value that the innovation provides over the current method); compatibility (i.e., how easily the innovation incorporates into the current routine), simplicity (i.e., whether the innovation is difficult to use); trialability (i.e., how easy it is to try the innovation without commitment); and observability (i.e., how visible the innovation is in a community of the adopter's peers). Considering these five factors and the adopter categories, several categories of motiv-

ators and capabilities must be addressed to prompt adoption of cybersecurity capability maturity models by a given operator.

For example, increased observability of vulnerabilities by a critical-infrastructure operator peer group can inform executives on the will and direction of their association and may form the impetus for adoption by the industry. Similarly, enhancing the regulatory frameworks shown in Table 1 or brand damage resulting from exploitation can inform executives on their obligations to securing critical infrastructure and form the impetus for adoption. The availability of applicable capability maturity models for the operator and competent staff may address the factors of simplicity and trialability. We contend that applying diffusion of innovation theory to assess adoption methods will help build a cybersecurity capability maturity model for operators of interdependent critical infrastructure such as municipal governments.

Conclusion

Modern society has become increasingly dependent on the computers and systems that control our critical infrastructure and in doing so have created a scenario whereby a cyber-attack can have serious impacts on our way of life. In the case of municipal governments that operate a network of interdependent systems, the impacts of such a cyber-attack could be far reaching. The unique properties and criticality of these entities constitutes a new category of critical infrastructure provider that warrants study.

Our review of the current cybersecurity capability maturity models highlighted that, although many models exist, none are specifically crafted to address the scenario of an operator of multiple interdependent systems. Rather, they are focused on federal infrastructures or specific industry sub-sectors, and are all at a high level. The absence of a cybersecurity capability maturity model for municipal governments provides an opportunity for further research to industry experts and researchers of cybersecurity capability maturity models.

Although the regulatory frameworks shown in Table 1 provide clear definitions of critical infrastructure and the need to secure them, they lacked a focus on adoption of cybersecurity capability maturity models, relying on operators to define and adopt best practices. We postulate that Rogers' (1983) diffusion of innovation theory can be applied when building and facilitating industry adoption of a cybersecurity capability maturity model for municipal operators of critical infrastructure, and this topic may be worthy of further study.

This article contributes to the literature in two ways.

1. It identifies a new category for operators of *interdependent networks of critical infrastructure*, highlighting the need for a cybersecurity capability maturity model for operators such as municipal governments.

2. It highlights a gap in the literature relative to the adoption of cybersecurity capability maturity models, particularly at the municipal level, providing an opportunity for further research.

In summary, this article discussed critical infrastructure, cybersecurity capability maturity models, and factors affecting their adoption. We found that there is an opportunity to develop a cybersecurity capability maturity model that better addresses the unique properties of operators of interdependent critical infrastructures. Researchers may seize the opportunities for further study on cybersecurity capability maturity models and their adoption. Operators should consider Rogers' five-factors when reviewing their plans for augmenting their cybersecurity readiness.

About the Authors

Walter Miron is a Director of Technology Strategy at TELUS Communications, where he is responsible for the evolution of their packet and optical networks. He has over 20 years of experience in enterprise and service provider networking conducting technology selection and service development projects. Walter is a member of the research program committee of the SAVI project, the Heavy Reading Global Ethernet Executive Council, and the ATOPs SDN/nFV Working Group. He is also Chair of the Venus Cybersecurity Corporation and a board member of the Centre of Excellence for Next Generation Networking (CENGN) in Ottawa, Canada. Walter is currently a graduate student in the Technology Innovation Management (TIM) program at Carleton University in Ottawa, Canada.

Kevin Muita is a graduate student in the Technology Innovation Management program at Carleton University in Ottawa, Canada. He has a Bachelor's degree in Technology from Africa Nazarene University in Nairobi, Kenya. He has co-founded two technology startups: a network consultancy company and a systems installation and maintenance company. He has experience in logistics and supply chain management, having managed a Coca-Cola distribution network in Kenya, overseeing a successful 300% increase in sales volume, operations, and service delivery.

References

Agresti, W. 2010.The Four Forces Shaping Cybersecurity. *Computer*, 43(2): 101-104.
http://dx.doi.org/10.1109/MC.2010.53

Becker, J., Knackstedt, R., & Pöppelbuß, J. 2009. Developing Maturity Models for IT Management. *Business & Information Systems Engineering*, 1(3): 213-222.
http://dx.doi.org/10.1007/s12599-009-0044-5

Chaplin, D. A., & Akridge, S. 2005. How Can Security Be Measured? *Information Systems Control Journal*, 2.

Debreceny, R. S. 2006. Re-Engineering IT Internal Controls: Applying Capability Maturity Models to the Evaluation of IT Controls. *Proceedings of the 39th Annual Hawaii International Conference on System Sciences:* 196c.
http://dx.doi.org/10.1109/HICSS.2006.407

Dupont, B. 2013. Cybersecurity Futures: How Can We Regulate Emergent Risks? *Technology Innovation Management Review*, 3(7): 6-11.
http://timreview.ca/article/700

European Commission. 2013. Critical Infrastructure. European Commission, Home Affairs. July 20, 2014:
http://ec.europa.eu/dgs/home-affairs/what-we-do/policies/crisis-and-terrorism/critical-infrastructure/index_en.htm

Grau, D., & Kennedy, C. 2014. TIM Lecture Series – The Business of Cybersecurity. *Technology Innovation Management Review*, 4(4): 53-57.
http://timreview.ca/article/785

Lahrmann, G., Marx, F., Mettler, T., Winter, R., & Wortmann, F. 2011. Inductive Design of Maturity Models: Applying the Rasch Algorithm for Design Science Research. In H. Jain, A. P. Sinha, & P. Vitharana (Eds.), *Service-Oriented Perspectives in Design Science Research:* 176–191. Berlin: Springer.
http//dx.doi.org/10.1007/978-3-642-20633-7_13

Office of the US President. 2003. *National Strategy for the Physical Protection of Critical Infrastructures and Key Assets*. Washington, DC: The White House.
http://www.dhs.gov/national-strategy-physical-protection-critical-infrastructure-and-key-assets

Public Safety Canada. 2009. *National Strategy for Critical Infrastructure*. Ottawa: Government of Canada.
http://www.publicsafety.gc.ca/cnt/rsrcs/pblctns/srtg-crtcl-nfrstrctr/index-eng.aspx

Rahman, H. A., Martí, J. R., & Srivastava, K. D. 2011. A Hybrid Systems Model to Simulate Cyber Interdependencies between Critical Infrastructures. *International Journal of Critical Infrastructures*, 7(4): 265–288.
http://dx.doi.org/10.1504/IJCIS.2011.045056

Rogers, E. M. 1983. *Diffusion of Innovations*. New York: Free Press.

Siponen, M. 2002. Towards Maturity of Information Security Maturity Criteria: Six Lessons Learned from Software Maturity Criteria. *Information Management & Computer Security*, 10(5): 210–224.
http://dx.doi.org/10.1108/09685220210446560

U.S. Department of Energy. 2014. *Oil and Natural Gas Subsector Cybersecurity Capability Maturity Model (ONG-C2M2 v1.1)*. Washington, DC: U.S. Department of Energy.
http://energy.gov/oe/downloads/oil-and-natural-gas-subsector-cybersecurity-capability-maturity-model-february-2014

U.S. Department of Homeland Security. 2013. What Is Critical Infrastructure? Washington, DC: U.S. Department of Homeland Security. July 20, 2014:
http://www.dhs.gov/what-critical-infrastructure

Wendler, R. 2012. The Maturity of Maturity Model Research: A Systematic Mapping Study. *Information and Software Technology*, 54(12): 1317-1339.
http://dx.doi.org/10.1016/j.infsof.2012.07.007

Xiao-Juan, L., & Li-Zhen, H. 2010. Vulnerability and Interdependency of Critical Infrastructure: A Review. *Third International Conference on Infrastructure Systems and Services: Next Generation Infrastructure Systems for Eco-Cities (INFRA):* 1–5.
http://dx.doi.org/10.1109/INFRA.2010.5679237

Yusta, J. M., Correa, G. J., & Lacal-Arántegui, R. 2011. Methodologies and Applications for Critical Infrastructure Protection: State-of-the-Art. *Energy Policy*, 39(10): 6100–6119.
http://dx.doi.org/10.1016/j.enpol.2011.07.010

Keywords: cybersecurity, critical infrastructure, capability maturity models, municipalities, standards, compliance, protection, regulation, framework, adoption

7

Challenges in Maritime Cyber-Resilience

Lars Jensen

" *Maritime cyber-attacks are no longer the stuff of* "
science fiction. They are happening now, and the
threats are growing.

Fred Roberts
Professor of Mathematics and Director of CCICADA

The maritime industry has been shown to be under increasing levels of cyber-attack, with future attacks having the potential to severely disrupt critical infrastructure. The industry lacks a standardized approach to cybersecurity, a national approach will be counterproductive, and a global mandatory standard, while needed, will take a long time to implement. In the shorter term, this article recommends that the industry coalesce around a set of voluntary guidelines in order to reduce the risk profile and increase resilience. To provide context for these recommendations, this article examines the specific characteristics of the maritime industry in relation to cybersecurity. Examples of existing vulnerabilities and reported cyber-attacks demonstrate that the threat is current and real.

Introduction

The maritime industry is the foundation for the efficient functioning of all aspects of modern society, from the supply of raw materials such as oil, iron, and grain to virtually every product on the shelves of the local stores and supermarkets – and it is wide open to disruptive cyber-attacks.

In the wake of the 9/11 attacks on the Twin Towers in New York, the maritime industry saw an escalation in physical security procedures aimed at reducing the risk of paralyzing vital infrastructure; in particular, there was a focus on port security (IMO, 2015). However, a similarly security-conscious approach is found to be lacking in relation to cyber-risks. As this article will demonstrate, a closer investigation of the landscape of both cyber-threats and actual incidents in the maritime sector, shows that risks are indeed real and that the impact of an attack can range far beyond the company being attacked.

A hypothetical scenario to illustrate the point would be a cyber-attack that involved the deletion of operational data in a few large container shipping terminals. Such an attack would choke the entire supply chain for tens of thousands of companies. The 100 largest container ports globally each handle in excess of one million 20-foot containers annually (Lloyds List, 2014). Shutting down just a handful within the same geographical region means that the overflow cannot be handled elsewhere. The economic impact on society would be large. In 2002, the key ports on the western coast of the United States were shut down for ten days due to a labour dispute. At that point in time, it was estimated that this had a cost to the United States economy of $1-2 billion USD per day due to disrupted supply chains (Cohen 2002). Since then, the volume of containerized trade has grown significantly, and hence a cyber-attack shutting down key ports can thus be expected to have an even larger impact on the national economy of the affected country – or countries.

Four key sources provide an overall perspective on this issue:

1. A study by the European Union Agency for Network and Information Security (ENISA, 2011) provides a baseline analysis of maritime cybersecurity and the related policy context.

2. A policy paper by The Brookings Institution focused on critical infrastructure cyber-vulnerabilities in port facilities in the United States (Kramek, 2013).

3. A United States Senate (2014) inquiry into cyber-intrusions emphasized the threat of cyber-attacks on the networks of the United States Transportation Command, which is responsible for Department of Defense transportation, including maritime transportation.

4. A whitepaper issued by the author's maritime cybersecurity company, CyberKeel (2014a), examined the vulnerability of the maritime industry to various cyber-risks and highlighted its lack of adequate defenses.

Generally, these studies all arrived at the same conclusion, albeit while covering different sub-domains. The various authors found the levels of cybersecurity to be very low and that significant and dedicated efforts were needed to improve the situation. They furthermore showed that the amount of publically reported incidents do not represent the actual amount of malicious activity ongoing in the industry – a fact particularly underscored by the US Senate inquiry, which revealed a large gap in reporting despite such reporting being mandatory in stated contractual terms with suppliers.

This article aims to propose immediate and longer-term steps the industry can take to improve its cyber-resilience. It will initially examine the specific characteristics of the maritime industry that are of importance in relation to cybersecurity. It will assess whether certain types of threats are to be considered theoretical or whether they have in fact already been seen, and then it will identify the likely entities behind the threats. Finally, the emerging view of the industry will be used to recommend how cybersecurity and cyber-resilience can be improved in the maritime industry in both the short and long term.

Industry Characteristics

In terms of cyber security, the maritime industry has a range of characteristics that makes it difficult to implement solid cyber-defenses. To illustrate the point, it is worthwhile examining how a generic container shipping line operates. A large container shipping line will have offices spread across 150 different countries. They own, and hence control, half of these offices, but for the other half, they rely on the services of local agents. The shipping line thus has to share access to key backend systems with a large number of local agents who have their own IT infrastructure, and where the shipping line usually has extremely limited insight, and influence, on the cybersecurity standards.

Additionally, the shipping line may be operating a fleet of 300 vessels of which they own 150. The other 150 vessels are chartered from a wide range of vessel-owning companies for short- or medium-term duration. The shipping line will not have the ability to control the IT structure onboard vessels chartered for a shorter period. Even for the vessels the shipping line owns, cybersecurity on vessels tend to be an issue. In many shipping companies, the IT department located at headquarters tends to be in charge of land-based IT systems, whereas the vessel-based IT systems fall under the purview of the marine technical department – who often have very limited IT background knowledge. Adding to the challenges, the shipping line may not be the one fully in control over the crewing of the vessel, hence opening an avenue for social engineering intrusion on board the vessels themselves. A tangible example of such a scenario was shared with CyberKeel by a physical maritime security company. They had experienced a vessel approaching the Gulf of Aden, which at the time had a significant piracy risk. However, prior to entering the Gulf of Aden, it was discovered that a person onboard the vessel had been uploading significant amounts of images to a Facebook account – images that provided a detailed look into the safety measures in place on the vessel. The ability to do this is a consequence of the recent, rapid roll-out of "crew welfare", which is the term most often used to indicate making Internet access available to crew using satellite connections.

Finally, when a container is moved from point A to point B, the information related to this movement may pass through between 10 and 50 different systems, each being controlled by different entities such as ports, customs offices, trucking companies, banks, shared-service centres, and industry information portals. These entities do not share a common IT infrastructure, nor do they have any agreed cybersecurity standards. At CyberKeel, we have asked several of the major players in the industry who provide IT systems or IT services how often their customers ask about the cybersecurity aspects of a link-up. The answers are that this is not the norm, the discussion is basically focused on functionality. Given that the successful movement of illicit cargo, or the theft of cargo, only requires successful penetration of one or two of these many hand-over points, it is easy to see how this system can be utilized by criminal elements.

The industry is hence characterized by companies who may have solid control of central parts of their own IT landscape, but have limited – or no – control over more "remote" parts of the landscape. These remote parts thus present an easy access approach to attacks directed at the central elements of the IT landscape.

Is the Threat Genuine?

As CyberKeel approached management layers in many maritime companies in the first half of 2014 on the topic of cybersecurity, many voiced the opinion that the threats appeared to be more theoretical than real. After all, the fact that something can be done is not the same as somebody actually going through the trouble of doing it.

As a consequence, CyberKeel issued a whitepaper (Cyberkeel, 2014a) and subsequently started a monthly newsletter called Marine Cyberwatch (tinyurl.com/ozxukd5) including an identifications of actual attacks across the maritime sector. Some attacks had already been known, particularly within the cybersecurity sector, but still appeared to be relatively unknown by maritime managers. Additionally, a number of attacks were described that, until then, had been relatively unknown.

One such incident was a cyber-attack against the Iranian shipping line IRISL, which took place in August 2011 (cited in CyberKeel, 2014a). The attacks damaged all the data related to rates, loading, cargo number, date and place, meaning that "no-one knew where containers were, whether they had been loaded or not, which boxes were onboard the ships or onshore" (CyberKeel, 2014a). Although the correct data was eventually restored, the company's operations were significantly impacted: the company's internal communication network was disrupted, cargo was sent to the wrong destinations, and the company suffered severe financial losses in addition to losses of actual cargo. A similar attack on a major international container line would have a crippling effect on the supply chains of thousands of international companies.

Another incident was first reported by CyberKeel based on a forensic analysis performed by Clearsky, a cyber-intelligence company (CyberKeel, 2014b). A number of maritime companies – principally shipping lines and bunker fuel suppliers – were infiltrated with a remote access tool. This remote access was used to monitor email communication and subsequently spoof the communication resulting in a change of bank account information pertaining to large payments. This type of incident is also known in other industries, but was first reported in the maritime sector in late 2014.

In addition to identifying actual attacks, CyberKeel made a simple investigation of the 50 largest container shipping lines who collectively control 94% of the global container vessel fleet (CyberKeel, 2014a). The investigation was simple in the sense that only two aspects were tested. One test was for potential SQL injection vulnerabilities; the other was a simple Shodan search for accessible hardware running a systems version with known exploits available. The results were that 37 out of the 50 carriers exhibited vulnerabilities.

Who Performs the Attacks

The motivations of the attackers in the maritime sector appear no different than in a number of other industry sectors. Some attacks are motivated by financial gain, though from various angles. Some, as illustrated earlier, aim at stealing money directly from the targeted companies. Others are aimed at, for example, contraband cargo. A widely publicized cyber-intrusion enabled a drug smuggling operation through the port of Antwerp (Bateman, 2013), where the terminal operation system had been penetrated, allowing smugglers to extract containers from the terminal using manipulated data.

Another type of attack is aimed at potentially infiltrating, controlling, or damaging critical infrastructure. The global shipping industry is undeniably an element of critical infrastructure to all nations, given that a disruption could have a significant impact on national economies – not to mention the ramifications of disrupting shipping services related to military operations. The report from the US Senate inquiry described earlier documented 50 intrusions into suppliers for the United States Transportation Command in a span of one year (United States Senate, 2014). In terms of shipping, the report also noted that commercial vessels handled 95% of all military dry cargoes in 2012.

Conclusion

In the context of cyber-crime related to the theft of money, the maritime industry is fundamentally no different from other industries. Criminals will use weaknesses to obtain a financial payoff, and the main victim of such attacks is the company losing the money. However, the nature of shipping also results in a situation where cyber-attacks, even those "only" aimed at a single company, can have significant ripple effects into entire national economies. As an example, a ransomware attack against a few key container terminals can cripple an entire national or regional supply chain, resulting in losses significantly out of proportion with the loss suffered by the company under attack. Or, even worse, remote tampering with on-board vessel systems – something that has been demonstrated as feasible – can result in catastrophic effects with not only economic but also significant environmental impacts.

In order to improve the situation, it is important that the maritime industry rapidly develops a set of best practice guidelines to improve the situation, while at the same time working on a longer-term plan to introduce global cybersecurity standards. National governments in many places need to increase their awareness of the critical vulnerabilities of their port infrastructure systems and provide the necessary support to allow for an improvement in cybersecurity.

The current challenge is that no practical guidelines are in place for the maritime sector, and given the global nature of the maritime industry, nationally mandated guidelines are highly likely to become conflicting and hence counterproductive as vessels move across different national jurisdictions.

Reaching a consensus on standards would require the involvement of the International Maritime Organization (IMO; www.imo.org); however, this process will likely take many years to come to fruition. In the interim, a practical approach would be the rapid establishment of voluntary global guidelines that heighten security industry-wide, and such an approach could be beneficially anchored with industry-wide best practice forums such as the Baltic and International Maritime Council (BIMCO; bimco.org). Such anchoring would allow maritime companies to pool their resources related to the necessary analysis and research, as well as attract the attention of IT companies towards dedicated maritime cybersecurity solutions. This approach would further support the adoption of voluntary guidelines.

Maritime organizations should then be encouraged to adopt these voluntary guidelines using three principal tools: i) informational campaigns directed at the maritime companies in terms of the cyber-risks they face; ii) pressure from customers who are made increasingly aware of the risk to their cargo in cases where maritime companies lack cyber-defenses; and finally iii) "cyber-premiums" on insurance policies that reflect the degree to which maritime companies adhere to the voluntary guidelines. Also, national governments could play a key role in helping identify and map out the cyber-risks faced by maritime companies within their own domain, and make such analyses readily available to maritime companies. Additionally, governments could emphasize collaboration with the IMO to fast-track the development and adoption of more binding cyber-standards in the future. Together, these steps would bring us greater cyber-resilience for the efficient functioning of the maritime industry, upon which we all depend.

About the Author

Lars Jensen is CEO and Co-Founder of CyberKeel, an international maritime cybersecurity company based in Copenhagen, Denmark. He is a recognized global expert in container shipping markets, having worked initially working for Maersk Line, where he was responsible for global intelligence and analysis as well as e-Commerce. In 2011, he founded SeaIntel Maritime Analysis, and he is currently the CEO of SeaIntel Consulting in addition to being CEO of CyberKeel. He holds a PhD in Theoretical Physics from the University of Copenhagen, and he has received strategy and leadership training from the London Business School and the Copenhagen Business School.

References

Bateman, T. 2013. Police Warning after Drug Traffickers' Cyber-Attack. *BBC News*, October 16, 2013. Accessed April 1, 2015: http://www.bbc.com/news/world-europe-24539417

Cohen, S. S. 2002. *Economic Impact of a West Coast Dock Shutdown.* Berkeley, CA: Berkeley Roundtable on the International Economy. http://www.brie.berkeley.edu/publications/ships%202002%20final.pdf

CyberKeel. 2014a. *Maritime Cyber-Risks: Virtual Pirates at Large on the Cyber Seas.* Copenhagen: CyberKeel. http://www.cyberkeel.com/images/pdf-files/Whitepaper.pdf

CyberKeel. 2014b. Shipping Companies Successfully Penetrated for Money Transfers. *Marine Cyberwatch*, October: 1. http://www.cyberkeel.com/images/pdf-files/Oct2014.pdf

ENISA. 2011. *Cyber Security Aspects in the Maritime Sector.* Heraklion, Greece: European Union Agency for Network and Information Security. http://www.enisa.europa.eu/activities/Resilience-and-CIIP/critical-infrastructure-and-services/dependencies-of-maritime-transport-to-icts/cyber-security-aspects-in-the-maritime-sector-1

IMO. 2015. Frequently Asked Questions on Maritime Security. *International Maritime Organization.* Accessed April 1, 2015: http://www.imo.org/OurWork/Security/Guide_to_Maritime_Security/Pages/FAQ.aspx

Kramek, J. 2013. *The Critical Infrastructure Gap: U.S. Port Facilities and Cyber Vulnerabilities.* Washington, DC: Brookings Institution. http://www.brookings.edu/research/papers/2013/07/03-cyber-ports-security-kramek

Lloyds List. 2014. *One Hundred Ports.* London: Informa Publishing. http://europe.nxtbook.com/nxteu/informa/ci_top100ports2014/#/6

United States Senate. 2014. *Inquiry into Cyber Intrusions Affecting U.S. Transportation Command Contractors.* Washington, DC: United States Senate Committee on Armed Services. http://www.armed-services.senate.gov/imo/media/doc/SASC_Cyberreport_091714.pdf

Keywords: maritime, cyber-resilience, cyber-risk, cybersecurity, CyberKeel, container, terminal, vessel

8

Cybersecurity Metrics and Simulation

George Cybenko

" *Given the continual onslaught of successful cyber-attacks against* " *banks, governments, and retailers, one has to wonder whether any progress is being made in computer security at all. How is it possible to reconcile the huge investments that have been made in securing networks and computers with the fact that attackers are still routinely breaching what should be highly protected networks? What metrics can explain the situation and how can we evaluate those metrics through simulation or other means?*

George Cybenko
Professor of Engineering, Dartmouth College

Overview

The TIM Lecture Series is hosted by the Technology Innovation Management program (timprogram.ca) at Carleton University in Ottawa, Canada. The lectures provide a forum to promote the transfer of knowledge between university research to technology company executives and entrepreneurs as well as research and development personnel. Readers are encouraged to share related insights or provide feedback on the presentation or the TIM Lecture Series, including recommendations of future speakers.

The sixth TIM lecture of 2014 was held at Carleton University on October 8th, and was presented by George Cybenko, the Dorothy and Walter Gramm Professor of Engineering at Dartmouth College in New Hampshire, United States. In the first part of his lecture, Cybenko provided an overview possible security metrics together with their pros and cons in the context of current IT security practices. In the second part of the lecture, Cybenko presented a modelling and simulation approach that produces meaningful quantitative security metrics as the basis for a more rigorous science of cybersecurity.

Summary

To begin his lecture, Cybenko highlighted the many high-profile cyber-attacks that dominate headlines today, which stand in contrast to massive investments in cybersecurity research and practices, as well as the creation of many cybersecurity companies, over the past 10 to 15 years. Thus, he then challenged the research community – himself included – to demonstrate

greater progress over the next 10 years in terms of our capacity to mitigate the impacts of cyber-attacks. And, in introducing the key subject of his lecture, he pointed to the potential for cybersecurity metrics and simulation as a promising avenue to facilitate such progress.

To be effective, cybersecurity metrics should be:

1. *Reproducible:* when measuring a particular phenomenon, two people should be able to independently arrive at the same results.

2. *Relevant:* organizations must find the metrics operationally relevant and actionable.

3. *A basis for comparison:* metrics must facilitate comparisons between architectures, applications, systems, networks, etc.

4. *A basis for claims:* metrics must facilitate evaluations of systems and architectures to quantify their suitability to particular applications.

In developing metrics, we must also take into account the computer security lifecycle, which progresses from security concepts (i.e., an understanding of the technology and relevant threats), to architecture (i.e., an abstraction of the design), to implementation (i.e., code, hardware, support, and access), and then to operations (i.e., forensics on past events, real-time monitoring and patching of present conditions, and predicting future events). Metrics must be considered at each step in the lifecycle so that they can be effective once the operations stage is reached.

Next, Cybenko recognized a common skeptical view of security metrics, which, in its extreme form, rejects the need for metrics altogether, arguing that a system is either secure or it is not. However, when challenged to provide an example of a secure system, such skeptics struggle to come up with definitive examples. Thus, in practice, it is worthwhile recognizing a spectrum of computer security and using metrics to try to evaluate just how secure a given system is.

Proposed approaches to cybersecurity metrics include:

1. *Penetration testing:* automated tools that run a set of exploits against a network; by definition, penetration tests use only known exploits and cannot assess vulnerabilities or weaknesses that might be revealed by a human attacker.

2. *Red teams:* expert hackers hired to assess or attempt to break into a system; however, the perceived protection level is limited to the expenditure on testing (i.e., a company may pay a "Red Team" $X to assess a system, but hackers would expend effort exceeding $X to reach assets of greater value, and much greater human effort may expended for the same cost in countries where the labour rate is much lower).

3. *Compliance:* controls and standards for development, software, architecture, etc.; the protection level is only as good as the compliance standards; can redirect an organization's security expenditure away from novel and up-to-date approaches.

4. *Response times:* how quickly is a system patched? How quickly does an organization identify and respond to incidents? What is the optimal policy for disclosing vulnerabilities?

5. *Software size, complexity, and constructs:* may be indicators of security vulnerability

Each of these approaches has its benefits and shortcomings; however, it may be more useful to think about the field of cybersecurity metrics within the context of risk analysis. Thus, the expected cost of security may be calculated based on the probability and costs of potential losses. For example, in cases where expected losses due to fraud and intrusions exceed the costs of technology updates, the justification for improved technology becomes clear.

Next, in the second part of the lecture, Cybenko presented an alternative, simulation-based approach to cybersecurity metrics, which attempt to quantify cybersecurity. In particular, he focused on the QuERIES methodology, which was also detailed in Cybenko's 2013 article in the TIM Review (Hughes & Cybenko, 2013). The QuERIES methodology quantifies cybersecurity risk following an analogy from physical security, where the "time to compromise" in a system is a measureable performance metric. In cybersecurity, the time it takes an attacker to complete a successful attack against a protected software system provides a similar metric, which can be simulated and then presented in a probability distribution.

The QuERIES methodology simulates the value of success to an attacker if they are able to succeed within a particular amount of time. Thus, the value of the asset to an attacker changes over time because there is a cost to continued effort, and at some point, no amount of effort may be worth the value of the target asset. And, this type of risk-analysis approach is used to assess the progression of cyber-attack, it becomes possible to calculate the optimal time for an attacker to abandon an attack based on the cost of the attack and the value of the asset. Ideally, cybersecurity defenses could be sufficiently robust that the attacker's cost of attacking would be prohibitively high, and an attack would not even be initiated.

For a fuller explanation of the QuERIES methodology, see:

Hughes, J., & Cybenko, G. 2013. Quantitative Metrics and Risk Assessment: The Three Tenets Model of Cybersecurity. *Technology Innovation Management Review,* 3(8): 15–24. http://timreview.ca/article/712

About the Speaker

George Cybenko is the Dorothy and Walter Gramm Professor of Engineering at Dartmouth College in New Hampshire, United States. He has made multiple research contributions in signal processing, neural computing, information security, and computational behavioural analysis. He was the Founding Editor-in-Chief of both IEEE/AIP Computing in Science and Engineering and IEEE Security & Privacy. He has served on the Defense Science Board (2008–2009), on the US Air Force Scientific Advisory Board (2012–2015), and on review and advisory panels for DARPA, IDA, and Lawrence Livermore National Laboratory. Cybenko is a Fellow of the IEEE and received his BS (Toronto) and PhD (Princeton) degrees in Mathematics.

This report was written by Chris McPhee.

Keywords: cybersecurity, metrics, simulation, modelling

9

Formulating an Executive Strategy for Big Data Analytics

Gopalakrishna Palem

" Without big data analytics, companies are blind and "
deaf, wandering out onto the web like deer on a freeway.

Geoffrey Moore
Organization Theorist and Author

The recent surge in big data technologies has left many executives, both of well-established organizations and emerging startups, wondering how best to harness big data. In particular, the analytics aspect of big data is enticing for both information technology (IT) service providers and non-IT firms because of its potential for high returns on investment, which have been heavily publicized, if not clearly demonstrated, by multiple whitepapers, webinars, and research surveys. Although executives may clearly perceive the benefits of big data analytics to their organizations, the path to the goal is not as clear or easy as it looks. And, it is not just the established organizations that have this challenge; even startups trying to take advantage of this big data analytics opportunity are facing the same problem of lack of clarity on what to do or how to formulate an executive strategy. This article is primarily for executives who are looking for help in formulating a strategy for achieving success with big data analytics in their operations. It provides guidelines to them plan an organization's short-term and long-term goals, and presents a strategy tool, known as the delta model, to develop a customer-centric approach to success with big data analytics.

Introduction

The idea of analyzing terabytes of data in under an hour was, for most people, unimaginable just a few short years ago. But, thanks to big data, it is a reality today. But what is big data? When trying to understand what big data is all about and how it helps any organization, the concept can be represented in two different ways: i) big data as a storage platform and ii) big data as a solution enabler.

As a storage platform, big data is a means of storing large volumes of data from a variety of sources in a reliable (i.e., fault-tolerant) way. For example, big data solutions can reliably store real-time data from sensors, RFID tags, GPS locators, and web logs, thereby enabling near real-time access to millions of users simultaneously.

As a solution enabler, big data offers distributed computing using a large number of networked machines to re-duce the total "time-to-solution". For example, exploratory analysis on large volumes of credit card data to identify any signals of fraud, known as fraud detection, usually requires hours or even days to complete. But, with big data techniques, such complex and large computations are distributed across multiple networked machines all running in parallel, thereby reducing the total time it takes to arrive at a solution.

These two representations big data – as a storage platform and as a solution enabler – go hand-in-hand and lead to what is commonly referred to as "big data analytics". Thus, big data analytics enables an organization to reliably collect and analyze large volumes of data. Furthermore, by being domain neutral, the applications of big data transcend verticals, meaning that these concepts can benefit all domains.

Some of the prominent examples where big data analytics have been used successfully by the author include:

1. Usage based insurance: Why should an aggressive driver and a decent rule-abiding driver pay the same amount of insurance premium? What if a good driver could receive discounts on their insurance as an incentive for following safety regulations that not only save lives but also reduce the driver's total carbon footprint? Usage-based insurance implements that concept by calculating the insurance amount based on the actual usage behaviour and not on preset calculations, made possible by monitoring the driver behaviour and providing incentives to the driver based on their driving habits, including even infrequent hard braking or sudden acceleration. As will be discussed in this article, big data's cloud-storage and stream-processing architecture makes this scenario possible.

2. Predictive maintenance: What if fleet managers knew beforehand how many of their vehicles were going to break down, say, in the next 100 days? And further, what if they not only knew how many vehicles, but they also knew which exact vehicles were going to break down and with which exact failure reason? Can they make alternative arrangements and save extra labour costs and repair costs and improve productivity? Thanks to big data analytics, it is all possible. Once again, the stream-processing architecture described in this article can be used to predict machine component availability and minimize downtime.

3. Epidemic outbreak detection: What if public health officials could analyze disease-causing factors and detect epidemics in real-time before they can spread out of control? One of our recent case-studies on public health data lead us to model the disease-causing factors and create an epidemic outbreak detection mechanism, all of which was made possible through the real-time stream-processing architecture for big data.

4. Sentiment Analysis: Retailers thrive on capturing market share with promotions, discounts, and sales leads. But often the voice of the customer is lost somewhere in the social media feeds and the real sense of "what works and what does not?" and "who is the potential customer and who is not?" is left uncaptured. What if an organization could capture all the social media data and monetize all the intentions to buy? What if they could gain unprecedented levels of insight into what exactly the customers are thinking about their products and which one of their competitors' products are stealing their market share? Text-mining algorithms applied to large social feeds make this possible when facilitated by big data analytics facilitates.

This list is by no means exhaustive, but each example draws upon the approach to big data analytics described in this article and depicted in Figure 1. And, these examples illustrate why big data analytics is one of the most prominent opportunities to emerge into mainstream computing in recent years. It promises easy adaptation "straight out of the box" to almost all sectors, such as healthcare, banking, retail, manufacturing, and so on, making it a very interesting opportunity for both information technology (IT) service providers and non-IT service consumers.

The cost-saving potential and new revenue opportunities big data analytics promises for businesses is another driving factor for its adoption. For example, a few of my own clients from the automotive domain that implemented big data analytics to manage their spare-part inventory and work-labour schedules based on condition-based monitoring and predictive maintenance in the recent years have reported an average of approximately 25% lower maintenance costs and 75% less machine downtime, along with overall productivity increases of 25% due to predictable work schedules and work-life balance. Similarly, customers from the retail and finance sectors are seeing new opportunities to gain customers through big data social media analytics and advanced recommendation engines capable of profiling and analyzing customers' shopping behaviours in real time. All these innovative cost-saving and revenue-generation opportunities are encouraging solution providers to include big data analytics in their service and product portfolios.

Although the general approaches to analytics have become familiar to most executives, the integration of analytics with big data presents new challenges. The key challenge is that this integration must occur in two places: i) with the real-time streaming data and ii) with the persistent historical data. Analytics then uses one or both of these datasets depending on the nature of the problem being solved and the depth of the solution.

For example, as shown in Figure 1, real-time streaming data collected from vehicles (e.g., to analyze driver behaviour) or shopping carts (e.g., to analyze the shopper behaviour) or patient health records (e.g., to detect epidemic outbreaks), is usually processed against a pre-stored historic profile data containing information such as other drivers' profiles, shoppers' profiles, disease-factor profiles, etc. The historic data is often large in volume, ranging from terabytes (1012 bytes) to petabytes (1000 Terabytes) based on the domain in question, and resides in a reliable cloud storage that is readily accessible across all data centres.

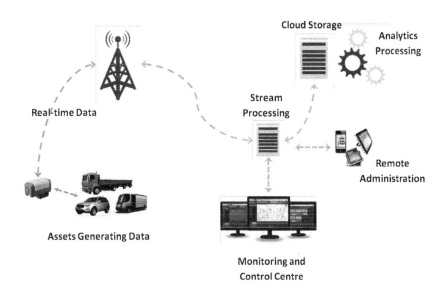

Figure 1. A typical schematic of a big data analytics solution

Processing the real-time data to identify any patterns similar to patterns in historic data is achieved through what is called stream processing. During stream processing, algorithms known as complex event processing (CEP) engines crunch the data that is streaming in real time to detect observable patterns of anomaly or significance in relation to the old data. However, sometimes, the old data may not be in a ready-to-use format (e.g., missing data points or un-normalized data set) and hence, has to be pre-processed before it can be used in the stream processing. This problem is resolved by having a dedicated analytics-processing unit that runs alongside the cloud storage, taking care of scheduling batch processes at regular time intervals to ensure all the data collected is pre-processed correctly and is in a readily usable state for the real-time stream-processing calculations.

The results of the stream-processing algorithms are then converted into statistical scores for computing a numeric index that can point to an actionable business insight, such as the eligibility of a driver for insurance based on an assessment of risk, recommendations or discounts for shoppers, alerting health administrative departments, and so on. The results are also stored in the cloud storage to act as the historical data for future data that comes in later.

A central administrative command centre will keep track of the whole operation to ensure operational compliance, and also take care of any alerts, such as taking actions to implement quarantine measures in case of epidemic outbreak signals, sending repair personnel to the breakdown spot in case of any machine or vehicle breakdown, etc. A well-designed big data analytics platform also allows remote administration capabilities, in addition to the centralized command centre, to allow the concerned personnel to be notified about any important alert or event no matter where they are, through the use of a mobile short message service (SMS) or other similar techniques, and let them take corrective action in real time, thereby reducing the total time to respond.

Big data architectures such as these have been proven to work reliably in a wide range of business cases irrespective of the domain, and they are the most basic setup required for any organization dealing with big data analytics. In the following sections, we discuss how to build such executive capabilities into their organization so that they can build similar architectural models and tools into their own operations, and how they can implement the required strategy using a customer-centric approach. Next, guidelines on laying out the short-term and long-term goals are presented, followed by competency-measure criteria to evaluate what it means to be successful in this big data analytics field. We conclude the article with a few remarks on some of the pitfalls to watch out for when implementing these techniques.

The Vision

A typical vision statement for any big data analytics organization or division would be: "to become established as the leading big data analytics solution provider in the industry". However, there is one primary challenge that needs to be resolved before such vision can be realized. Although big data analytics transcends verticals in scope, with applications to almost all sectors ranging from automotive to retail to energy and utilities, operators in the respective sectors usually lack sufficient knowledge of its usage or benefits. Thus, many organizations have become aware that they need big data, but they do not know exactly what they need it for.

This gap between an organization's perceived need for big data analytics and its level of understanding about the domain creates a unique situation where the solution providers are now responsible for thinking about the requirement for the customers, instead of customer coming up with their own requirements as happens in traditional projects. This situation puts extra burden on the providers, because they have to provide not only solutions, but also the problems!

Even if the big data analytics solution provider somehow understands the customers' needs and comes up with a solution, there is no guarantee that the existing methodologies or solutions in place for the customer are compatible with big data solutions. Most of the operators in the field still use traditional systems and databases that are geared towards traditional processing and that are not suitable for real-time analytics or large-scale data processing. The cost and effort of integration alone can turn away many customers from embracing any kind of big data solution.

Such a challenge requires solution providers to educate their customers on the applications of big data analytics to their respective domains and provide solutions that are easy to integrate into their existing infrastructure. Thus, in the initial stages, an organization's focus should be on the *solution enablers* – either building solutions in-house or adapting open source solutions, such as: i) a stream-processing framework that enables customers to rapidly adapt their existing infrastructure for real-time analytics, and ii) an Internet of Things (IOT; tinyurl.com/5qr2nq) platform that enables solutions for cloud storage and big data analytics, seamlessly bridging the gap between their existing systems and big data solutions.

However, owning the solution enablers is just a small step towards building a foundation, and it alone cannot make the vision statement come true. A full and solid foundation has to be built upon and followed-up with medium- and long-term strategy goals to realize the grand outcome. The subsections that follow illustrate a sample set of short-, medium-, and long-term goals and the steps to be taken to realize each of these goals. Short-term goals are aimed at laying out the technology foundation and building a strong customer base for sustainable revenue generation, whereas the medium-term goals strive to support the delivery functions for retaining the acquired customer base and reinforcing the customer bond with high-quality outputs and optimal schedules. Long-term goals are aimed at leading the market with innovative solutions and strategic partnerships.

Short-term goal: Lay the foundation
The following immediate activities focus on establishing the foundation upon which solutions will be built:

1. Platform building: The stream-processing and Internet of Things platform should act as the foundation for big data analytics solutions to be built upon for customers from various segments. It should encompass complete end-to-end workflow starting from real-time event capture to end-user analytics and cloud storage in a demonstrable form to clients. Targeted list of customers should be used for marketing campaigns and workshops to showcase the platform capabilities in a way that is customized to their needs. Proposals for a proof of concept also should be developed.

2. Competency building: Big data analytics is a cross-domain endeavour, and competencies need to be built for various domains for which solutions are being targeted. Competency building should focus on filling the gaps between the customer requirements and resource competencies on identified verticals. This task primarily involves increasing the analysts' comfort level with the big data technologies and the platform workflow. The integration between the two technologies happens at this stage, and analysts should proactively build customer solutions in a demonstrable form while working closely with the big data platform leaders, and the big data teams should take the analysts' feedback into account when planning platform improvements.

Short-term goal: Market penetration
Other immediate actions should focus on market penetration by improving the customer base and reach of solutions with pro-active solutions and promoted brand identity:

1. Proactive solutions: Initial response time is one of the key factors for high customer satisfaction ratings. Proactively identifying customer requirements and planning the solutions ahead, improves initial response times enormously and gives the impression of thought leadership. To start with, use cases should be identified and solutions should be proactively built for one particular vertical (e.g., automotive, healthcare) that the firm knows well and, once reasonable customer foundation is achieved, activities for the remaining verticals can be slowly expanded. Of course, if the organization is well established with enough resources and budget, it is also possible to start with multiple verticals in parallel, though in such cases, accountability and success tracking becomes a major and unnecessary burden. It is always suggested to start with identifying a core field of skill and then expand, rather than trying to tackle them all at the same time. Table 1 lists solutions that can be built for each different vertical and can be used as a starting point.

2. Brand name promotion: Brand loyalty often dictates market penetration and customer reach. Webinars, whitepapers, and research articles are a good way to expand the customer reach: they not only educate the customers but also promote brand name and associate leadership status to brand identity. Brand identity and customer education can be enriched by cultivating a publication culture among engineers. Organizations should also incorporate knowledge triage systems and encourage open knowledge sharing among teams both internally and externally, where possible. By putting their people first, creating an identity for them, and making them leaders, companies become identified as leaders in the market.

Medium-term goal: Architectural standardization
Organizations can improve the quality of the solutions and shorten the time to market through architectural standardization, as follows:

1. While developing cross-vertical solutions, recurring problem patterns should be identified and reusable tools and middleware frameworks should be created.

2. Variety in data is one of the main challenges for big data when dealing with cross-vertical solutions. In such scenarios, schema-neutral architectures capable of supporting dynamic ontologies should be designed and used for establishing standards.

3. Best-practice guidelines should be widely published and enforced among all teams to standardize the offerings and improve the solution quality.

4. Big data technologies are vast in scope, starting from large-volume data storage to real-time, high-velocity streaming and analytics. A culture of subject matter experts should be promoted and efforts should be made to increase the pool of specialist talent. These subject matter experts should be held accountable for the quality of solutions their respective teams deliver.

Long-term goal: Drive the leadership message
The organization's long-term goals should be aimed at establishing a leadership position in the market:

1. Big data technologies are still evolving and their integration with analytics platforms remains challenging. There is an urgent need for research on creating more seamless integration possibilities. Any organization that takes the lead in such research and produces viable options is bound to become a de facto integration leader.

2. Organizations should promote internal architectural practices and best-practice guidelines as industry standards. New optimized protocols for low-latency, real-time near-field communications are good examples of opportunities in the big data standards arena, which can serve as architectural best practice guidelines. Companies that promote and drive these standards in the initial days of the big data evolution can become established as industry leaders.

3. Partnerships should be sought with leaders in various segments and open challenges should be identified. Success in big data analytics requires strong cooperation between big data technology experts and leaders from various customer segments.

4. By developing innovative solutions for the identified open challenges, organizations can lead their industry.

Table 1. Example list of big data analytics solutions for diffent verticals

Industry	Solution

Automotive	Fleet management
	    • Predictive maintenance
	    • Optimal workforce scheduling and inventory control
	Eco-routing
	    • Sensor-based traffic monitoring
	    • Emergency response and passenger safety

Healthcare	Public health
	    • Real-time disease progression monitoring and epidemic outbreak detection
	    • Healthcare cost predictions based on living conditions and dietary habits
	Clinical decision support
	    • Health information exchange with electronic health records
	    • Diagnostic assistance

Retail	Real-time asset tracking Supply chain monitoring
Finance	Usage-based insurance Real-time fraud detection Credit-score modelling
Energy/Utilities	Smart-grid usage prediction and dynamic load generation based on smart sensors Real-time monitoring of operational metrics for failure prediction

The Strategy

Clearly stated business goals lie at the centre of any successful organization. But what defines success? How should an organization be measured on its achievements? Typically, an organization is judged based on the quality of its "4Ps": people, partners, processes, and products. Although people and processes are internal to organizations, partners and products are external indicators of success, and more often than not, they serve as cross-comparison criteria. For organizations dealing in big data analytics, there are three broad categories of such comparison criteria:

1. Current offerings
   • Solution architectures
   • Data handling capabilities
   • Discovery and modeling tools
   • Algorithms
   • Model deployment options
   • Lifecycle tools
   • Integration capabilities
   • Support for standards

2. Solution strategy
   • Licensing and pricing
   • Resources dedicated to the solutions
   • R&D spending
   • Ability to execute the strategy
   • Solution roadmap

3. Market presence
   • Financials
   • Global presence
   • Client/customer base
   • Partnership with other vendors

Based on the span of operations fulfilled from the above criteria, the capabilities of solution providers are broadly categorized into three levels, which progress with increasing complexity and indicate the maturity of an organization in being able to deliver solutions around analytics:

Level 1. Data analysis services
• The customer provides data and pays for analysis insights derived from that data.

- The insight outputs delivered to the customer are not reusable and are valid only for the particular dataset provided.

- If there is new data, the customer has to use the service again (and hence pay) for insights on the new data.

- The customer will not be aware of the tools used or methodologies applied in deriving the insight.

- There is no lock-in. When new data becomes available, the customer is free to choose any other service provider.

Level 2. Model-building services
- The customer provides a business problem and a sample dataset related to that problem, and pays for a model that solves the problem.

- The model output delivered to the customer is reusable for different datasets for the same problem.

- If there is a new business problem, the customer has to use the service once again (and hence pay) for new models that can solve the new problem.

- The customer will be somewhat aware of the tools used and methodologies applied, given that the model will be deployed onto customer systems and their staff will be trained to use it with different data.

- The customer is locked in only for the duration of the model validity. For new business problems, the customer is free to choose other providers for model building.

Level 3. Expert systems production
- The customer defines the business nature and pays for expert systems that can build models of any business problem that can possibly arise in the course of stated business operations.

- The expert system delivered to the customer is reusable for the lifetime of the business.

- The expert system will be capable of solving not only the present business problems stated explicitly by customer, if any, but will also be capable of predicting potential future problems and helping alleviate them even before they happen.

- Based on the licensing criteria, the expert systems delivered to the customer also would be capable of being applied to other business domains because the domain knowledge is separated from business data right in the architecture.

- The customer will have to be fully aware of the modelling techniques and methodologies to be able to derive most benefit out of the delivered expert system.

- The customer is locked in for the lifetime of their business. Switching providers is not easy or feasible.

Leaders in predictive analytics solutions are expected to offer a rich set of *algorithms* to analyze data, *architectures* that can handle big data, and *tools* for data analysts that span the full predictive analytics lifecycle. This diversity of offerings is achieved through competency building, architectural standardization, research drive cultivation, and other strategic drives, as presented below:

1. People
   - Competency building
   - Recognition and proliferation of subject matter experts
   - Research drive cultivation

2. Processes
   - Architectural review processes
   - Best practice guidelines
   - Reusable frameworks and tools for standardizing solutions

3. Partners
   - Educate customers on what is possible with big data analytics
   - Bridge the gap between existing customer solutions and big data requirements
   - Market penetration by laying out new industry standards
   - Brand name promotion with whitepapers, blogs, research articles, and webinars

4. Products
   - Reduce the initial response time with proactive solution approaches
   - Lead the pack by researching and implementing solutions for open challenges

The grand strategy that encompasses all these activities can be summarized, for brevity, as a three-point triangle known as the delta model (Figure 2). The three options represented in the triangle are the milestones for the strategic vision. The strategy starts by aiming for the first point, at the right-hand side of the triangle, the *Best Solution* positioning.

Best Solution positioning
This positioning aims to become the best solution provider in the market. It acts as the base for attaining sustainable revenue for targeting next positions and instills a brand-name presence in the market with reasonable customer base. This, however, cannot be the final position for various reasons:

1. The position is rather inward and narrow, based on the prevailing product economics. Frequently the solutions are standardized and only restricted to Level 1, and the customers are faceless.

2. The way to attract, satisfy, and retain the customer is through the inherent characteristics of the solution itself. Quality of insights delivered and quick turnaround time are what make the customers come back.

3. Yardsticks for success at this level are the relevant competitors that the organization is trying to surpass or equate.

4. Commoditization is a real threat and is often an unavoidable outcome, because there is not much scope for innovation or creativity at this level; delivering Level 1 insights is vulnerable to imitation.

5. The measure of success is product share, which ultimately can fragment the business activities into a set of solution or product offerings.

Total Customer Solutions positioning
In the left-hand side of the triangle sits the option of *Total Customer Solutions*, which represents a 180-degree departure from the *Best Solution* positioning. In this phase, rather than selling standardized and isolated services/products to depersonalized customers, the organization will be providing Level 2 solutions consisting of a portfolio of customized products and services representing unique value proposition to individualized customers. This positioning improves the customer bonding and provides a continuous stream of revenue to enable experimentation, as follows:

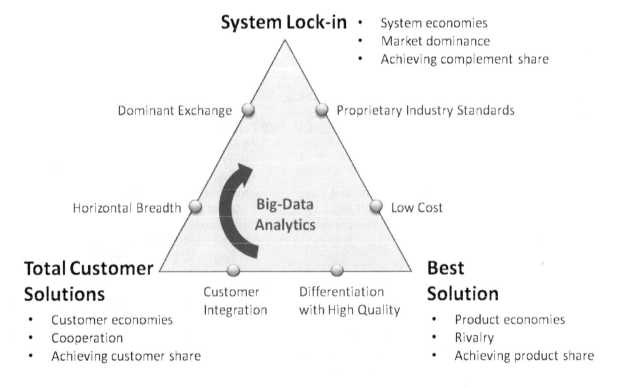

Figure 2. Strategy for the big data analytics business drive

1. Instead of acting alone, the organization engages the relevant set of partners that constitute the extended enterprise.

2. The relevant overall measure of performance becomes the total customer share.

3. Not limited by the internal product development capabilities, the joint efforts become the key success factors, such as contributing to the open source big data frameworks and driving their proliferation.

4. Although this position is relatively safe, with reasonable customer lock-ins, it is not safe enough given that the competitors are not locked-out yet and they can still take away the customers with better offerings.

System Lock-in positioning
At the top of triangle stands the most demanding strategic option that every organization craves for, the *System Lock-in*. In this stage, the organization will be addressing the full customer network as the relevant scope, with gaining of complementor's share as the ultimate objective, and the system economics as the driving force, as follows.

1. Those who are successful in reaching this position gain de-facto dominance in the market that not only assures a customer lock-in but also a competitor lock-out.

2. Complementors play key roles, because they are the basis for consolidation of the success. For example, application developers are the complementors for Microsoft, who are not on the payroll of Microsoft but contribute to the success of its products. Similarly, Android developers contribute to the success of Android, and so on. A Level 3 expert system with open standards and third-party plugin application programming interface (API), for example, can provide such system lock-in.

The *Best Solution* strategy rests on the classical form of competition, which dictates that there are only two ways to win: either through low-cost provisioning or through high-quality differentiation. The problem, however, is that differentiation is seldom a source of sustainable advantage because, once the strategy is revealed and becomes publicly known, technology often allows a quick imitation that neutralizes the sought-after competitive advantage. In the big data analytics case, everyone has access to the same set of tools for

building Level 1 solutions. The low-cost provisioning option does not provide much room for success either. After all, how low can one go and how many players can enjoy simultaneous low cost advantage?

The transformation toward a *Total Customer Solutions* positioning requires a very different way to capture the customer and a very different mindset. To achieve this shift, the organization has to engage three options that need to be pursued simultaneously:

1. Segmenting the customers carefully, arranging them into proper tiers that reflect distinct priorities, and providing differentiated service to each tier based on the identified priorities. For example, customers looking for Level 1 analytics solutions cannot benefit from preferential treatment as much as those who are looking for Level 3 analytics solutions.

2. Pro-actively identifying the challenges in the customer's business domain and proposing solutions to alleviate them even before they happen, thereby displaying thought leadership and gaining customer trust.

3. Expanding the breadth and reach of the solutions to provide full coverage of services to the customers.

Once in the *Total Customer Solutions* position, the organization is left with the final, hard-to-reach positioning on the top of triangle: the *System Lock-in*. One powerful way to achieve this position is through the development and ownership of the standards of the industry, perhaps with open API and third-party solution compatibility.

Another way to achieve system lock-in is through *dominant exchange* strategy. For example, by designing the solution as domain-neutral and schema-invariant, the Internet of Things system will be capable of becoming a dominant data exchange platform, poised towards achieving a system lock-in strategic positioning in the long run, when envisioned and executed correctly.

Conclusion

The present-day challenges in big data analytics require solution providers to first educate their customers on the applications of big data analytics to their respective domains, and then provide solutions that are easy to integrate and amenable to their existing infrastructure. A good roadmap to get started in the big data analytics market includes short-term goals aimed at laying out the technology foundation and building a strong customer base for sustainable revenue generation, with medium-term goals striving to support the delivery functions for retaining the acquired customer base and reinforcing the customer bond with high-quality outputs and optimal schedules. The long-terms goals aim for leading the market with innovative solutions and strategic partnerships.

The delta model outlined in this article is a customer-based approach to strategic management. It is based on customer economies and, as such, is well suited for both established organizations and initial startups, because the emphasis is on achieving success by customer bonding, rather than on working against the competition. Implementing this delta model thus requires thorough understanding of the customer needs and openness towards partnerships. Big data technologies, at least in today's world, thrive on open source efforts and hence are aptly suited for such a model of partnerships, where crowdsourcing and open development are the fundamental mode of business.

Some of the pitfalls one may encounter in implementing such a strategy, however, are: lack of customer interest in cooperation, limited partnership opportunities, and a scarce pool of capable technical resources. Especially for startup companies who are yet to establish their brand, the prime opposition towards any innovative big data analytics solution comes directly from the customers' apathy towards such solutions. Skeptical and suspecting, many a customer today is not yet ready to share the business data with the big data analytics entrepreneurs. A question of security for their data on the open plains of big data cloud architectures is the major contributor for these suspicions on the customer's part. Adding to this is the scarcity of qualified technical resources capable of innovating on these big data technologies, making the companies treat the competitors more and more as opponents than as prospective partners. Such a heavy inward focus towards attracting, engaging, and retaining the customers and resources, is making the companies lose global focus, rendering them as just another group of disconnected functional silos. Until the technology platforms mature and become capable of resolving such customer security concerns, and until the technical resources become available in abundance, this situation continues to present both a challenge and opportunity for big data entrepreneurs.

About the Author

Gopalakrishna Palem is a Corporate Technology Strategist specialized in distributed computing technologies and advanced predictive analytics solutions. During his 12-year tenure at Microsoft and Oracle, he helped many customers build their executive strategy for various technology initiatives, driving the brand-name promotions and improved revenue targets. He offers consultations for C-level executives in technology management strategy and is actively engaged in guiding researchers and entrepreneurs in knowledge modelling systems, algorithmic information theory, and systems control and automata. He can be reached at gopalakrishna.palem.in/

Keywords: big data, predictive analytics, executive strategy, IT entrepreneurship, business vision

10

Building Cyber-Resilience into Supply Chains

Adrian Davis

❝*Today's CISO focuses on tier 1 or direct suppliers.*❞
Tomorrow's CISO will need to focus on the supply chain.

Chief information security officer (CISO) of a major
international bank

The article discusses how an organization can adopt an information-centric approach to protect its information shared in one or more supply chains; clearly communicate the expectations it has for a direct (Tier 1) supplier to protect information; and use contracts and measurement to maintain the protection desired. Building on this foundation, the concept of resilience – and that of cyber-resilience – is discussed, and how an information-centric approach can assist in creating a more cyber-resilient supply chain. Finally, the article concludes with five steps an organization can take to improve the protection of its information: i) map the supply chain; ii) build capability; iii) share information and expertise; iv) state requirements across the supply chain using standards, common frameworks, and languages; and v) measure, assess, and audit.

Introduction

Supply chains – and the organizations involved in them – are now targets for hackers. There are several reasons behind this: one is that supply chains contain a wealth of information that may be sold or may embarrass one or more organizations in the supply chain; another is that one organization can be used as a route to attack another organization in the same supply chain, as was seen in the 2013 attack on the retailer Target in the United States (Krebs, 2014).

Information, just like the physical components of supply chains, is vital for the continued efficient operation of supply chains. Indeed, for some supply chains to operate, the constituent organizations may need to share trade secrets, proprietary data, and other sensitive information. However, the role and protection of information in supply chains has received less attention than the physical aspects of those supply chains. That situation is changing.

Much effort has been invested in reducing the risks associated with the physical aspects of supply chains – and improving their resilience overall – but less attention has been paid to the overall resilience and security of the cyber-related aspects of supply chains. This article will examine that key issue: how an organization can protect its information in one or more supply chains, and use that as the basis to build cyber-resilience across one or more of its supply chains.

The information-centric approach, which provides an organization with a powerful tool to protect the information it does and does not share, is presented as a solution to this key issue. How the approach can be adopted and used with direct – or Tier 1 – suppliers is discussed. From this foundation, the article looks at the concept of resilience and how cyber-resilience can be defined: the role of the information-centric approach is highlighted as a component of cyber-resilience. Finally, five steps an organization can take to build both an information-centric approach and cyber-resilience are listed and described.

Protecting Information in the Supply Chain

The ubiquity of information technology (IT) and the availability of information has placed all organizations in a dilemma. For a supply chain to work effectively and efficiently, information – some of it sensitive or confidential – must be shared between many organizations.

Yet, at the same time, one or more of those organizations may not want to share that information or may have external obligations, such as those set out in law or regulation, to protect the same information. Certain types of information, for example, personally identifiable information and medical records, are subject to legal or regulatory obligations concerning their protection and use. These obligations may preclude sharing – yet such sharing is essential to supply chain success. This requirement to share is a key risk in today's digitally connected, information-dependent supply chain. Sharing information has become easier with the advent of IT and the Internet but, paradoxically, has also become harder with the proliferation of technologies and services made available by IT and the Internet. As a result, information can be shared in many forms and in many formats (including paper), multiplying the number of copies in existence and, in some cases, multiplying the possibility of error.

Across a supply chain, the capability and desire of suppliers to expend resources on cybersecurity and cyber-resilience will vary significantly. Some suppliers will possess the expertise, knowledge, and ability to address cyber-related issues in a consistent and comprehensive manner. Other suppliers will not. From the perspective of an acquiring organization (hereafter "the acquirer" in accordance with the ISO/IEC 27036-1:2014 [ISO, 2014; Part 1]), a key issue is that, despite a lot of hard work and significant expenditure, the acquirer cannot negotiate, agree, measure, and assess the cybersecurity and associated risks of its suppliers and across a supply chain. For an acquirer, various factors may combine to make up this issue, including the inability to:

1. State cybersecurity requirements to suppliers using a common framework and language.

2. Integrate cybersecurity into the acquirer procurement process.

3. Devote resource to investigate the makeup of the supply chain (i.e., which supplier organizations make up the supply chain).

4. Understand how a supplier meets the acquirer's requirements when not using a common, shared, framework, and language.

5. Identify acquirer information shared between the acquirer and its direct suppliers, and acquirer information shared between direct and indirect suppliers.

6. Specify cybersecurity requirements for indirect suppliers (i.e., the suppliers to the direct suppliers).

7. Measure the effectiveness of cybersecurity arrangements at suppliers and across the supply chain using a consistent set of indicators.

8. Identify and quantify cyber-related risks across the supply chain.

9. Identify the use of technology (such as the cloud) and technology providers by the acquirer and suppliers across the supply chain.

10. Control the confidentiality, integrity, and availability (CIA) of information once shared with suppliers and the supply chain.

These factors may vary in their significance across a supply chain. It worth noting that an acquirer may have multiple supply chains and that the issues and factors may vary in their significance across each supply chain. If we look at a simplified supply chain from an information or cybersecurity perspective, we can highlight where the ten factors listed above often occur.

Figure 1 shows that the factors can be grouped into two types:

1. Acquirer-focused

2. Supply-chain-focused

Acquirer-focused factors (numbered 1 to 4 in the list and in Figure 1) are internal to the acquirer and, to a degree, can be actively managed and addressed by the acquirer's management and staff. Typically, these factors fall under information security, third-party (i.e., supplier) security and data privacy programmes, and projects run by the organization's staff or by consultants.

Supply-chain-focused factors (numbered 5–10) are outside of the acquirer's control. Once acquirer information is passed to a supplier, then that information can be shared, copied, stored, changed, deleted, and so on without the acquirer's knowledge or permission. The acquirer thus has no idea how its information is being protected, who its information is shared with, where that information is – physically and electronically – and who may have seen or used that shared acquirer information. Once this situation occurs, it is very difficult to regain (or gain) any control over the protection of in-

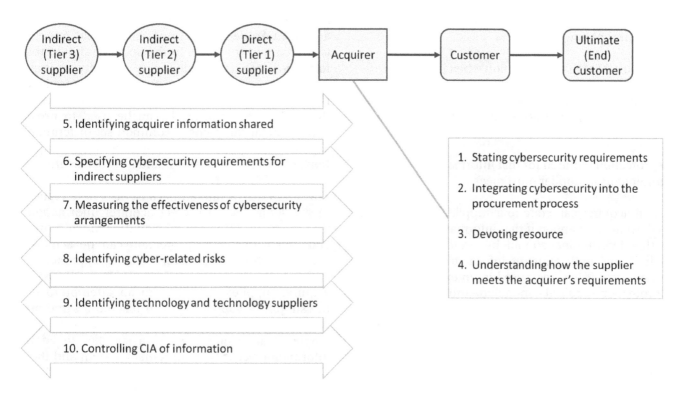

Figure 1. Factors that can impact the ability of an acquirer to protect its information using a simplified supply chain model

formation and to assess the risks to that information. Because the acquirer typically has little or no ability to work with, or influence, its indirect suppliers (e.g., if there is no contract in place), the acquirer cannot set out its requirements for the protection of its information at those indirect suppliers, which makes it difficult to measure the effectiveness of the cybersecurity arrangements across the supply chain and may significantly impact the overall cybersecurity risk associated with sharing. Sub-contracting by the supplier – especially to technology or service providers offering cloud, mobile device, and social media services – can also significantly impact the risks of sharing, protecting information, and controlling the CIA of acquirer information.

Securing Information in Supply Chains

Given the requirements to share and protect information, and the issue and factors discussed above, acquirers have made efforts to address how best to share and protect information they make available to suppliers. Typically though, these efforts are focused at Tier 1 suppliers, occur late in the procurement cycle, and apply "one size fits all" information security approaches. Thus, an acquirer will specify certification or compliance with an information security management system

(e.g., ISO/IEC 27001:2013 [ISO, 2013a]), the "right to audit" and requiring a supplier to meet the requirements of the acquirer's internal policy documents, irrespective of the information being shared or the goods and services being supplied. Such an approach may not provide the best protection to shared information, because information risks may not have be adequately addressed, and so risk treatment may be overly strong in one area and weak in another. Acquirers have also struggled to identify what information they actually share, further dispersing their efforts in terms of protection.

To protect information shared with Tier 1 suppliers in the manner the acquirer is expecting requires an information-centric approach. In this approach, the acquirer determines at the start of the procurement cycle what information has to be shared to purchase a particular good or service. Knowing what information is to be shared will allow the acquirer to understand the harm it may suffer should the information be compromised at a supplier and the risk treatment the supplier should put in place at a minimum. This information-centric approach allows the acquirer to indicate:

• what information is being shared

- its importance to the acquirer (the organization sharing the information)

- the sensitivity of that information when it is shared

- the harm to the acquirer should that information have its confidentiality, integrity, or availability compromised

- the protection required for that information – and the requirements a supplier must meet

Thus, an acquirer can state to a supplier what is being shared, what can happen if that information is lost, and how that information should be protected. This approach is the application of information risk assessment, but now it has been used in an external context. The protection required can include processes, technologies (such as encryption), and the ability to assess and audit that the supplier is actively implementing the protection required. Figure 2 illustrates how information – and its protection – can be built into a typical procurement cycle.

Once the information to be shared has been determined, the protection of information can be worked into all procurement documents used by the acquirer (such

as the Expression of Interest and Invitation to Tender) and to make decisions. Importantly, what information is shared and the harm to the acquirer should that information lose its confidentiality, integrity, or availability can be used to drive the protection required using a risk-based approach. Standards such as the multi-part ISO/IEC 27036 (ISO, 2014) can be used to provide a common starting point, a common set of terminology, and a common understanding of how each organization approaches its business and its cybersecurity.

This approach is limited because it is only focused on Tier 1 suppliers. To protect acquirer information further upstream (Tier 2 and beyond) is much more difficult, but a degree of protection can be achieved by using pass-through clauses, technical approaches, and auditing. Pass-through clauses, which are placed in the acquirer-supplier contract, are an attempt to ensure the supplier's suppliers put in place the same protection as the contract requires the supplier to do. For example, if an acquirer wants a supplier to adopt an information security management system and the supplier's suppliers to do the same, a pass-through clause could be inserted into the acquirer-supplier contract stating "all suppliers of the contracted supplier that are likely to handle the information provided by the acquirer must have an information security management

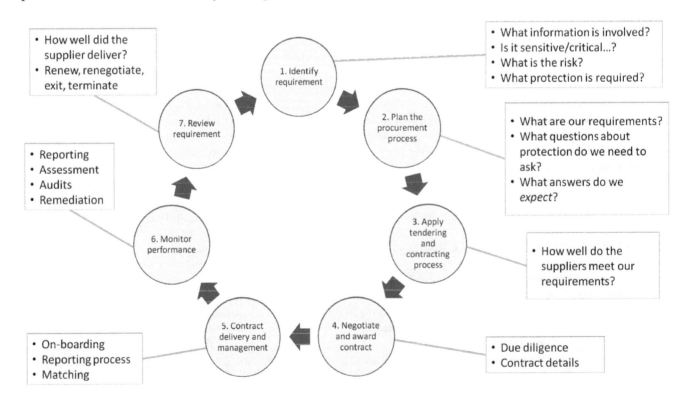

Figure 2. Integrating information into a typical procurement cycle

system in place. The contracted supplier will be held responsible for ensuring compliance with this clause." Needless to say, pass-through clauses are not necessarily popular with suppliers, because such clauses place obligations on them. Pass-through clauses typically only reach Tier 1 and Tier 2 suppliers. Technical approaches, such as digital rights management, offer a partial solution, which may extend to upstream suppliers. Allowing suppliers to connect to the acquirer's infrastructure to access information is another control mechanism, because a control over who sees acquirer information and what is copied can be exercised, thus hopefully limiting wider exposure to the supply chain. However, there are both management and technical overheads to these approaches, which an acquirer may feel outweigh the protection offered. Finally, a thorough audit of the supplier and its communications will also allow the acquirer to understand how its information is being shared. Audits of this nature are time consuming and expensive and also rely on the supplier having kept records of such communications and of the goodwill of the supplier in sharing them. Resource, cost, time, and other constraints often mean that audits such as these are performed very infrequently. Figure 3 summarizes how the approaches discussed in this section can be applied and illustrates the reach of those approaches across a model supply chain.

Being able to protect information at a Tier 1 supplier, let alone upstream, is a major step forward, but to achieve true cyber resilience, other steps are necessary. First of these is to understand and then create resilience.

Resilience

The concept of resilience takes many forms and has been applied to supply chains, organizations, and IT. Unfortunately, there are many definitions of resilience itself, which are then appropriated to fit specialist disciplines. As a starting point, we will use this definition of resilience: "[…] the ability of a system to return to its original [or desired] state after being disturbed" (Peck et al., 2003). Resilience can be viewed from several broad perspectives, which are briefly discussed here. The first approach views resilience from an organizational viewpoint and is concerned with preparing for and reacting to an incident and reducing the harm or impact. The second approach, which is narrower, views resilience as the ability of an organization's IT to keep running in the event of error, failure, or incident. These two approaches share much in common and are intertwined, because organizations are typically dependent on IT to carry out and support their business operations: a failure in IT could significantly harm an organization. The third perspective is that of business continuity, which views business continuity plans and disaster recovery as

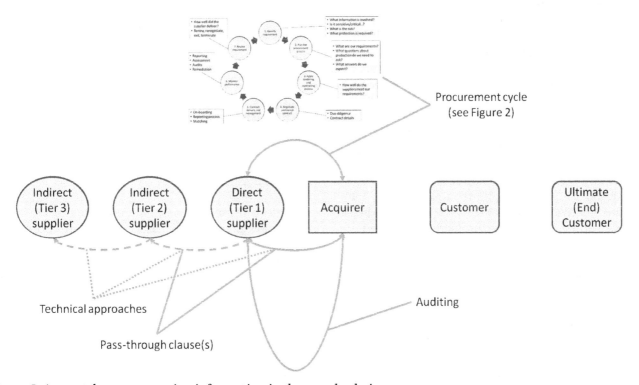

Figure 3. Approaches to protecting information in the supply chain

an essential component of resilience (Davis & Skelton, 2014) and provides the basis upon which an organization can plan and execute its responses to an incident. Importantly, resilience has a time component; for example, the concepts of "recovery time objective" and "maximum tolerable downtime" are taken from business continuity (Tipton & Hernandez, 2013). These three perspectives are typically organizationally-focused and inward-looking to a great extent.

Supply chain resilience is "the ability of the supply chain to cope with unexpected disturbances" (Christopher, 2011) and one of its characteristics is a business-wide recognition of where the supply chain is most vulnerable. Supply chain management, design, and business continuity all have a role to play in creating resilience (Waters, 2011).

Finally, resilience is a developing concept in cyberspace. Again, various perspectives can be taken. The broadest looks at the resilience of the physical and virtual components of the Internet – the hardware, software, processes, and communication links – and how that entire system of systems could still operate if there were failures, attacks, or other incidents. Another perspective examines how an organization could continue to do business if its access to its information, the Internet, or the services delivered via the Internet were interrupted or impaired. This is what the author takes to be "cyber-resilience": the ability of a system that is dependent on cyberspace in some manner to return to its original [or desired] state after being disturbed.

So, cyber-resilience is more than just an IT or information security issue (Information Security Forum, 2012; World Economic Forum, 2012). It is a business issue and should be woven into business or enterprise risk management, it should be considered across all business operations, and it has special relevance to an acquirer's supply chains. Attacks against information – and the systems that process, store, and transmit that information – strike at the resilience (cyber- or otherwise) of the supply chain. Thus, protecting information can be regarded as a fundamental component of building cyber-resilience.

Building Cyber-Resilience in the Supply Chain

Good cybersecurity and cyber-resilience in the supply chain starts "at home". An organization that understands, in the broadest sense, which information it holds is sensitive, critical, or damaging should it be compromised will be able to protect its information

and start to create resilience. Techniques such as classifying or labelling information and educating users about the utility and value of information will create or enhance a security-positive approach to how information is handled. Senior executives will need to champion this cause and ensure that resources are committed to achieving this information-centric approach. Hand in hand with this approach is the need for information security governance (as laid out in ISO/IEC27014: 2013[ISO, 2013b]) and information security strategy, to direct, manage, and deliver the approach inside the organization. Key to the success of this approach will be the ability to categorize, group, or define groups of related information – for example, trade secrets, intellectual property, legal documents, and commercial documents – and then express the harm caused should information in each group be compromised. Once this harm can be expressed, risk treatment options can be selected, using published or in-house processes and methodologies.

Protecting information is one part of this task. To build cyber-resilience across the supply chain, each organization needs to build a set of capabilities, both internal- and external-facing. A summary list for an organization, based on material published by the World Economic Forum (2012), is presented here:

1. Implement a cybersecurity (or information security) governance framework and place a member of the executive management team at its head.

2. Create a cybersecurity programme.

3. Integrate the cybersecurity programme with enterprise risk management approaches.

4. Communicate, share, and apply the cybersecurity programme with suppliers, educating them where necessary.

To achieve these four steps requires significant effort. The achievement can be assisted by the adoption of standards, the sharing of cyber-related information, such as threats, attacks, weaknesses, and mitigations – a point made in several publications (Information Security Forum, 2012; World Economic Forum, 2012). For many organizations, they do not have the resources, expertise, or time to act on cyber-related information, or they may be reliant on a supplier to act for them. This is where education and, if necessary, actually investing in a supplier's capabilities may be required and may yield a return.

Conclusion

So, building cyber-resilience starts at the organization. This article has discussed components of organizational cyber-resilience such as an information-centric approach, adopting a governance framework, a strategy of integrating information into the procurement cycle. To extend cyber-resilience to the supply chain, an acquirer needs to take the following further actions:

1. **Map the supply chain.** Many organizations do not actually understand the make-up of their supply chains. Even Toyota, often held up as an example of supply chain excellence, could not map its chain (Supply Chain Digest, 2012). Mapping is complicated by the resources available, the number of suppliers an organization may have, the willingness of suppliers to reveal their suppliers, and the linear and lateral nature of the supply chains themselves. As an acquirer, understanding who is in a supply chain at Tier 1 and Tier 2 (even if partially) – and the information they may need from the acquirer – means that information risk and risk treatment can be better identified and addressed. Additionally, knowing the risks in the supply chain builds resilience, because the acquirer can prepare for incidents and interruptions. The acquirer can also spot potential weak links in the supply chain where information may be compromised. Mapping past Tier 2 may be very difficult for many acquiring organizations but some may have to do so for regulatory or other requirements.

2. **Build capability.** Both the acquiring organization and its suppliers may not have the resources, expertise, or knowledge to protect information. If a supplier cannot protect information or its systems, then it may provide a route for attackers to compromise both the supplier and the acquirer, thus causing harm and directly undermining the cyber-resilience of the supply chain. For an acquirer, helping suppliers to protect acquirer information is a win-win, because the costs of remediation after a breach and failure of resilience (perhaps including fines levied by regulators and any legal costs) will probably far exceed the costs of assisting a supplier to correct any deficiencies. Building capability does not necessarily mean employing experts to work in silos: integrating cybersecurity questions and checklists into procurement documents, or better yet, integrating cybersecurity professionals into the procurement process and function is an alternative and value-adding approach many organisations can take easily. Adopting standards such as the ISO/IEC 27036 series (ISO, 2014) discussed above and enhancing supply chain risk management to include information security- and privacy-related questions (such as PAS 7000:2014 [BSI, 2014]) can also raise an acquirer's capability and increase awareness in the supplier community. Acquirers and suppliers may wish to jointly invest in staff training as well.

3. **Share information and expertise.** Both acquirers and suppliers should share information about threats, attacks, and incidents – anything that may adversely affect their combined cyber-resilience. These organizations may also want to share information about the protective mechanisms they have in place – and their effectiveness – to further enhance their resilience. Sharing information about cyber-resilience can take many forms including joining government information-sharing networks, discussion and presentation within membership or other trusted groups, direct communication between individuals, and using social media. Sharing expertise may involve both acquirers and suppliers cross-posting staff, sharing best practice, recommending the use of standards or creating joint ventures to promote best practice across their supply chains and upstream suppliers. Acquirers may wish to provide education and training, to both on-boarded and prospective suppliers, about standards and frameworks that can be used.

4. **State requirements across the supply chain using standards, common frameworks, and languages.** Acquiring organizations should ensure that, whenever they work with suppliers, they follow standards and use a common language to promote understanding with their suppliers. Additionally, if the same standards, language, and frameworks are used with all suppliers, then the acquirer will have a basis for comparison between suppliers, which may assist risk management, supplier measurement, and associated efforts. Similarly, when an acquirer shares information, the requirements for protection should be couched in the same language for all suppliers. Using pass-through clauses and technology solutions, such as digital rights management may have a role to play here, as does education and training.

5. **Measure, assess, and audit.** All organizations in the supply chain will have to be able to measure their cybersecurity, their cyber-resilience, the cyber-risks in their supply chain and their governance. Additionally, organizations will need to be able to share and interpret these measurements, so they understand

their own cyber-resilience, their partners, and the supply chain as a whole. Acquirers may need to define performance indicators for suppliers, based on their internal measurement systems, or they may have to create new measures in conjunction with their suppliers. Both acquirers and suppliers may need to create continuous monitoring and measurement systems to overcome the rather static nature of audits, and to allow the detection and prevention of and reaction to attacks in real time or near real time.

Cyber-resilience – the ability of a system that is dependent on cyberspace in some manner to return to its original [or desired] state after being disturbed – is an evolving and important concept. When applying cyber-resilience to the supply chain, the protection of information and its associated attributes (such as confidentiality, integrity, and availability), understanding information and cyber-risks across the supply chain and building a collaborative approach are important concepts. Yet, it is these areas where much work needs to be done, because information and cyber-risk assessment across supply chains are emerging fields of research; there is thus little to guide organizations and little best practice for them to study and adapt.

About the Author

Adrian Davis, PhD, MBA, FBCS CITP, CISSP, heads the Europe, Middle East, and Africa (EMEA) team for $(ISC)^2$, the global, not-for-profit leader in educating and certifying information security professionals throughout their careers. His role is to deliver the $(ISC)^2$ vision of inspiring a safe and secure cyber-world and its mission of supporting and providing members and constituents with credentials, resources, and leadership to secure information and deliver value to society. Before working for $(ISC)^2$, Adrian delivered practical business solutions to over 360 blue-chip multinational clients for the Information Security Forum. His expertise included: managing information security in supply chains; information security governance and effectiveness; the relationship between information security and business continuity; and possible near-term threats to organizations. Adrian regularly attends and chairs conferences and contributes articles for the press. He also contributed to the development of *ISO/IEC 27014: Governance of Information Security* and currently acts as a co-editor for *ISO/IEC 27036 Information Security in Supplier Relationships, Part 4: Guidelines for Security of Cloud Services.*

References

BSI. 2014. *PAS 7000 Supply Chain Risk Management – Supplier Prequalification*. The British Standards Institution. Accessed March 26, 2015:
http://www.bsigroup.com/en-GB/PAS7000/

Christopher, M. 2011. Logistics and Supply Chain Management (4th ed.). London: FT Prentice Hall.

Davis, A., & Skelton, E. 2014. Engaging the Board: Resilience Measured. In L. Bird (Ed.), *Operational Resilience in Financial Institutions*. London: Risk Books.

Information Security Forum. 2012. *Cyber Security Strategies: Achieving Cyber Resilience*. London: Information Security Forum.

ISO. 2013a. *ISO/IEC 27001:2013 Information Technology – Security Techniques – Information Security Management – Requirements*. International Organization for Standardization. Accessed February 9, 2015:
http://www.iso.org/iso/catalogue_detail.htm?csnumber=54534

ISO. 2013b. *ISO/IEC27014: 2013: Information Technology – Security Techniques – Governance of Information Security*. International Organization for Standardization. Accessed February 9, 2015:
http://www.iso.org/iso/catalogue_detail.htm?csnumber=43754

ISO. 2014. *ISO/IEC 27036: Information Technology – Security Techniques – Information Security for Supplier Relationships*. International Organization for Standardization. Accessed February 9, 2015:
Part 1: Overview and Concepts:
http://www.iso.org/iso/catalogue_detail.htm?csnumber=59648
Part 2: Requirements:
http://www.iso.org/iso/catalogue_detail.htm?csnumber=59680
Part 3: Guidelines for Information and Communication Technology Supply Chain Security:
http://www.iso.org/iso/catalogue_detail.htm?csnumber=59688
Part 4 (under development): Guidelines for Security of Cloud Services:
http://www.iso.org/iso/catalogue_detail.htm?csnumber=59689

Krebs, B. 2014. Target Hackers Broke in via HVAC Company. *Krebs on Security*, February 5, 2014. Accessed April 1, 2015:
http://krebsonsecurity.com/2014/02/target-hackers-broke-in-via-hvac-company/

Peck, H., Abley, J., Christopher, M., Haywood, M., Saw, R., Rutherford, C., & Strathern, M. 2003. *Creating Resilient Supply Chains: A Practical Guide*. Bedford, UK: Cranfield School of Management, Cranfield University.

Supply Chain Digest. 2012. Global Supply Chain News: Toyota Taking Massive Effort to Reduce Its Supply Chain Risk in Japan. *Supply Chain Digest,* March 7, 2012. Accessed February 9, 2015: http://www.scdigest.com/ontarget/12-03-07-2.php?cid=5576

Tipton, H. F., & Hernandez, S. (Eds.) 2013. *Official (ISC)² Guide to the CISSP CBK* (3rd ed.). Boca Raton, FL: CRC Press.

Waters, D. 2011. *Supply Chain Risk Management* (2nd ed.). London: Kogan Page.

World Economic Forum. 2012. *Partnering for Cyber Resilience.* World Economic Forum. Accessed February 9, 2015: http://www.weforum.org/projects/partnership-cyber-resilience

Keywords: cyber-resilience, cybersecurity, supply chain, resilience, direct suppliers, Tier 1 suppliers, indirect suppliers, procurement, information-centric approach, requirements

11

The Business of Open Source Software: A Primer

Michael "Monty" Widenius and Linus Nyman

" *Ideology isn't what has sold the open source model.* "
It started gaining attention when it was obvious that
open source was the best method of developing and
improving the highest quality technology.

Linus Torvalds
Software Engineer and creator of the Linux kernel

This article is meant as a primer for those interested in gaining a basic understanding of the business of open source software. Thus, we cover four main areas: i) what motivates businesses to get involved in open source; ii) common open source licenses and how they relate to community and corporate interests; iii) issues regarding the monetization of an open source program; and iv) open source business models currently employed. This article is particularly suitable for people who want a general understanding of the business of open source software; people who want to understand the significant issues regarding an open source program's potential to generate income; and entrepreneurs who want to create a company around open source code.

Introduction

In a world built on openness, in which licensing dictates that the product is not only free of charge, but can be freely copied, modified, and redistributed by enthusiasts and competitors alike, how *can* anyone possibly make money on open source? The question of how one can monetize open source software is a significant one. The quest for, and dissemination of, its answer was the spark that started what was to become the *Technology Innovation Management Review* (Lavigne, 2007: timreview.ca/article/92; McPhee, 2011: timreview.ca/article/465).

Although much has been learned during the years since the emergence of open source and the business that grew to surround it, there are still few articles that attempt to summarize its dynamics. Perhaps the most well known of those efforts is Hecker's "Setting up Shop" (1998; tinyurl.com/28n7o3), which largely focused on what strategies could be employed utilizing open source. Now that open source is a much more mature field than it was back then, we can focus on documenting what entrepreneurs have done rather than could do.

The goal of this article is to concisely explain the nuts and bolts of how the business of open source works, including sufficient detail to serve as a useful primer on

the topic – a springboard for further reading. Our focus is on approaches that generate income based on open source software and its development (e.g., not hardware manufacturers with an open source involvement).

The article is structured as follows. First, we offer a brief look at some of the main corporate motivations in open source. Second, we cover the most common types of open source licenses and the main aspects and concerns for businesses and programmers regarding licensing. Third, we outline the most significant points in a piece of software's earning potential. Finally, we briefly describe the more common business models in use today, and we examine their pros and cons from the standpoints of both the developers and entrepreneurs. Included at the end of the article is a list of recommendations for further reading.

Background: Corporate Motivations

The adoption of open source code allows businesses to harness the creativity and labour of both their employees and their customers in a way that is not available to firms employing only proprietary software licenses. Indeed, where developer motivations include many social motivations, firms have tended to emphasize economic and technological reasons for entering and contributing to open source (Bonaccorsi and Rossi, 2003; tinyurl.com/lfx847l). In addition to the possibility of a shortened development time (e.g., Dahlander, 2007; tinyurl.com/kg8wdd6), open source projects commonly report a wider adoption of their code (e.g., West, 2003; tinyurl.com/6s68jno) and receive more high-quality feedback and bug reports than closed source projects (see Schindler [2007; tinyurl.com/mv8eea9] for a comparison). Open source licensing also enables a faster average time from discovery to solution (Schindler, 2007; tinyurl.com/mv8eea9). Indeed, open source products have been often shown to be superior to their proprietary counterparts (e.g., Wheeler, 2007; tinyurl.com/r1yk). Furthermore, companies can see development of their product in directions they did not realize was significant to their users, as well as the development of features that are too far from the firm's core business to receive in-house funding for development. As an example, only two of the more than 20 language connectors for MySQL were programmed in house; the rest were developed and submitted by the community.

By joining an open source development effort, corporations can also influence the direction of its development. Furthermore, open source has been identified as a strategy for implementing long-term sustainable software systems (e.g., Lundell and Gamalielsson, 2011; tinyurl.com/n24dw4u). Open source can also be adopted as a competitive strategy, for example through making the functionality of a competitor's product freely available (Fitzgerald, 2006; tinyurl.com/al995aj). Open source can also be of value to companies that offer products other than software, for example by promoting open source in areas that facilitate the deployment of their hardware (Fitzgerald, 2006; tinyurl.com/al995aj).

Open Source Licenses

A basic understanding of licensing is important for entrepreneurs and programmers alike. License choice decides what can be done with a program and what other programs (or, rather, licenses) it can and cannot be combined with. All open source licenses guarantee users the rights to use the program, access the source code, modify the source code, and redistribute the program in its original or modified form. However, beyond these basic rights, licenses differ in significant ways. Based on these differences, open source licenses are commonly divided into three main categories: i) permissive licenses, ii) weak copyleft licenses, and iii) strong copyleft licenses. The licensing requirements of copyleft licenses are only triggered upon distribution.

This means that, for personal use, one can do largely whatever one wants with open source code, but if and when one distributes a program the stipulations of the license are triggered and must then be complied with. Note, however, that the AGPL license has some minor restrictions, which will be discussed later.

One of the most important elements of, and differences between, open source license types relates to a concept called *license compatibility*. License compatibility is a term used to describe the issue of which licenses can be combined. Particularly, from a business perspective, license compatibility considers which licenses can be combined with proprietary software. A further issue, though one of lesser interest, is that of the right to change the license, in particular whether one is allowed to change an open source license to a proprietary one. For businesses, this may be of interest as a source of free code. The issue of changing to a proprietary license splits the developer community into two camps. Those who are for it generally want to ensure (or at the very least do not mind) that their code is as valuable to corporate interests as possible. Those who are against it generally want to ensure that the open source project remains a freely available community good in perpetuity. The issue of license combining (including embedding) and license change is summarized in Table 1.

Permissive licenses
Permissive licenses allow a high degree of freedom to use and reuse (or fork) the code. It is not an extreme oversimplification to distil the permissive licenses down to the message: "here's the code, do whatever you want with it". (Commonly, one needs to distribute a copy of the copyright with the code, but in practice,

Table 1. Post-distribution rights of open source license types

Rights	Permissive	LGPL	GPL
Can it be combined with proprietary programs?	Yes	Yes	No
Does it allow the license to be changed to a proprietary license?	Yes	No	No
Does it guarantee access to source code?	No	Yes	Yes

this need not be more complicated than including a readme file.) In other words, it is possible to fork a permissively licensed program and make it closed source. (As an example, both Apple's OS X and iOS operating systems contain code that was copied from permissively licensed open source projects, most notably BSD: tinyurl.com/kffrf.) An issue which sets the permissive licenses apart from the copyleft licenses is that, once the source code is compiled, one does not need to distribute the original source code with the compiled (i.e., binary) version of the program. Among the more common permissive licenses are the Apache (tinyurl.com/kmenxch), MIT (tinyurl.com/3vfsyal), and BSD (tinyurl.com/lejoxn7) licenses.

Weak copyleft licenses (LGPL)
Weak copyleft licenses, such as the GNU Lesser General Public License (LGPL; tinyurl.com/mp4w4lw), can be combined with proprietary code, but cannot be relicensed under a proprietary license. So, although a firm's proprietary program can remain proprietary, even when combined with the LGPL, the LGPL-licensed program cannot be made proprietary. Furthermore, any modifications to an LGPL program must also be licensed under the LGPL. The Mozilla Public License (MPL; mozilla.org/MPL/) is also a weak copyleft license.

Strong copyleft licenses (GPL)
Much like the LGPL is synonymous with *weak* copyleft, the GNU General Public License (GPL; tinyurl.com/2459b5) is synonymous with *strong* copyleft. Hence, we will focus our discussion of strong copyleft licenses on the GPL. Although use of the GPL is in decline (Aslett, 2011; tinyurl.com/7ujq7sj), as of the writing of this article, it is still the most common open source license overall (Black Duck Knowledgebase; tinyurl.com/nl4z94t). The GPL requires any modifications to the code to also be licensed under the GPL. From a business perspective, the key issue to be aware of is that combining or embedding a program with the GPL necessitates the (re)licensing of all connected software so that it is also under the GPL. In practice, this means open sourcing any proprietary programs connected to a GPL-licensed program, and is therefore something many firms seek to avoid. Importantly, programs licensed under a GPL license cannot be re-licensed under a more permissive license (i.e., neither as LGPL or permissive).

A general comment regarding license change is that one can commonly change a license to a more restrictive license type but not to a more permissive one. Furthermore, only the permissive licenses can be changed to proprietary.

With the rise of cloud computing, a variation of the GPL license worth special mention is the Affero General Public License (AGPL; tinyurl.com/lzmmq8n). The AGPL differs from the GPL in that online use of a program is considered distribution, thus triggering the requirement for license compliance (i.e., source code access is required) even though a physical copy of the program has not been distributed. In other words, using an AGPL-licensed program in the cloud necessitates distribution of source code.

Choosing a license
Open source licensing is a more complex topic than can be covered in detail here. Furthermore, because legal precedent is rather limited, there are issues regarding licensing that are still subject to interpretation and that are coloured, among other things, by pragmatic versus ideological concerns. Thus, what may and may not be done under certain conditions is to some extent a matter of opinion. We recommend a close study of licensing before any final licensing decisions are made. For further reading, please refer to the links at the end of this article.

On the Business of Open Source

Establishing a sufficient, steady income is a significant challenge in creating a company around open source software. Thus, although open source is a superior development model, there is no guarantee that one's program will make enough money to fund its continued development. Of particular significance to the business of open source are the questions of program ownership and location in the software stack, because these factors affect what business models one can choose from. In particular, the answers to these questions help decide whether one can employ what is arguably the most lucrative open source business model: dual licensing.

Ownership of code
A company or person that owns the rights to the code they develop can sell closed source copies of the code, which is a standard practice with proprietary programs. The dual licensing, business source, and (to a lesser extent) open core business models, which will be described in further detail later, require ownership of the code.

Location in the software stack (and "embedded" programs)
Most software relies on other software to run. This concept of software codependence is most apparent in the so-called software stack. On the top of the stack is the application: a word processing program, a photo ed-

itor, a game, etc. Digging deeper, one can find elements such as databases, middleware, and an operating system. It is not important for the purposes of this article to understand the layers or functions of a software stack; it is merely enough to know that such layers exist and that a program's location in the stack is significant to its overall importance to the stack. Programs higher up in the stack rely on programs lower down to function, but not the other way around. Whereas a word processor needs an operating system to be able to run, an operating system does not need a word processor for it to function. One way for an open source program to gain potential value is having other programs rely on it: by being embedded in the software stack and by being a required component for applications and other programs to function properly – or even run at all.

Business Models

Although a business model can usefully be seen as something much more complex than merely a revenue source (e.g., West, 2007: tinyurl.com/dxsemd; Bailetti, 2009: timreview.ca/article/226), at its essence is the question of how the firm can create value for the customer while simultaneously extracting some of that value for itself (West, 2005; tinyurl.com/ov69jb8). For the purposes of this article, we make use of very broad brush strokes in our interpretation, using the term "business model" to indicate the way in which a company delivers value to a set of customers at a profit (e.g., Johnson, 2010; tinyurl.com/m9uf6xe). Recommended reading for more in-depth analyses of questions related to business models are offered at the end of the article.

The business models of open source can be divided in two main categories: those that require complete (or at least partial) ownership of the code and those that do not. Table 2 outlines the criteria for selecting an open source business model; however, it should be noted that these business models need not be mutually exclusive.

Support contracts and services

Support and services are closely related approaches; in fact, companies that provide one commonly also provide the other. Thus, although they could be separated, we have chosen to group them under one heading. The services business model is one in which income is generated by offering services in the form of, for example, training, consulting, or extensions development around an open source product. Companies that offer services will commonly also offer long-term support contracts, thereby achieving a more stable income than by merely focusing on one-off services. Two of the main challenges with the support and services approach are the lack of scalability and that the typical profit margin of 20–30% is not enough to pay for full-time developers for the project.

The availability of support and services is an important factor for customers (e.g., Shanker, 2012; timreview.ca/article/635) and can be considered a necessary element for software to become truly successful. Bear in mind that, although support should be offered, it need not be provided by the same company that develops the software. Examples of a support and services providers are Red Hat (redhat.com) and SkySQL (skysql.com). For more information on Red Hat's approach, see Suehle (2012; timreview.ca/article/635).

Open core or commercial extensions

Open core is a business model in which the core of a program is open source, with additional closed source features provided for a fee. Open core has gained much momentum over the past few years. However, it is an approach primarily focused on appealing to the venture capitalist rather than the end user (Prentice, 2010; tinyurl.com/pqpmptk). The economic rationale is clear-cut, but the reaction of the community and customers may not be as easy to estimate. Although pragmatic firm motivations are accepted by the community provided they comply with the rules of the community (Bonaccorsi and Rossi, 2003; tinyurl.com/lfx847l), some developers see

Table 2. Criteria for business model selection

Criteria	Support and Services	Open Core	Business Source	Dual Licensing
Can I choose this business model even if I do **not** own the code?	Yes	No*	No	No
Can I choose this business model even if my program is **not** embedded?	Yes	Yes	Yes	No

*Ownership is required for the closed source extensions

the open core approach a breach of those rules. The proponents of free software criticize it on ideological grounds and proponents of open source software criticize it on technical grounds, due to the restrictions to the development model caused by limited access to the code. From the perspective of the end user, open core forces vendor lock-in and is furthermore faulted with not delivering and sustaining the cost savings and flexibility of open source software (e.g., Phipps, 2012; tinyurl.com/9tjv8c9). Potential outcomes of adopting this model may include problems in attracting and maintaining developers (see Dahlander and Magnusson, 2005: tinyurl.com/88djuec; 2008: tinyurl.com/6w6k95q), or even the emergence of a competing fork (Nyman, 2013; tinyurl.com/mahze3o).

However, it should be noted that there are successful open core projects, which show that the approach can work. If considering an open core approach, it is worth bearing in mind that the more useful the core product is, the greater the potential community interest will be. Thus, making non-critical parts of the program closed will lessen the potential negative effect on developer interest in the project. A time-limited hybrid licensing (Sprewell, 2010; tinyurl.com/n8zeoqr), in which the closed source components of open core become open source after a 1–5 year delay, has been proposed to help meet the demands of both users and developers. However, we posit that the business source approach explained below may be a more mutually beneficial means to the same end. Examples of open core are not as easy to come by as the frequent discussion of the topic over the past few years would imply. Perhaps the best-known example is MySQL (mysql.com), which offered dual licensing of an identical product (a closed source and a GPL version) under its previous owners, but has changed to an open core approach for its free version after it was purchased by Oracle (Young, 2011; tinyurl.com/3hyxttc).

Business source

Business source is a business model that employs two different licenses with a time delay. In this business model, the source code is openly distributed and freely editable. However, for a set amount of time, a predefined segment of users (0.1–1% is suggested) have to pay to be allowed to use it. After this initial time period (3 years is suggested), the license automatically changes to an open source license. Business source is a new entrant in the field of open source licensing, which we first detailed in the June 2013 issue of the *Technology Innovation Management Review* (Widenius and Ny-

man, 2013; timreview.ca/article/691). It was created to help simultaneously meet the needs of both the open source community and the open source entrepreneur; being too restrictive in one's licensing can harm community growth, whereas being too permissive can harm business growth. Though a newly introduced concept, there are already reports of companies switching to business source, with both developers and owners pleased with the results (Widenius, 2013; tinyurl.com/mkurs58). For a more in-depth presentation of the business source approach, with a sample license, see Widenius and Nyman (2013; timreview.ca/article/691).

Dual licensing

Dual licensing is a business model in which a program is offered under two separate licenses, commonly one version under a copyleft, GPL-style license and another under a commercial, closed source license allowing for proprietary use (and combining with other proprietary software). Traditionally, the source for both versions is identical, except for changes in the copyright. Dual licensing is the best option for programs that are embedded, and for which one owns the code. The primary customers are companies who want to include software in their own packages, but who do not want to release their code under open source, as is required by the GPL. Its excellent scalability makes dual licensing the most potentially lucrative of the business models presented herein. The first ever program to adopt a dual licensing approach was Ghostscript (tinyurl.com/2p6zmt); MySQL (msql.com) – (before and during its ownership by Sun – was the second program to utilize this approach, and the first to use GPL as the open source license.

Software as a service

Software as a service (SaaS) is a fairly new business model in which connectors and application programming interfaces are open source but the server code they connect to is not accessible to the end user. For instance, one may use an application that can access certain data on a server, but not be able to access the actual source code (of, for example, the database management system) on the server one accesses. Although SaaS is not directly related to open source, it is included here because it can incorporate open source components. Examples of SaaS businesses are Salesforce (salesforce.com) and Web of Trust (mywot.com); in building their service, they may use open source software on their servers, but this software is not distributed to their users.

Managerial Implications

When deciding whether or not to start an open source project, the following managerial implications should be considered:

1. Before starting a new open source project, check if a similar project already exists. Participating in an active program is preferable to starting a new fork. If there are similar programs that have been abandoned, do some research to find out why they were abandoned. Repositories such as GitHub (github.com) and SourceForge (sourceforge.net) have a myriad of abandoned programs.

2. Find a company or a group of users that want to work with you to define the scope of the project. From the start, you will want to have users using the product while it is still in development.

3. Two of the most important decisions will be business model and license. If you are planning on relying on community participation, be mindful of their reactions to both business model and license choices. See the end of this article for further reading on community.

4. In choosing a business model, consider these questions: Do you want to concentrate on services or development? Do you plan to have a big community or work with a few big companies? Do you plan to take in investors? And, if so, what is your exit plan?

5. In choosing a license, consider these questions: What will your business model be? How much control do you want to have over the use (and potential forks) of your code? What kind of community do you want to attract around the product?

6. If you plan to rely on community participation, remember to use community-creating tools to reach and communicate with them: web pages, a forum or knowledge-base, email lists, bug system, build systems, source code repository, etc. You can start by hosting your project on GitHub, SourceForge, or another repository, but you will eventually want to host it yourself.

7. Significant enabling factors for creating a successful business around open source are ownership of code and embeddedness (a program's location in the software stack). These same factors also largely determine what business models one can choose from. Figure 1 provides a flowchart to help choose a business model based on ownership, embeddedness, and intentions for further development. If the flowchart recommends against starting a business, consider either partnering, or releasing the code (e.g., under an Apache or BSD license) for someone else to continue developing the software.

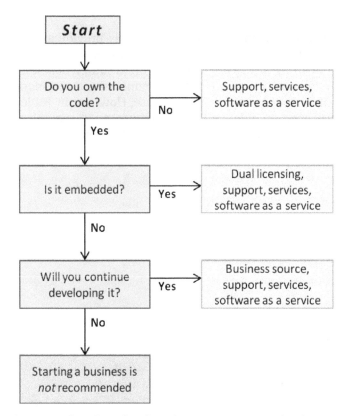

Figure 1. Flowchart for choosing an open source business model

Conclusion

Through this primer, we have given a brief answer to the question: "How can one make money on open source?" To the uninitiated, financing a business based solely around the development of open source code may perhaps seem somewhat enigmatic. Although challenging, it is nonetheless possible. Our goal in this article was to clarify this enigma by explaining some of its most significant parts.

The possibilities for monetization of a program are dependent on many factors, and key among them are ownership of code, choice of license (including the issue of license compatibility), and location in the software stack. These factors in turn affect the choice of business model.

As a primer, this article will hopefully provide a useful introduction to the business of open source. It is not intended to cover every aspect of open source businesses in full detail, nor can it provide conclusive recommendations that will apply in every case. However, in Table 3, we have included a list of recommended reading for those that want to dive deeper into the topic.

About the Authors

Michael "Monty" Widenius is the founder and original developer of MySQL and MariaDB. He has been an entrepreneur since 1979 and is the founder of MySQL Ab, Monty Program Ab, SkySQL, the MariaDB Foundation, and Open Ocean capital.

Linus Nyman is a doctoral researcher at the Hanken School of Economics in Helsinki, Finland, where he is researching code forking in open source software. A further research interest of his is free-to-play gaming. He also lectures on corporate strategy, open source software, and the new business models of the Internet age. Linus has a Master's degree in economics from the Hanken School of Economics.

Keywords: open, open source business models, open source software development, open source licenses, dual licensing, business source, open core, entrepreneurship

Table 3. Recommended reading

Topic	References
Open source licensing	• Välimäki (2005; tinyurl.com/ahljzwu) • International Free and Open Source Software Law Review (ifosslr.org)
Open source license selection in relation to business models	• Daffara (2011; timreview.ca/article/416)
License compatibility, compliance, and legality concerns	• Wheeler (2007; tinyurl.com/cbc579) • Hammouda et al. (2010; tinyurl.com/bfp82mw) • Lokhman et al. (2013; tinyurl.com/n64q3wm)
Popularity of various licenses	• Black Duck Knowledgebase (tinyurl.com/kp25s8s)
More on specific licenses	• Open Source Initiative (opensource.org/licenses) • Free Software Foundation (tinyurl.com/4e7wm)
Open source and business models	• West (2007; tinyurl.com/dxsemd) • Bailetti (2009; timreview.ca/article/226) • Hecker (1999; tinyurl.com/28n7o3) • Prowse (2010; timreview.ca/article/366) • Suehle (2012; timreview.ca/article/513)
Matching licenses with business models	• Lindman et al. (2011; tinyurl.com/na3e6fd)
Business source	• Widenius and Nyman (2013; timreview.ca/article/691)
Partnership strategies	• Riekki-Odle (2010; timreview.ca/article/364)
Business models for companies partnering with an open source vendor	• Groganz (2011; timreview.ca/article/463)
Collaboration models between open source projects and their communities	• Noori and Weiss (2013; timreview.ca/article/647) • Weiss (2011; timreview.ca/article/436)
Customer value propositions for corporate open source software	• Shanker (2012; timreview.ca/article/635)
Open source support and its requirements	• Peters (2007; timreview.ca/article/54)
Establishing a community	• Byron (2009; timreview.ca/article/258)
Participation architecture in corporate open source	• West and O'Mahoney (2008; tinyurl.com/66fly95)

12

Cyber-Resilience: A Strategic Approach for Supply Chain Management

Luca Urciuoli

" Business is all about risk taking and managing "
uncertainties and turbulence.

Gautam Adani
Business magnate

Risk management and resilience strategies in supply chains have an important role in ensuring business continuity and reliability in a cost-efficient manner. Preventing or recovering from disruptions requires access and analysis of large amounts of data. Yet, given the multiple stakeholders, operations, and environmental contexts in which a global supply chain operates, managing risks and resilience becomes a challenging task. For this reason, information and communication technologies (ICT) are being developed to support managers with tailored tools and services to monitor disruptions, enhance instantaneous communication, and facilitate the quick recovery of supply chains. Hence, the objective of this article is to shed light on managerial strategies to improve the resilience of supply chains and thereby to point out how these could be automated by means of innovative ICT systems. In particular, this article concludes by warning about existing challenges to implementing such systems. If these challenges are not correctly addressed by managers, there is a major risk of further jeopardizing supply chains.

Introduction

Recent catastrophic events, such as terrorist attacks, natural disasters, and pandemics, have drawn attention to the vulnerability of global supply chains to risks (Jüttner, 2005). Vulnerability means that supply chains are susceptible to disruptions, meaning interruptions in business operations that result in undesirable consequences such as delayed deliveries or lost sales (Svensson, 2002). For example, the earthquake that hit Taiwan in September 1999 had a severe impact on the personal computer industry worldwide – 10% of the world's computer chips and 80% of the world's motherboards were produced in Taiwan – resulting in lost revenues of more than 200 million dollars due to production shut-downs (McGillivray, 2000). Supply chain trends such as globalization, specialization, complexity, and lean processes have been largely indicated as the main drivers of these risks (Pfohl et al, 2010; WEF, 2012). Hence, in such a scenarios, supply chain managers are asked to improve their risk management skills in terms of identifying, analyzing, mitigating, and finally monitoring risks.

Supply chains are often described as sets of organizations joining a virtual network through which flows of services/products, information, and money are moved and exchanged. The common goal of these networks is to transform raw materials into components and products that are delivered to final consumers, at the right time, quantity, quality, and place. In these networks, strategies to manage risks and resilience have an important role in ensuring business continuity, delivery reliability, responsiveness, etc.

To ensure the optimal management of risks and resilience, managers of supply chains need to identify, access, and analyze large amounts of data through different information technology platforms and sources. In particular, specific ICT systems based on a combination of push and pull services are indicated as the most promising approaches to support risk management and resilience in a cost-effective manner. The principle behind these systems is very simple: such systems consists of web-services providing common and consistent access to data for all the different actors in the supply chain (e.g., suppliers, transport providers, manufacturers, distributors, importers, retailers) but also for governmental agencies worldwide (Williams et al., 2002). Yet, given their novelty, there is still much uncertainty about how these systems should be best integrated in companies.

Hence, the objective of this article is to provide a general overview of resilience strategies applied in supply chains and thereby shed light on how ICT systems can be exploited. By understanding and putting into practice these conceptual links, this article aims to contribute a visionary perspective of cyber-resilience in supply chains, illustrating how resilience in supply chains can be enhanced through the exploitation of innovative information technology services.

The article is structured in a manner to build up and lead to the cyber-resilience topic: after the introduction, it provides an overview of risk management and resilience strategies in supply chains. Next, it enumerates known challenges of these approaches, and thereafter it sheds light on the role of ICT in cyber-resilience. Finally, the article concludes by providing managerial implications and recommendations.

Risk Management and Resilience Strategies in Supply Chains

Besides risk management strategies, both researchers and practitioners point out that particular attention has to be given to strategies improving the resilience of supply chains, that is, the capability of supply chains to bounce back to stable conditions after a disruption. Resilience is important for two reasons: first of all, sooner or later, companies will have to face unexpected risks, for which no mitigation strategies have been planned in advance. Hence, the capabilities to respond to these events need to be built into the management of the companies. Second, the reactions of governmental agencies triggered after large catastrophes (e.g., terrorist attacks, earthquakes, hurricanes) may also give rise to unexpected events that supply chain companies need to deal with in order to ensure business continuity and survival (Sheffi, 2001).

Looking at the literature, diverse strategies to manage resilience have been enumerated. Some of those are:

- **Diversification of suppliers:** The access to a wider supply base enables firms to exploit additional production lines and quickly shift volumes and production in case of a disruption (Sheffi, 2006; Tang, 2006; Tomlin, 2006).

In addition, companies may use flexible contract agreements, inspections to qualify suppliers, and make-and-buy strategies to split production across different factories (Sheffi, 2006).

- **Inventory management:** Safety stocks can be increased in order to avoid stock-outs in case of missed demand. Inventory redundancy may build additional capacity in firms, yet they are well known to generate additional costs as obsolescence, product lifecycles, and inventory holdings (Sheffi, 2006; Tang, 2006; Tomlin, 2006).

- **Ensure additional transport capacity and multiple consignment routes:** Plan in advance possibilities to transport cargo by means of multiple transportation modes, multiple carriers or providers, and consequently multiple routes and distribution channels (Tang, 2006; Tomlin, 2006). Additional transport capacity can also be ensured by investing in and maintaining a dedicated transportation fleet (Sheffi, 2006).

- **Product-centric design:** Aligning the design of the products with the supply chain efficiency targets. This process cannot happen in isolation, but it implies vertical cooperation and early involvement of suppliers in product concept development and design (Khan et al., 2012; Zsidisin et al., 2000). Multiple designs of products can become useful in emergency situations, for example, in case a specific raw material or component is unexpectedly not accessible (Sheffi, 2006).

- **Information sharing:** Information sharing may improve flexibility of supply chains or enable monitoring of risks and the establishment of preventive actions (Skipper & Hanna, 2009; Tomlin, 2006).

Challenges in Managing Risks and Resilience

Given the multiple stakeholders, operations, and environmental contexts in which a global supply chain operates, managing risks and resilience is a challenging task. These challenges are especially acute in the domain of cross-border trade, where the organizations in the virtual network need to be managed as single entities across national borders, and where several regulatory compliance frameworks exist. In practice, this means that supply chain companies need to deal with different cultures, geopolitical and organizational issues, regulatory compliance frameworks, and ultimately with different ICT systems, standards, and technologies operated by different actors and under different business logics (Urciuoli et al., 2013).

The latest R&D initiatives are putting their efforts on the development of ICT tools that may support companies with this complex process. These tools aim to enhance visibility of risks along the supply chain by enabling information collection through sensor technologies, sharing of data, and application of advanced business intelligence rules to analyze data; in particular, data are not being shared merely between the supply chain companies, but also between the supply chains and the governmental agencies. This practice is fundamental to reduce the administrative costs that cross-border supply chains entail (Urciuoli et al., 2013).

To give a sense of the burden experienced by companies, it can be reminded that, to import goods into a country, companies have to produce export and import declarations, with licenses and other permits to be attached, in order to demonstrate compliance with customs regulatory frameworks. In Europe alone, customs administrations are processing almost 200 million declarations every year; for example, in 2007, it was 183 million (IBM, 2008). Each of these declarations consists of roughly 40 typologies of documents and in total about 200 data elements need to be exchanged between business and governmental entities, resulting in highly complex and costly data transfer, processing, and storage challenges (ADB, 2005).

The Role of ICT: Towards Cyber-Resilient Supply Chains

Cyber-resilience may be achieved by smartly combining technologies and services that exist today on the marketplace or that are being developed in R&D projects. These are presented in this section as ICT systems for B2B (Business to Business) and B2G (Business to Government) information sharing and analysis.

B2B information sharing
Several IT companies are struggling to develop multiple data interfaces in order to guarantee full interoperability and access to data to supply chains stakeholders. Data is actually being shared between companies in a supply chain, however, often in paper and sometimes in electronic format. In particular, the usage of paper-based information exchange has been indicated as not effective, because of the risk for mistakes, data loss, as well as redundant transfer and collection of the same data. Hence, the usage of sophisticated electronic systems to collect, store in a common repository ecosystem, and analyze data has received a lot of attention because of the abundant cost savings that could be earned. For instance, in an international shipment, files of data containing bills of lading, invoices, packing lists, country of origin, cargo quantity and type, etc. need to be shared by supply chain companies in order to improve the prediction of estimated times of arrival (ETAs). According to ETA estimations, transportation and diverse resources can be optimally scheduled and allocated, market campaigns can be punctually started to strategically retain major market shares, etc. Likewise, customs declarations in import and export countries can be submitted simultaneously by different stakeholders (Urciuoli et al., 2011).

Nowadays, web-services based on service-oriented architectures (SOAs) seem to be widely exploited to ensure connectivity of the supply chain in a plug-and-play fashion. These services enable electronic data sharing, and with it may reduce the risk for mistakes or incomplete data. In addition, web-based push and pull services can be exploited to avoid data redundancy and speed up response procedures in case of unexpected disruptions:

- **B2B pull services:** Data may be pulled by a supply chain company in order to obtain the current status of a consignment/container or to interrogate the inventory levels of suppliers, distribution centres/wholesalers, retailers, transport infrastructure capacity, traffic conditions, etc.

- **B2B push services:** Push services are instead used to trigger alerts to companies whenever the status of inventory levels, demand, containers conditions. or position change in an unexpected manner. In other words, the service is able to sense whenever data outrange previously established upper and lower control limits (UCLs and LCLs). These data ranges can be determined by means of advanced business intelligence techniques.

The combination of the above push and pull services enables full visibility and control in the supply chain. By pulling key data, managers may monitor, in real time, inventory levels, shipping statuses, environmental conditions of cargo and containers, arrival time at specific nodes in the supply chain network, etc. This information improves decision making in terms of optimizing inventory levels, scheduling and planning transport assignments, allocating resources, designing networks, etc. On the contrary, push services are more suitable to handle risks and manage resilience. Hence, in case of deviations from planned routines, alerts may be triggered to recover or activate response procedures. Examples of push services could be alerts triggered by environmental sensors in containers, alarms installed in vehicles, panic buttons, geofences, timefences, etc.

B2G information sharing
Nowadays, to enable resilience strategies, supply chain companies work with different contract typologies and portfolios of suppliers located in various countries across the globe. However, despite contracts being in place, in case of a disruption, companies will suddenly need to deal with several different regulatory frameworks and customs procedures. Not only that, different countries require different data formats or usage of different information technology interfaces, implying higher costs in terms of translation and adaptation efforts needed to bridge between different national systems. Experts believe that future information technology systems will ensure that companies' systems can easily connect to customs administrations' web-platforms (i.e., e-Customs) and facilitate filing of customs declarations or provide easy access to international trade-related documentation (Urciuoli et al., 2013). In addition, push and pull services developed in prototype platforms may play a fundamental role in managing resilience:

- **B2G pull services:** Pull services connected to e-Customs platforms may be used to control existing trade regulations, necessary documentation for import/export procedures, status of release and clearance of containers, customs declarations, licenses, etc.

- **B2G push services:** Push services are instead planned to include alerts in case of changed trading regulations, tariffs or taxes, deviations of containers inspections and release, etc. These systems may eliminate unnecessary delays, reduce paper redundancy, and in this way, reduce costs to companies and governments.

Conclusion

ICT has already been indicated as playing a major role in controlling and managing more complex value networks in a cost-efficient manner. However, additional capabilities, mainly aiming to improve cyber-resilience, may be exploited to ensure quick response to risks and disruptions in supply chains. These capabilities are supported by the development of common repository IT ecosystems where B2B or B2G push and pull web services are created and contemporarily accessed by supply chain actors, but also governmental agencies.

Enabling B2B and B2G data sharing may allow companies to access an unimaginable amount of data and services that can enhance the cyber-resilience of the whole supply chain. For instance, companies will be able to easily manage and control portfolios of suppliers online, make more accurate ETA estimations, monitor in real time the transport infrastructure capacity, learn and apply any sudden changes in trading regulations, rapidly submit electronic orders and comply with regulatory frameworks, etc.

Despite the promising future visions, there is still much work to be done in order to ensure that these ICT systems will be fully accepted and integrated into supply chain companies. Many challenges are being encountered and need to be solved in order to move a step forward towards cyber-resilient supply chains. These are, in sequential order, the following:

1. **Exploit/develop reliable and robust information collection and sharing (both B2B and B2G).** Collection and sharing of information is still a major concern, especially for small companies, both in terms of technical development, know-how, and monetary investments.

2. **Exploit business intelligence rules.** Develop tailored push and pull web services that enable cyber-resilience. Yet, to develop reliable business intelligence rules, resources need to be allocated to identifying, modelling, and assessing risks in a systematic manner.

3. **Ensure public–private partnerships.** Partnerships should focus on the implementation of ICT systems to exchange data with public agencies and aim at developing up-to-date standards and legislative frameworks.

4. **Solve potential data confidentiality issues.** Sharing information implies that data will need to be held in repositories or remote locations. For obvious reason, this requirement is not accepted by many business companies that fear their business strategies will be disclosed to competitors.

5. **Ensure cybersecurity.** In several instances, it has been pointed out that, although the information technology layer of supply chains is relevant to optimizing supply chain management, it may also expose companies to criminal actions (e.g., theft, fraud, forgery, industrial espionage) or sabotage, hackers, and terrorists aiming to promote ideological issues and hurt the economy of a nation or a single industry (e.g., hacktivism, sabotage). Hence, this risk naturally implies that cyber-resilience strategies should be followed by information technology security management systems.

In conclusion, it is strongly believed that, without common data access, managers may struggle to fully develop, apply, and coordinate resilience operations in companies. Resilience becomes even more challenging in global supply chains, where managers need to deal with threats and recovery operations outside their companies and in different and multi-faceted environmental contexts. Current R&D initiatives are demonstrating that ICT systems for B2B and B2G data exchange, when combined with business intelligence techniques, may provide supply chain managers with advanced capabilities to improve resilience. Hence, supply chain companies could be only "a click away" from fully automated cyber-resilience.

Acknowledgements

The author of this paper would like to thank the CORE project (Consistently Optimised Resilient Secure Global Supply Chains, Grant Agreement No. 603993), a project funded under the European Union's Seventh Framework Programme for research, technological development, and demonstration. This publication reflects the views only of the author, and the EU Commission cannot be held responsible for any use which may be made of the information contained therein.

About the Author

Luca Urciuoli is an Associate Research Professor in the MIT International Logistics Program within the Zaragoza Logistics Center in Spain, where he teaches and performs research in supply chain network design, supply chain risk, and security management. He holds an MSc degree in Industrial Engineering from Chalmers University of Technology in Gothenburg, Sweden, and a Doctorate in Transportation Security from the Engineering University of Lund, Sweden. He has been working at the research unit of the Volvo group as a project manager developing on-board transport and telematics services. He also led the research of the Cross-border Research Association in Switzerland and collaborated in several FP7 research and consultancy projects, with a focus on topics such as e-Customs, trade facilitation, supply chain security, waste security, and postal security. He is also an editorial board member for the *Journal of Transportation Security*, and he has published his research in several scientific and practitioner journals.

Contact: lurciuoli@zlc.edu.es

References

ADB. 2005. *ICT for Customs Modernization and Data Exchange.* Manila, Philippines: Asian Development Bank.

IBM. 2008. *Implementing e-Customs in Europe: An IBM Point of View.* Somers, NY: IBM Corporation.

Jüttner, U. 2005. Supply Chain Risk Management: Understanding the Business Requirements from a Practitioner Perspective. *International Journal of Logistics Management,* 16(1): 120–141. http://dx.doi.org/10.1108/09574090510617385

Khan, O., Christopher, M., & Creazza, A. 2012. Aligning Product Design with the Supply Chain: A Case Study. *Supply Chain Management,* 17(3): 323–336. http://dx.doi.org/10.1108/13598541211227144

McGillivray, G. 2000. Commercial Risk Under JIT. *Canadian Underwriter,* 67(1): 26–30.

Pfohl, H.-C., Köhler, H., & Thomas, D. 2010. State of the Art in Supply Chain Risk Management Research: Empirical and Conceptual Findings and a Roadmap for the Implementation in Practice. *Logistics Research,* 2(1): 33–44. http://dx.doi.org/10.1007/s12159-010-0023-8

Sheffi, Y. 2001. Supply Chain Management under the Threat of International Terrorism. *International Journal of Logistics Management,* 12(2): 1–11. http://dx.doi.org/10.1108/09574090110806262

Sheffi, Y. 2006. Resilience Reduces Risk. *Logistics Quarterly,* 12(4): 12–14.

Skipper, J. B., & Hanna, J. B. 2009. Minimizing Supply Chain Disruption Risk through Enhanced Flexibility. *International Journal of Physical Distribution and Logistics Management,* 39(5): 404–427. http://dx.doi.org/10.1108/09600030910973742

Svensson, G. 2002. A Conceptual Framework of Vulnerability in Firms' Inbound and Outbound Logistics Flows. *International Journal of Physical Distribution & Logistics Management,* 32(2): 110–134. http://dx.doi.org/10.1108/09600030210421723

Tang, C. S. 2006. Robust Strategies for Mitigating Supply Chain Disruptions. *International Journal of Logistics Research and Applications,* 9(1): 33–45. http://dx.doi.org/10.1080/13675560500405584

Tomlin, B. 2006. On the Value of Mitigation and Contingency Strategies for Managing Supply Chain Disruption Risks. *Management Science,* 52(5): 639–657. http://dx.doi.org/10.1287/mnsc.1060.0515

Urciuoli, L., Hintsa, J., & Ahokas, J. 2013. Drivers and Barriers Affecting Usage of E-Customs — a Global Survey with Customs Administrations Using Multivariate Analysis Techniques. *Government Information Quarterly,* 30(4): 473–485. http://dx.doi.org/10.1016/j.giq.2013.06.001

Urciuoli, L., Zuidwijk, R., & van Oosterhout, M. 2011. Adoption and Effects Extended SICIS. In *Proceedings of the 2011 Hamburg International Conference of Logistics (HICL)*.

WEF. 2012. *New Models for Addressing Supply Chain and Transport Risks*. Geneva, Switzerland: World Economic Forum.

Williams, L. R., Esper, T. L., & Ozment, J. 2002. The Electronic Supply Chain: Its Impact on the Current and Future Structure of Strategic Alliances, Partnerships and Logistics Leadership. *International Journal of Physical Distribution & Logistics Management*, 32(8): 703–719.
http://dx.doi.org/10.1108/09600030210444935

Zsidisin, G. A., Panelli, A., & Upton, R. 2000. Purchasing Organization Involvement in Risk Assessments, Contingency Plans and Risk Management: An Explorative Study. *Supply Chain Management*, 4(4): 187–197.
http://dx.doi.org/10.1108/13598540010347307

Keywords: IT, ICT, supply chain management, cross-border trade, cyber-resilience, risk management

The Business of Open Source

Michael Weiss

" *Today, if you don't think of open source as part of your* " *technology business, you are doing something wrong.*

Michael Weiss
Associate Professor, Carleton University

Overview

The TIM Lecture Series is hosted by the Technology Innovation Management program (carleton.ca/tim) at Carleton University in Ottawa, Canada. The lectures provide a forum to promote the transfer of knowledge from university research to technology company executives and entrepreneurs as well as research and development personnel. Readers are encouraged to share related insights or provide feedback on the presentation or the TIM Lecture Series, including recommendations of future speakers.

The seventh TIM lecture of 2013 was presented by Michael Weiss, Associate Professor in the Technology Innovation Management program at Carleton University, who examined the business of open source, with a focus on common patterns followed by open source businesses. The event was held at Carleton University on December 12th, 2013.

In the first part of his lecture, Weiss provided an overview of the business of open source, described the key elements of early-stage open source businesses, and presented common patterns followed by open source businesses. In the second part of the lecture, he closely examined late-stage open source businesses, the impact of licensing and architecture, and what the future may hold for open source. The slides from this lecture are available here: tinyurl.com/loz5yof

Summary

Open source has become an integral part of commercial software development. Whereas in the past, open source software development was considered to be driven by volunteer effort, today most of it is carried out by companies. How companies leverage open source ranges from the adoption of open source development practices, the use of open source development tools, and the integration of open source components into products to active contributions to existing open source projects, and the initiation of their own company-led open source projects. Open source furthermore enables companies to collaborate on the creation of common assets that they can jointly use in product development.

An open source business is a business built around an open source offer. Thus, open source is not by itself a business model; rather, it used by the business as a strategy to strengthen its business model (Bailetti, 2009; timreview.ca/article/226). Typically, open source businesses use open source to: i) develop new products; ii) build products or services around open source offers; iii) initiate their own open source projects; or iv) leverage open source as a form of co-opetition (i.e., cooperation with competitors). Indeed, close study of the way in which businesses have leveraged open source has led to the identification of common patterns used by open source businesses.

Patterns are proven solutions to common problems, and have been popular in the fields of architecture and software design. More recently, they have also been used to document business strategies, including those used by open source businesses. The patterns that Weiss described in this lecture aimed to provide entrepreneurs, managers, and students of business models with a language for creating new business models around open source, and for incorporating open source into existing business models. Some of these patterns are unique to the stage of a company's engagement with open source (i.e., from primarily just using open source assets, to contributing to projects, to championing particular development projects, and finally to collaborating strategically within the ecosystem), whereas a given pattern relating to licensing and architecture typically may be used in all stages (Figure 1).

Examples of open source business patterns discussed in the lecture include:

1. **Bootstrap:** This use-stage pattern refers to the reuse of existing open source components to develop products. This pattern allows a company to shorten the time it takes to create a first version of their product, while keeping costs low; however; it also increases the complexity of the software and the breadth of knowledge needed.

2. **Contribute back:** By contributing resources (e.g., code, people, money) to the projects they use, companies can: i) build trust with the community, ii) influence the development of the project, and iii) demonstrate their competence.

3. **Credible promise:** When championing a project, building a critical mass of functionality into the project from an early stage can mobilize contributors to a company's project – it helps the company demonstrate that the project is doable and has merit.

4. **Feed the community:** A company can build legitimacy with a project community by nurturing the community without any expectation of immediate return, for example by: i) giving to the community (e.g., contributing code, writing documentation, participating in the discussion forum); ii) establishing a clear licensing practice; iii) establishing a clear process for making contributions; iv) making decisions in the open; and v) not treating community members as prospects.

5. **Sell complements:** An open source product can be monetized through the selling of services (e.g., hardware or support) that complement the open source product.

6. **Run a tight ship:** To keep control of a project's direction, companies often retain full ownership of the code.

7. **Dual product (open core):** To entice commercial users to pay for an open source software product, a company may sell a commercial version of the open source produce with exclusive features.

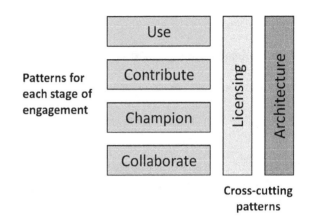

Figure 1. Open source business patterns

8. **Pool resources:** To optimize the use of resources in the collaboration stage, a company may jointly develop a common stack of open source assets with other companies. Each company can then develop their own differentiated products based on these common assets.

9. **Foundation:** A company can attract other companies to contribute its open source project by transferring ownership of the code to an independent foundation. A foundation creates an arms-length relationship between the project creator and the project itself, and it centralizes common functions that all members can access (e.g., legal, marketing, project management). Creating a foundation builds trust and facilitates collaboration among the contributors.

Examples of patterns related to licensing include:

1. **Play by the rules:** The risk of a licensing problem arising after a product is released can be mitigated by ensuring license compliance for open source components that are combined.

2. **Dual license:** To encourage commercial users to pay for an open source software product, a company can offer the same product under two licenses: commercial and open source. Non-commercial users still benefit from the rights under the open source license, and buyers of the commercial license are released from some of the obligations of the open source license.

3. **IP modularity:** Alignment of its intellectual property with the product architecture can help a company manage the complexities of having both open source and proprietary versions of a dual product.

Examples of patterns related to architecture include:

1. **Modular architecture:** External contributors may have difficulty contributing if they require deep knowledge of the project. A company can overcome this problem by partitioning the code base so that different parts (or modules) can be worked on and managed independently.

2. **Manage complements:** A governance model and regulatory tools can help manage the quality of complements developed by the community.

To conclude the lecture, Weiss speculated about what the future might hold for open source. The discussion focused on the shift away from desktops and servers onto what are – for open source – non-traditional platforms of mobile, embedded systems, and hardware. The role of open source in the "Internet of Things" (tinyurl.com/5qr2nq) was also explored. Finally, Weiss reflected upon the ongoing growth of "open" beyond software (e.g., open hardware, open data, and open science).

Lessons Learned

In the discussions that followed each portion of the presentation, audience members shared the lessons they learned from the presentation and injected their own knowledge and experience into the conversation.

The audience identified the following key takeaways from the presentation:

1. Patterns help you recognize and find solutions beyond your expertise, and they help you collaborate

2. There are now real and practical examples of companies employing these strategies – open source business is now a well-travelled road.

3. Different patterns are suited to different contexts/opportunities.

4. Although open source can reduce costs, the increased complexity it often brings is a challenge.

5. The value to companies is significant if they share R&D for non-core development; they can then focus their efforts on what makes them different from the competition.

6. Companies go though phases in their engagement with open source. They start out as users, then start contributing. Eventually, they may champion their own project and then collaborate with other companies, perhaps even by forming a foundation. It's a learning curve.

7. Community management only works when you have appropriate governance in place.

8. The value of the code is a function of: i) how quickly you can learn about it; ii) how modular it is; and iii) how many applications it can serve. These factors determine how quickly you can ramp up.

9. Companies have options and can make conscious choices about how to use open source in their strategies and business models.

10. The value of the disruption that open source represents is threefold: i) it allowed companies to make money in new ways; ii) it enabled software to be produced and distributed in completely new ways; and iii) it reduced the barriers to entry while increasing the potential for collaboration.

11. There is a trend towards the creation of open source toolsets that allow for the early and simple creation of applications. This technical capability enables others to quickly solve real-world domain-specific problems.

12. In the future, we need new ways of innovating around business models. The landscape is now different; we need to look forward and not worry about what did or did not work in the past.

Additional Resources

1. Slides from this lecture: tinyurl.com/loz5yof

2. Related papers by Michael Weiss:

   - "Performance of Open Source Projects"
     (2009; tinyurl.com/l2zf8qz)

   - "Profiting from Open Source"
     (2010; tinyurl.com/m974nya)

   - "Profiting Even More from Open Source"
     (2011; tinyurl.com/ktt37jy)

This report was written by Michael Weiss and Chris McPhee.

About the Speaker

Michael Weiss holds a faculty appointment in the Department of Systems and Computer Engineering at Carleton University in Ottawa, Canada, and is a member of the Technology Innovation Management program. His research interests include open source, ecosystems, mashups, patterns, and social network analysis. Michael has published on the evolution of open source business, mashups, platforms, and technology entrepreneurship.

Keywords: open source software, business models, patterns, engagement, entrepreneurship, licensing, architecture, community

14

Effective Digital Channel Marketing for Cybersecurity Solutions

Mika Westerlund and Risto Rajala

"Why kick the man downstream who can't put the parts together because the parts really weren't designed properly?"

Philip Caldwell (1920–2013)
Former CEO of the Ford Motor Company

Smaller organizations are prime targets for hackers and malware, because these businesses lack cybersecurity plans and the resources to survive a serious security incident. To exploit this market opportunity, cybersecurity solution providers need to leverage the power of downstream channel members. We investigate how a supplier's digital channel marketing can encourage value-added resellers to sell that supplier's cybersecurity solutions. Our analysis of survey data from 109 value-added resellers of a multinational supplier shows that resellers are more committed to stock and sell cybersecurity products and services if the supplier's digital channel marketing provides tools that help them sell the solutions to end customers. This support is likely needed because cybersecurity offerings are technologically complex and systemic by nature, as supported by the finding that value-added resellers pay little attention to supplier's campaigns and price discounts. Thus, cybersecurity suppliers should maintain trusted and informative relationships with their resellers and provide them with hands-on sales tools, because a reseller's commitment to selling cybersecurity solutions is linked with their ability to understand the offering and with the extent of their supplier relationship. These findings are in line with previous literature on the challenges perceived by salespeople in selling novel and complex technology.

Introduction

According to The 2112 Group (2014), the volume and severity of cyber-threats and malware represent the second highest operational risk for small and midsized businesses, behind only economic uncertainty. Yet, four out of five such businesses have no cybersecurity plans, meaning there is a substantial market opportunity for cybersecurity providers. One of the most effective ways to reach these numerous potential customers is to leverage the power of downstream channels (cf. Sreenivas & Srinivas, 2008; Chung et al., 2012). Value-added resellers are systems integrators that can work either with a single vendor that offers most of the technology needed to build end-to-end offerings, or multiple vendors to integrate and craft more comprehensive solutions. Although many value-added resellers prefer working with a single vendor, a growing number show better returns by creating holistic solutions using multiple "best-of-breed" technologies (The 2012 Group, 2014). Given that value-added resellers have choices in sourcing, assembling, and deploying hardware and software solutions for customers, cybersecurity suppliers need to build brand awareness to maximize the popularity of their products as a part of the reseller's total solutions.

Digitization has redefined how contemporary businesses communicate across their channels of distribution (Rapp et al., 2013). Holden-Bache (2011) refers to a study by BtoB Magazine in which more than 93 percent of business-to-business marketers were found to use one or more forms of social media to interact with their downstream channel members. According to Kalyanam and Brar (2009), designing a channel-management system that enables value-added resellers to sell solutions to end users is an important strategy, particularly in the information and communication technology industry. Furthermore, Jerman and Zavrsnik (2012) suggest that the success of an organization can result from the effectiveness of its marketing communication. Hence, a firm should have a business model that tracks how marketing communication influences what its customers know, believe, and feel, and how they behave.

Much of the current research on downstream channel marketing focuses on value propositions associated with products or services. In addition, many studies on marketing communications have focused on the consumer market, with little regard for the business-to-business market (Jerman & Zavrsnik, 2012). The determinants of perceived value associated with complex products and services, such as cybersecurity, remain unclear and largely under-explored (Menon et al., 2005). Hence, the existing literature offers limited empirical and theoretical insight into marketing communications effectiveness in business-to-business marketing. Specifically, there is little help for marketing managers when planning effective communications strategies and understanding the impact of their suppliers' channel marketing activities (Jerman & Zavrsnik, 2012).

To address these gaps in the literature, we investigate the effectiveness of digital channel marketing in the context of business-to-business cybersecurity solutions. We consider that cybersecurity is an interesting context given the growing demand for cybersecurity solutions, especially among small and midsized businesses, and acknowledge that the marketing activities of suppliers in downstream channels are increasingly digital by nature. Craigen and colleagues (2014) define cybersecurity as "the organization and collection of resources, processes, and structures used to protect cyberspace and cyberspace-enabled systems from occurrences that misalign *de jure* from *de facto* property rights." Bearing this definition in mind, our study aims to improve the current understanding of how cybersecurity solution providers can increase the impact of their digital channel marketing by focusing on the paramount marketing activities and by allocating their marketing resources accordingly. Further, our study draws on the view of Johanson (2013), who defines cybersecurity products as software, hardware, and ser-

vices that help users protect themselves from cybersecurity threats related to information sharing, security risks, cyber-incidents, and cybercrime, as well as cyber-intrusions. Thus, we investigate cybersecurity solutions as the offerings consisting of products and related expertise provided to meet the customers' cybersecurity needs and posit a research question: How can suppliers of cybersecurity solutions use digital channel marketing effectively to promote their products in the downstream channel?

To answer our research question, we investigate the effects of digital channel marketing by cybersecurity solution providers in terms of its functional, informative, and relational qualities, as well as the influence of marketing abundance on the effectiveness of digital channel marketing by cybersecurity solution providers. According to Kalyanam and Brar (2009), there are many ways in which channel partners such as resellers can help generate demand. Resellers are often deeply embedded in the customer's decision-making processes and are able to create and offer solutions to customer's specific business situation and technology needs. Thus, suppliers need to focus on creating top-of-mind awareness among their value-added resellers to ensure them becoming a preferred supplier when resellers are in a position to sell cybersecurity solutions to the end customers.

The article is structured as follows. After this introduction, we discuss the objectives and activities of digital channel marketing on the basis of prior literature. Then, we present our research model and methodological approach. Thereafter, we present the results, limitations, and future research opportunities regarding our empirical inquiry. We conclude by discussing the implications for research and practice.

Digital Channel Marketing

A supplier's success in the marketplace is at least partly contingent on their ability to energize downstream channel members to resell their products and services, according to Hughes and Ahearne (2010). Moreover, Danaher and Rossiter (2011) argue that digital marketing communication is a vital part of the relationship between a supplier and a value-added reseller. Contemporary marketers face an increasingly wide and diverse choice of digital media channels through which they aim to energize their brokers, agents, wholesalers, and retailers to sell their products and services effectively to other channel members, and, ultimately, to the end users. As Internet technologies have become an every-day part of the workplace for millions of people around the globe, current marketing channels feature many digital elements such as banner ads, email and blogs, social software, and text messaging (SMS). Lindgreen and colleagues (2006) show that many suppliers increasingly use digital communications to interact with their resellers rather than face-to-face interaction.

To be effective, channel marketing communications should create value for channel partners. According to Simpson, Siguaw, and Baker (2001), the objective of creating value for channel partners and the desire to capture part of that value are the reasons suppliers enter into relationships with value-added resellers. Barry and Terry (2008) point out that the determinants of value have an economic, technical, and functional dimension. Economic value refers to pricing (how much something costs), while technical value points to deliverables (what is received) and functional value refers to delivery (how it is received). Payne and Holt (2001) argue that, according to the augmented product view, competition between companies is not based solely on products and services, but also on advertising and customer advice that create value for the downstream channel members. Edwards, Battisti, and Neely (2004) anticipate that the benefits of digital channel marketing for value-added resellers depend upon the quality and extent of activities the supplier generates through digital marketing. The benefits of digital channel marketing may be realized by communicating the value of factors beyond the core product or service (Lilien et al., 2010).

The effectiveness of marketing communications can be measured in several ways, although in terms of economic measures, the most common indicator of marketing performance is the volume of sales. Danaher and Rossiter (2011) investigate supplier-initiated marketing communication and measure the effect of promotional offers in an electronic medium on intentional customer behaviour. Thus, marketing effectiveness in supply chains can be measured as the reseller's intention and increased efforts to sell a supplier's products and services (Johnson et al., 2001). Kalyanam and Brar (2009) found that, because resellers in the dynamic information technology industry are typically selling many technologies, they lack the time to focus and learn specific technologies or product information. Following Jerman and Zavrsnik (2012), we see that it is important for marketers to understand the contribution of different marketing objectives to the overall effectiveness of their marketing communications.

Relational qualities
The relational qualities of digital channel marketing focus on strengthening the supplier's relationships with the members in the downstream channel. This notion is concordant with the thesis by Webster (2000), according to which, in the relationship between the supplier, reseller, and end customer, the quality of the relationship for any given actor will depend on the quality and strength of the relationship between the other two actors. The value of the supplier relationship, as perceived by the reseller, usually refers to the net benefits realized through the supplier's offerings or the supplier-reseller relationship (Kumar et al., 1992). It builds on the assumption that value-added resellers want to maximize the perceived benefits and minimize the perceived sacrifices (Lindgreen & Wynstra, 2005). A supplier's business marketing communications have great potential to produce such value to the value-added reseller. According to Andersen (2001), marketing communication is connected with relationship development, and the receiver's commitment to the sender is preceded by awareness and persuasion.

Relationship marketing scholars have found that communication is a fundamental aspect of relationship development – it is the glue that holds together the channel of distribution (Anderson, 2001). Andersen also notes that communication has a direct impact on central aspects of relationship marketing such as trust, coordination, and commitment. Communication is seen as an independent or mediating variable for partnership success (Mohr & Spekman, 1994). The essence of these activities is to decrease exchange uncertainty and to encourage customer collaboration and commitment through gradual development and ongoing adjustment of mutual norms and shared routines. If customers are retained over several transactions, both buyers and sellers may profit from the experience gained through previous transactions (Andersen, 2001). Accordingly, we developed the following hypothesis:

Hypothesis 1: *Digital channel marketing that strengthens the relationship between supplier and value-added reseller is positively linked with the reseller's intention to sell the supplier's cybersecurity solutions.*

Informative qualities
The informative qualities of channel marketing ensure that value-added resellers are kept up to date with campaigns and product developments. Jerman and Zavrsnik (2012) posit that marketing communications

aimed at downstream channel members play more of an informational and supportive role than do those that target end consumers. Marketing communications need to provide clear, pertinent, and timely information, so that good decisions can be made (Jerman & Zavrsnik, 2012). Hansen and colleagues (2008) suggest that information sharing increases the value of the supplier-reseller relationship, as perceived by the value-added reseller, and it fosters adaptation and trust in that relationship. Moreover, Edwards, Battisti, and Neely (2004) found that suppliers can be a key source of information for buyers, exceeded only by the company's internal knowledge acquisition. Hansen, Samuelsen, and Silseth (2008) point out that suppliers may inform their value-added resellers about the product-related information relevant for the relationship, including changes in pricing, changes in market, new products and services, as well as organizational changes that may affect the supplier-reseller relationship. In particular, sales promotion is an informative type of communication that consists of a set of short-term motivational tools used to encourage buyers to buy more and promptly (Rahmani et al., 2012).

According to Kalyanam and Brar (2009), high-tech companies such as Cisco, which has invested significantly in digital channel marketing, training, and certification programs for its downstream channel members, have enjoyed increased sales volumes. Therefore, Simpson, Siguaw, and Baker (2001) argue that the supplier's activity as a provider of information can serve as a critical informational resource for the reseller. One-way oriented communication, such as advertising, branding, and other traditional tools, may help the supplier develop an attractive personality profile (Andersen, 2001). Hence, if a supplier has developed an attractive image in the mind of the prospective buyer, it may cause the decision maker to look for information on this particular supplier first: a top-of-the-mind effect (Andersen, 2001). Hence, we developed the following hypothesis:

Hypothesis 2: *Digital channel marketing that is informative of supplier's campaigns and price discounts is positively linked with the reseller's intention to sell the supplier's cybersecurity solutions.*

Functional qualities

Functionally motivated communication supports the capability of downstream channel members to resell the suppliers' products. For example, suppliers may possess specific expertise, which the downstream channel partners may not have in-house or may not want to

acquire (Ulaga, 2003). This benefit is especially important with complex technology such as cybersecurity products and services. Therefore, a supplier of cybersecurity products can provide benefit to value-added resellers by educating and helping them improve their skills and competences to sell the supplier's products. Supplier-provided facilities and tools are among the key factors that augment the value perceived by downstream channel partners (Simpson et al., 2001). In addition, Simpson, Siguaw, and Baker (2001) contend that product and service related training is perceived valuable by resellers. These tools include point-of-sale scanner data for inventory, promotion and payment management, customer management database tools, and an online presence for Internet marketing. According to Simpson and colleagues (2001), research has shown that these supplier-provided tools improve the sales performance of value-added resellers. Also, Lindgreen and colleagues (2006) suggest that the value of channel marketing goes beyond the immediate value of goods or services, given that the education the supplier provides is part of that value.

We consider the functional objectives to be instrumental by nature, because the supplier helps its value-added resellers obtain something to improve their sales performance. In doing so, we comprehend the instrumental value of suppliers' digital channel marketing through two distinct aspects. First, it implies that value-added resellers perceive the digital marketing communications of their suppliers as useful, because it helps the resellers to develop and improve their selling skills and capabilities. Second, it gives the resellers new tools for selling complex products and services. Based on these notions, we consider it reasonable to suggest that digital channel marketing by suppliers can support resellers by providing them with professional skills or practical tools that improve their sales performance. Therefore, we developed the following hypothesis for the context of cybersecurity:

Hypothesis 3: *Digital channel marketing that provides functional support to resellers is positively linked with the resellers' intention to sell the supplier's cybersecurity solutions.*

Abundant digital channel marketing, sales intention, and stocking decisions

Previous research does not consistently show whether more digital marketing is better from the performance point of view. There may be a valuable premium in frequency and continuity of marketing messages to the customers. Danaher and Rossiter (2011) researched how customers perceive marketing communications and direct marketing messages they receive from suppliers in various ways, including different channels. Surprisingly, senders rate email more negatively than receivers do. That is, business receivers view email messages in a positive light, but senders are more cautious in fear of using it excessively. Thus, it makes sense, for instance, to send multiple waves of marketing emails, because marketers in the digital era cannot count on the recipients to open a particular email message. Consequently, we developed the following hypothesis:

Hypothesis 4: *Abundant digital channel marketing is positively linked with reseller's intention to sell the supplier's cybersecurity solutions.*

The theory of reasoned action developed by Fishbein and Ajzen (1975) and its successor, the theory of planned behaviour proposed by Ajzen (1985), are among the most predictive persuasion theories. They have been applied to studies of the relations among beliefs, attitudes, behavioural intentions and behaviours in various fields such as advertising, public relations, and marketing. The theory states that behavioural intention, which is a function of attitudes toward behavioural and subjective norms toward that behaviour, predict actual behaviour. Thus, we developed the following hypothesis:

Hypothesis 5: *The intention of value-added resellers to sell a supplier's cybersecurity solutions is positively linked with its stocking decisions.*

Model

Our research model is rooted in previous studies on the effectiveness of advertising on sales performance. One of them is the article by Hughes (2013) about the effects of advertisement on sales efforts and performance of resellers. Jerman and Zavrsnik (2012) confirm that marketing communications have a positive effect on the market performance of suppliers. With increasing calls for accountability of significant marketing communication spending, it is imperative to measure the contribution of marketing communication to firm performance (Jerman & Zavrsnik, 2012).

Lemmink and colleagues (1998) have proposed that customer value includes emotional, logical, and practical benefits. We amend their conceptualization for a better fit with channel marketing in supply chains, and anticipate that the supplier's digital channel marketing provides resellers with relational, informative, and functional benefits. These benefits comprise the perceived quality of digital channel marketing, whereas marketing abundance, referring to the extent and volume of marketing messages, reflects the quantity of marketing. In our research model, sales intention refers to a reseller's increased effort to sell the supplier's products and the reseller's stocking decision is understood as the actual purchase of the supplier's products to ensure its stock-and-sell availability. As the hypothesized model illustrates, we anticipate that both quality and quantity of a supplier's digital channel marketing contribute to the sales intention of its value-added resellers, and, ultimately, to their stocking decisions (Figure 1).

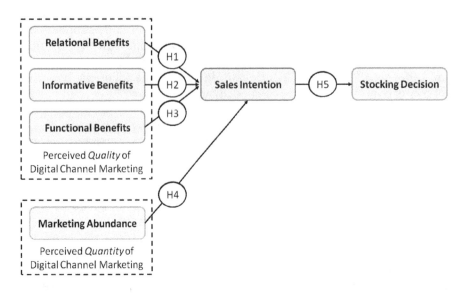

Figure 1. Research model, including the five hypotheses

Methodology

We conducted an online survey in late 2008 among Finnish retailers of an internationally operating supplier of cybersecurity products. The company provides a broad range of data security, cybersecurity, and infrastructure security solutions to value-added resellers in 15 countries in Europe and North America. To select the target companies for the survey, we administered it to the active resellers of the supplier's products. Our contact at the company sent an invitation to participate in the survey to 335 potential respondents by email. The questionnaire yielded 109 usable responses, thus giving a response rate of 32.5 percent. We measured all items on a five-point Likert scale (1="strongly disagree" to 5="strongly agree).

We chose the Partial Least Squares (PLS) path-modelling method for our empirical analysis. The advantages of PLS include the ability to model multiple constructs, to explore the relative importance of the independent variables, and the ability to handle their multicollinearity. In addition, the method provides us with robustness in the face of missing data; it poses minimum requirements on measurement levels and allows the creation of independent latent variables directly on the basis of cross-products involving the response variables (Chin et al., 2003; Tenenhaus et al., 2005). These concerns are important in our research setting, where there is no strong theory to test in order to explain the phenomenon. In practice, PLS helps to avoid biased and inconsistent parameter estimates for equations, which is appropriate when the research model is in an early stage of development (Teo et al., 2003). We performed the empirical analysis using the SmartPLS 2.0 software by Ringle Wende, and Will (2005).

Results

The results of our hypothesis testing show that H1, H3, and H5 are supported, whereas H2 and H4 are not supported. In other words, the results suggest that relational benefits (H1; β=.26, p<.05) and functional benefits (H3; β=.60, p<.001) of a cybersecurity suppliers' digital channel marketing are positively linked with the increased sales intention of the value-added resellers. Moreover, this sales intention (H5; β=.42, p<.001) is positively linked with the reseller's actual stocking behaviour. On the contrary, informative benefits (H2; β=-.09, n.s.) and the quantity of marketing in terms of abundant marketing messages (H4; β=.08, n.s.) are not linked with the increased sales intension of the value-added resellers. Table 1 presents the results of hypothesis testing, and Appendix 1 discusses the details of our analysis.

Every analysis has limitations, which provide opportunities for future research. First, we discussed the quality of digital channel marketing in terms of relational, informative, and functional benefits. An in-depth review of marketing communication theory may reveal other aspects, practices, or occasions that can affect the results. Further analysis could also reveal possible differences between new and established relationships between supplies and value-added resellers regarding the impact of supplier's digital channel marketing on the behavioural sales intention of resellers (cf. Andersen, 2001). Second, because our study was conducted in one European country only and focused on cybersecurity as a specific form of complex technology, future research may test our findings in other countries or market areas and in other domains beyond cybersecurity. Third, the results may be different if the effective-

Table 1. Results of hypotheses testing (n=109, bootstrap samples=1000, df=115)

Hypothesis	Relationship	β	t-value	p-value	Support
H1	RELATIONAL → SALES INTENTION	.26	2.70	.008	Yes
H2	INFORMATIVE → SALES INTENTION	-.09	1.30	.197	No
H3	FUNCTIONAL → SALES INTENTION	.60	6.87	.000	Yes
H4	ABUNDANT → SALES INTENTION	.08	.90	.370	No
H5	SALES INTENTION → STOCK	.42	3.96	.000	Yes

ness of the supplier's digital channel marketing is measured using other variables. Our analysis measured the stocking behaviour of value-added resellers in terms of subjective self-assessment. The behaviour should also be studied using objective financial and non-financial outcomes, such as actual sales figures, purchase frequency, or stocking volume. Thus, we call for empirical research on other variables that could explain a greater variety of reseller behaviour. It would be particularly interesting to examine if the simultaneous use of multiple marketing channels affected a reseller's behavioural sales intention and stocking behaviour.

Conclusion

The results of this study showed that two types of benefits determine the effectiveness of a cybersecurity supplier's digital channel marketing: relational and functional. The former refers to the perceived improvements in the quality of the relationship between suppliers and value-added resellers, and the latter refers to concrete tools and skills that the supplier can provide to the resellers. Conversely, the informativeness of communication, measured in terms of timely information about new offerings, upgrades, sales campaigns, and promotional offers does not increase the reseller's intention to sell the supplier's cybersecurity solutions. This finding is somewhat surprising, given that suppliers of IT products worldwide put a lot of effort into informing their resellers about price discounts and promotional campaigns. We believe that, because cybersecurity products are characteristically complex and difficult to comprehend by nature, price offers, campaigns, or even new product features are of little interest to value-added resellers. Rather, the resellers need to understand these solutions to be able to sell them at the first place. Cyber-threats are immense and beyond the control of the end customers, who are profoundly dependent on the knowledge of retailers who are selling cybersecurity solutions. In turn, these retailers become dependent on the supplier's technological and domain-specific expertise. Thus, we believe that cybersecurity solution providers, or providers of other complex technologies, who can assist their retailers to create clarity in technological complexity, will eventually gain respect and preferential status among the resellers.

Furthermore, the abundance of supplier's digital channel marketing does not seem to increase intention of value-added resellers to sell the supplier's cybersecurity products. It is likely that the ever-increasing complexity of cybersecurity solutions cause increased informational and cognitive demands for sales professionals, and the abundance of information per se – particularly related to provisional special pricing – does not alleviate their sales burdens. Again, value-added resellers are keen for practical sales tools that will improve their capability to understand and sell these solutions to end customers. Such tools may prove the most effective way of keeping the supplier's cybersecurity product and service brands at the forefront of the reseller's minds. In other words, we found that the marketing effectiveness of cybersecurity providers' digital channel marketing is contingent on the perceived quality rather than the quantity of digital channel marketing. These findings are important for cybersecurity providers, because the perceived quality of digital channel marketing has a direct influence on the intentions of value-added resellers to sell the supplier's cybersecurity products, which ultimately leads to stocking decisions. In addition, the findings support previous findings by, for example, Andersen (2001), who found that marketing communication is connected with relationship development, and a receiver's commitment to the sender is preceded by awareness and persuasion. The findings also support the work of Kauppila and colleagues (2010), who argue that social support from developers improves a salesperson's motivation and decreases their reluctance to sell new technology. Hence, our contribution to theory is that the extent to which digital channel marketing can strengthen the relationship between supplier and value-added reseller and improve the reseller's capabilities to sell cybersecurity solutions to end customers will ultimately determine the effectiveness of channel marketing.

The study offers some practical implications for cybersecurity solution providers, especially for those wishing to benefit from the growing market for cybersecurity products among small and midsized businesses. First, providers should leverage the power of resellers to better reach the fragmented market. However, they have to plan their marketing strategy appropriately. That is, instead of focusing on aggressive price discounts, promotional campaigns, and updates on new features and versions, cybersecurity providers should focus on helping their resellers to understand, communicate, and deliver the value of their cybersecurity solutions to the end customers in the first place. Also, they should pay attention to the quality of interaction with their value-added resellers, because it has the potential to strengthen or weaken supplier-reseller relationships. In particular, a supplier's digital channel marketing should focus on building reciprocal trust and commitment that would result in closer and deeper relationships. Second, cybersecurity suppliers should use digital channel marketing to provide their resellers with concrete sales tools and skills. Value-added resellers commit to sell a cybersecurity solution only if they are able to understand the solution and its value to end customers. The essence of digital channel marketing is to decrease technology and exchange uncertainty and to strengthen collaboration and commitment between suppliers and resellers for improved sales performance.

About the Authors

Mika Westerlund, D. Sc. (Econ.), is an Assistant Professor at Carleton University's Sprott School of Business in Ottawa, Canada. He previously held positions as a Postdoctoral Scholar in the Haas School of Business at the University of California Berkeley, in the United States, and in the School of Economics at Aalto University in Helsinki, Finland. Mika earned his first doctoral degree in Marketing from the Helsinki School of Economics in Finland. He is also a PhD student at Aalto University in the Department of Industrial Engineering and Management. His current research interests include user innovation, industrial ecology, business strategy, and management models in high-tech and service-intensive industries.

Risto Rajala, D.Sc. (Econ), is an Assistant Professor in the Department of Industrial Engineering and Management at Aalto University in Helsinki, Finland. Dr. Rajala holds a PhD in Information Systems Science from the Aalto University School of Business. His recent research concerns the management of complex service systems, development of digital services, service innovation, and business model performance. Rajala's specialties include management of industrial services, collaborative service innovation, knowledge management, and design of digital services.

References

Ajzen, I. 1985. From Intentions to Actions: A Theory of Planned Behavior. In J. Kuhl & J. Beckmann (Eds.), *Action Control: From Cognition to Behavior.* New York: Springer-Verlag.

Andersen, P. H. 2001. Relationship Development and Marketing Communication: An Integrative Model. *Journal of Business & Industrial Marketing,* 16(3):167-182.
http://dx.doi.org/10.1108/08858620110389786

Barry, J., & Terry, T. S. 2008. Empirical Study of Relationship Value in Industrial Services. *Journal of Business & Industrial Marketing,* 23(4): 228–241.
http://dx.doi.org/10.1108/08858620810865807

Bentler, P. M., & Chou, C.-P. 1987. Practical Issues in Structural Modeling. *Sociological Methods and Research,* 16(1): 78-117.
http://dx.doi.org/10.1177/0049124187016001004

Chin, W. W., Marcolin, B. L., & Newsted, P. R. 2003. A Partial Least Squares Latent Variable Modeling Approach for Measuring Interaction Effects: Results from a Monte Carlo Simulation Study and an Electronic-Mail Emotion/Adoption Study. *Information Systems Research,* 14(2): 189-217.
http://dx.doi.org/10.1287/isre.14.2.189.16018

Chung, C., Chatterjee, S. C., & Sengupta, S. 2012. Manufacturers' Reliance on Channel Intermediaries: Value Drivers in the Presence of a Direct Web Channel. *Industrial Marketing Management,* 41(1): 40–53.
http://dx.doi.org/10.1016/j.indmarman.2011.11.010

Corsaro, D., & Snehota, I. 2010. Searching for Relationship Value in Business Markets: Are We Missing Something? *Industrial Marketing Management,* 39(6): 986–995.
http://dx.doi.org/10.1016/j.indmarman.2010.06.018

Craigen, D., Diakun-Thibault, N., & Purse, R. 2014. Defining Cybersecurity. *Technology Innovation Management Review,* 4(10): 13–21.
http://timreview.ca/article/835

Danaher, P. J., & Rossiter, J. R. 2011. Comparing Perceptions of Marketing Communication Channels. *European Journal of Marketing,* 45(1/2): 6-42.
http://dx.doi.org/10.1108/03090561111095586

Diamantopoulos, A., & Siguaw, J. 2000. *Introducing Lisrel: A Guide for the Uninitiated.* London: SAGE.

Edwards, T., Battisti, G., & Neely, A. 2004. Value Creation and the UK Economy: A Review of Strategic Options. *International Journal of Management Reviews,* 5(3-4): 191–213.
http://dx.doi.org/10.1111/j.1460-8545.2004.00103.x

Eggert, A., Ulaga, W., & Schultz, F. 2006. Value Creation in the Relationship Life Cycle: A Quasi-Longitudinal Analysis. *Industrial Marketing Management,* 35(1): 20-27.
http://dx.doi.org/10.1016/j.indmarman.2005.07.003

Fishbein, M. & Ajzen, I. 1975. *Belief, Attitude, Intention, and Behavior: An Introduction to Theory and Research.* Reading, MA: Addison-Wesley.

Fornell, C., & Larcker, D. F. 1981. Evaluating Structural Equation Models with Unobservable Variables and Measurement Error. *Journal of Marketing Research,* 18(1): 39–50.
http://www.jstor.org/stable/3151312

Hansen, H., Samuelsen, B. M., & Silseth, P. R. 2008. Customer Perceived Value in B-to-B Service Relationships: Investigating the Importance of Corporate Reputation. *Industrial Marketing Management*, 37(2): 206-217.
http://dx.doi.org/10.1016/j.indmarman.2006.09.001

Holden-Bache, A. 2011. Study: 93% of B2B Marketers Use Social Media Marketing. *Social Media B2B*. October 1, 2014:
http://socialmediab2b.com/2011/04/93-of-b2b-marketers-use-social-media-marketing/

Hughes, D. E., & Ahearne, M. 2010. Energizing the Reseller's Sales Force: The Power of Brand Identification. *Journal of Marketing*, 74(4): 81-96.
http://dx.doi.org/10.1509/jmkg.74.4.81

Hughes, D.E. 2013. This Ad's for You: The Indirect Effect of Advertising Perceptions on Salesperson Effort and Performance. *Journal of the Academy of Marketing Science*, 41(1): 1-18.
http://dx.doi.org/10.1007/s11747-011-0293-y

Jerman, D., & Zavrsnik, B. 2012. Model of Marketing Communications Effectiveness in the Business-to-Business Markets. *Economic Research - Ekonomska Istraživanja*, 25(1): 364-388.

Johanson, D. 2013. The Evolving U.S. Cybersecurity Doctrine. *Security Index: A Russian Journal on International Security*, 19(4): 37-50.
http://dx.doi.org/10.1080/19934270.2013.846072

Kalyanam, K., & Brar, S. 2009. From Volume to Value: Managing the Value-Add Reseller Channel at Cisco Systems. *California Management Review*, 52(1): 94-119.
http://www.jstor.org/stable/10.1525/cmr.2009.52.1.94

Kumar, N., Stern, L. W., & Achrol, R. S. 1992. Assessing Reseller Performance From the Perspective of the Supplier. *Journal of Marketing Research*, 29(2): 238-253.
http://www.jstor.org/stable/3172573

Lemmink, J., de Ruyter, K., & Wetzels, M. 1998. The Role of Value in the Delivery Process of Hospitality Services. *Journal of Economic Psychology*, 19(2): 159-177.
http://dx.doi.og/10.1016/S0167-4870(98)00002-6

Lilien, G. L., Grewal, R., Bowman, D., Ding, M., Griffin, A., Kumar, V., Narayandas, D., Peres, R., Srinivasan, R., & Wang, Q. 2010. Calculating, Creating, and Claiming Value in Business Markets: Status and Research Agenda. *Marketing Letters*, 21(3): 287-299.
http://dx.doi.org/10.1007/s11002-010-9108-z

Lindgreen, A., & Wynstra, F. 2005. Value in Business Markets: What Do We Know? Where Are We Going? *Industrial Marketing Management*, 34(7): 732-748.
http://dx.doi.org/10.1016/j.indmarman.2005.01.001

Lindgreen, A., Palmer, R., Vanhamme, J., & Wouters, J. 2006. A Relationship-Management Assessment Tool: Questioning, Identifying, and Prioritizing Critical Aspects of Customer Relationships. *Industrial Marketing Management*, 35(1): 57-71.
http://dx.doi.org/10.1016/j.indmarman.2005.08.008

Menon, A., Homburg, C., & Beutin, N. 2005. Understanding Customer Value in Business-to-Business Relationships. *Journal of Business-to-Business Marketing*, 12(2): 1-38.
http://dx.doi.org/10.1300/J033v12n02_01

Mohr, J., & Spekman, R. 1994. Characteristics of Partnership Success: Partnership Attributes, Communication Behavior, and Conflict Resolution Techniques. *Strategic Management Journal*, 15(2): 135-52.
http://dx.doi.org/10.1002/smj.4250150205

Payne, A., & Holt, S. 2001. Diagnosing Customer Value: Integrating the Value Process and Relationship Marketing. *British Journal of Management*, 12(2): 159-182.
http://dx.doi.org/10.1111/1467-8551.00192

Rahmani, Z., Mojaveri, H.S., & Allahbakhsh, A. 2012. Review the Impact of Advertising and Sale Promotion on Brand Equity. *Journal of Business Studies Quarterly*, 4(1): 64-73.

Rapp, A., Beitelspacher, L. S., Grewal, D., & Hughes, D. E. 2013. Understanding Social Media Effects Across Seller, Retailer, and Consumer Interactions. *Journal of the Academy of Marketing Science*, 41(5): 547-566.
http://dx.doi.org/10.1007/s11747-013-0326-9

Ringle, C. M., Wende, S., & Will, S. 2005. SmartPLS 2.0 (M3) Beta, Hamburg.
http://www.smartpls.de

Simpson, P. M., Siguaw, J. A., & Baker, T. L. 2001. A Model of Value Creation – Supplier Behaviors and Their Impact on Reseller-Perceived Value. *Industrial Marketing Management*, 30(2): 119-134.
http://dx.doi.org/10.1016/S0019-8501(00)00138-3

Sreenivas, M., & Srinivas, T. 2008. Effectiveness of Distribution Network. *International Journal of Information Systems and Supply Chain Management*, 1(1): 80-86.
http://dx.doi.org/10.4018/jisscm.2008010105

Tenenhaus, M., Vinzi, V. E., Chatelin, Y.-M., & Lauro, C. 2005. PLS path modeling. *Computational Statistics and Data Analysis*, 48(1): 159-205.
http://dx.doi.org/10.1016/j.csda.2004.03.005

Teo, H. H., Kwok, K. W., & Benbasat, I. 2003. Predicting Intention to Adopt Interorganizational Linkages: An Institutional Perspective. *MIS Quarterly*, 27(1): 19-49.
http://www.jstor.org/stable/30036518

The 2112 Group. 2014. *The Power of Multiples: Best Practices for Selling Best-of-Breed Solutions*. Port Washington, NY: The 2112 Group.

Ulaga, W. 2003. Capturing Value Creation in Business Relationships: A Customer Perspective. *Industrial Marketing Management*, 32(8): 677-693.
http://dx.doi.org/10.1016/j.indmarman.2003.06.008

Walters, D., & Lancaster, G. 2000. Implementing Value Strategy through the Value Chain. *Management Decision*, 38(3):160-178.
http://dx.doi.org/10.1108/EUM0000000005344

Webster, F. E., Jr. 2000. Understanding the Relationships among Brands, Consumers, and Resellers. *Journal of the Academy of Marketing Science*, 28(1): 17–23.
http://dx.doi.org/10.1177/0092070300281002

Villarejo-Ramos, A. F. 2005. The Impact of Marketing Communication and Price Promotion on Brand Equity. *Journal of Brand Management*, 2(6): 431-444.
http://dx.doi.org/10.1057/palgrave.bm.2540238

Wold, H. 1982. Systems under Indirect Observation Using PLS. In: C. Fornell (Ed.), *A Second Generation of Multivariate Analysis*: 325-347. Praeger, New York.

Appendix 1. About the Research

We applied the partial least squares (PLS) method of analysis suggested by Wold (1982) to estimate the parameters. First, we ensured that our data of 109 companies and 15 indicators meets the guideline of five or more respondents per indicator (cf. Bentler and Chou, 1987). Second, we examined composite reliability values (ρc) and average variance extracted values (ρv) for each latent variable to assess the reliability and validity of the constructs. The scales seem to perform amply: ρc exceeded the recommended minimum level of .70 (cf. Fornell and Larcker, 1981) and ρv exceeded the .50 benchmark (cf. Diamantopoulos and Siguaw, 2000). Table 2 shows these values as well as means, standard deviations, and correlations for the constructs.

We examined the correlation matrix of the constructs in order to assess discriminant validity. Fornell and Larcker (1981) put forward that satisfactory discriminant validity among constructs is obtained when the square root of the average variance extracted is greater than corresponding construct correlations. In our data, the square root of the average variance extracted exceeded their correlations for each pair of first-order constructs (see numbers in parentheses in Table 1). All constructs met the criterion, which supports the discriminant validity of the constructs. The scale items used in the survey, as well as constructs and are listed in Table 3.

The PLS path modelling approach does not include proper single goodness of fit measure, but we used the global fit measure (GoF) suggested by Tenenhaus and colleagues (2005) to evaluate the goodness of fit in our model. Given that the criteria for small, medium, and large effect sizes are .10, .25, and .36, the GoF of our model (.46) indicates a good fit to the data. Furthermore, we assessed the explanatory power of the model for the dependent constructs by measuring their squared multiple correlations value (R^2). The independent variables were able to explain 62.3 percent of the variation in reseller's behavioural sales intention and 17.2 percent of the resulting stocking decision, both of which are considered appropriate.

Table 2. Construct correlations and descriptive statistics of measures

Construct	Mean	SD	ρ_v	ρ_c	1	2	3	4	5	6
1. Functional benefits	3.15	1.07	.86	.93	(.93)					
2. Informative benefits	3.69	0.83	.71	.88	.51	(.84)				
3. Stocking decision	1.94	0.91	.85	.92	.35	.12	(.92)			
4. Relational benefits	2.80	0.92	.84	.94	.60	.58	.23	(.92)		
5. Sales intention	2.64	0.98	.83	.91	.75	.42	.41	.63	(.91)	
6. Marketing abundance	2.39	0.76	.67	.86	.46	.59	.22	.72	.49	(.82)

Keywords: cybersecurity, retailer, value-added reseller, VAR, supplier, marketing, sales, digital channel marketing

Table 3. Scale items and constructs

Quality of Digital Channel Marketing

Item	Loading	Weight	Item description
RELATIONAL BENEFITS			*Modified from Walters & Lancaster (2000); Andersen (2001); Corsaro & Snehota (2010); Eggert et al. (2006).*
K12	.89	.35	Supplier's digital channel marketing (DCM) improves collaboration in our supplier-reseller relationship.
K13	.93	.36	Supplier's DCM builds our reciprocal trust
K14	.94	.38	Supplier's DCM augments long-lasting and close relationship with us
INFORMATIVE BENEFITS			*Modified from Martin et al. (2003); Villarejo-Ramos (2005); Eggert et al. (2006).*
K7	.92	.53	Receiving ongoing sales campaigns and promotional offers is important
K8	.90	.38	Information about new offerings and upgrades are valuable for us
K9	.68	.26	Information about upcoming events and seminars are valuable for us
FUNCTIONAL BENEFITS			*Modified from Lindgreen et al. (2006).*
K17	.93	.56	Supplier's DCM improves our sales skills and capabilities
K18	.92	.52	Supplier's DCM provides us with practical sales tools

Quantity of Digital Channel Marketing

Item	Loading	Weight	Item description
MARKETING ABUNDANCE			*Modified from Jerman & Zavrsnik (2012).*
K11	.89	.45	I prefer working with suppliers that are very active in digital channel marketing
K16	.80	.43	I highly value suppliers that send marketing messages frequently
K5	.78	.34	I receive marketing messages from the suppliers not too often

Sales Intention

Item	Loading	Weight	Item description
K19	.92	.58	I put extra effort in selling products that suppliers provide with plenty of information
K21	.90	.52	I prefer selling products we have obtained digital marketing messages of

Stocking Decision

Item	Loading	Weight	Item description
K20	.90	.51	I often buy to stock products actively marketed by the supplier
K22	.93	.58	I often buy to stock campaign products marketed by the supplier

Note: The response options ranged from 1 = "strongly disagree" to 5 = "strongly agree".

15

Identifying the Challenges in Commercializing High Technology: A Case Study of Quantum Key Distribution Technology

Anas Al Natsheh, Saheed A. Gbadegeshin, Antti Rimpiläinen,
Irna Imamovic-Tokalic, and Andrea Zambrano

" It is time for us all to stand and cheer for the doer, the " achiever – the one who recognizes the challenges and does something about it.

Vince Lombardi (1913–1970)
Player, coach, and executive of American Football

This article examines the challenges in commercializing high technologies successfully and sustainably using quantum key distribution (QKD) technology as a case study. Quantum communication is increasingly relevant to cybersecurity and nanotechnology, which will replace current technologies and change the way we live. To understand how such high technology could be successfully commercialized, we interviewed individuals from four metrology institutions and two international companies. The result revealed that scattered and small markets, supply chain development, technology validation/certification, a lack of available or adequate infrastructure, and after-sales services are the most serious challenges facing successful commercialization of quantum communication technology. To validate these challenges, we conducted a survey of 60 experts, 49 of whom agreed that above-mentioned factors could affect the commercialization success of QKD technology. Likewise, the survey revealed that technical development, customer orientation/awareness, and government regulations could also hinder the commercialization of QKD technology.

Introduction

One of the key drivers for economic growth nowadays is knowledge, and it involves high investment in education and training, research and development (R&D), and relationships between governments, academia, and industry (Lowe, 2005). To realize the benefits of knowledge and to receive returns from these investments, the resulting innovations or inventions must be sold, or commercialized (Meyers, 2009). Indeed, commercialization is an important contributor to economic growth (Tahvanainen & Nikulainen, 2011), and it makes technology available to end users. In essence, commercialization is an exchange of know-how for money (Speser, 2008), but it can be perceived in different ways, including:

- a series of activities for converting an invention to a product or service (Rosa & Rose, 2007)

- the process of taking the R&D of an organization to an industry (Cornford, 2002)

- the identification of a business opportunity for a certain scientific or engineering invention and subsequent steps to design, develop, and manufacture the invention to make it useful (Michael, 1990)

- the adoption of a new technology or service by customers (Tanev & Frederiksen, 2014)

- any scheme that permits members of a technological innovation team to receive economic gains from their efforts, including through patent licensing, research grants, and R&D joint ventures (Kalaitzandonakes, 1997)

Here, we focus on the definition of Pellikka and Malinen (2011) who state that commercialization brings high-technology innovations to the market and makes innovative products benefit of society. Commercialization is not a straightforward process; many challenges must be overcome. Although previous studies have outlined some challenges, this study also attempts to fill the perceived gap by identifying additional challenges of commercialization, particularly for high technologies. Usually, new technologies face many problems in the beginning of their lifecycle because they are new to the end users and they lack standardization or third-party certification. In this study, we examine quantum key distribution (QKD) technology as a case study because is a new high technology of increasing importance within the domain of cybersecurity.

QKD is a mean of sending and receiving safe information; it uses cryptographic keys to encode information at the point of dispatching and the keys are used by the receiver to decode or retrieve the information. Presently, QKD kits are commercially available but there are no any independent measurements and standards in the industry. Due to cybersecurity pressures, the European Union has funded a project named "Metrology for Industrial Quantum Communications" (MIQC). The MIQC project aims to develop and commercialize standards for the QKD technology systems. Most of the leading metrology centers in Europe participated in the development of new QKD standards and certification. However, in this article, we present the findings of the commercialization study, which examined how the new QKD technology would be available in the market. Although the case study focuses on QKD technology, the main motive for sharing the findings is that we believe that the study has broader implications and value for assisting researchers and innovators/inventors in many high-technology fields; the findings may help them become aware of and overcome hidden commercialization challenges.

This article is structured as follows. First, we review the literature on the challenges of commercializing high technology. Next, we describe the interview and survey methodology used in our QKD case study and then we present the results. Finally, we discuss the key findings and provide conclusions.

Literature Review: Commercializing High Technology

For a high-technology innovation to successfully reach the market, a company's commercialization team must identify, obtain, combine, and manage needed technological knowledge. The innovation must be developed into a product, which must then be manufactured, marketed, and distributed. Ongoing success with subsequent commercialization attempts can be facilitated by a growth strategy that exploits economies of joint costs and scale. Furthermore, an innovation can be successful if the innovation team or company can adhere to their learning paths and create and maintain a good network (Chandler, 2005). Additionally, the team must not only concentrate on a niche market but also focus on a wider (potential) market because a niche market may not be able to sustain the product in long run (Slater & Mohr, 2006).

Likewise, to successfully commercialize high technology, it is necessary to follow a market-oriented process: one that starts with market, ends with the market, and involves the market throughout the entire process (Valiauga, 2013). Nichols (2013) adds that commercialization is supposed to be a well-planned and well-implemented activity that improves product performance relative to its price and that focuses on competitors. Fletcher and Bourne (2012) state that there are 10 simple rules for successful commercialization: i) science must be differentiated from business; ii) know that there is no one specific way to commercialize; iii) know the company's rights and the rights of its partners, iv) consider the of implications of private and public business; v) decide what the company wants to give; vi) be realistic; vii) accept that a market may not exist in the beginning; viii) consider the difference between wants and needs; ix) make the invention comprehensive; and x) customers are the ultimate peer reviewers.

Pellikka and colleagues (2012) argue that the main difficulties of the commercialization process relate to marketing, resources, the business environment, and the planning and management of commercialization process. The marketing challenges relate to a failure to obtain sufficient and relevant market information, a failure to use it properly, insufficient knowledge about the international market and the business growth, and an inability to establish both local and international sales and distributions. These scholars explain further that the resource challenges of the commercialization process are an inability to acquire and assign resources, inadequate managerial and business skills, and insufficient funds to market the new product. In the business environment, they identify additional commercialization challenges, including a lack of available or adequate business infrastructure, low market potential, and insufficient business partners. Lastly, these authors mention that lack of a systematic model, time and materials for getting public funds, and insufficient knowhow threaten the planning and management of a commercialization process. However, these problems can be overcome through the effective pre-planning activities, better utilization of resources, and internal commercialization training of key staff.

Epting, Gatling, and Zimmer (2011) highlight common challenges with financing, production, distributing and marketing. The authors explain further that many innovators face the following problems in their commercialization adventures:

1. Undue delay caused by the inventor's attempts to "perfect" their product may allow a competitive, lower-quality product to enter the market, to the detriment of the inventor.

2. Licensing manufacturing to another company may hasten market entry, but at the expense of the inventor's control.

3. Funding may be exhausted in pre-sales activities.

4. Distribution and supply chains take time and expertise to establish.

In addition, Parker and Mainelli (2001) identify frequent mistakes made during technology commercialization, including: i) assuming that new features will be beneficial, ii) using top-down market analysis, iii) insufficient testing of the technology, iv) failure to assign a specific person or team to oversee the commercialization process, and v) an inability to value the new technology fully. Rosa and Rose (2007) add that financial problems due to insufficient funds to complete commercialization and human resource problems in the form of a lack of skilful people to sell and promote the innovating products are key obstacles facing technology commercialization.

Tahvanainen and Nikulainen (2011) found that a lack of time and interest, a negative attitude in the research environment, economic risks, conflicts of interest, bureaucratic disturbance, lack of business or commercialization knowledge, incompatibility of commercialization

with the ethics of science, and issues with ownership rights are challenges confronting commercialization. Similarly, Bulsara, Gandhi, and Porey (2010) outline difficulties with patent filing processes, commercialization interests, commercialization option selection, commercialization supports, obsolescence of technology, educational and business background of innovator, and the general business environment.

The above scholars hold a wide range of views regarding the challenges of commercialization. Others have identified specific challenges in particular industries. For instance, in focusing on commercialization biopharmaceutical knowledge in Iran, Nassiri-Koopaei and colleagues (2014) outline three main obstacles to commercialization in that country and industry: i) policy, ii) regulations, and iii) management. Likewise, Szuhaj and McCullough (2009) argue that supply chain management in the bio-pharmaceutical industry is a particularly critical aspect of commercialization in that industry.

Kaarela (2013), focusing on the nanotechnology, explains that the main processes of commercialization process are market validation in the planning phase and multidisciplinary team and mainstream customers in the execution phase. Although the author focuses on 64 cases in the Finnish-Russian nanotechnology commercialization alliance, he presents many problems associated with the technology commercialization. He notes that most of these challenges come from the business side rather than technology side. He also presents three main challenges: i) understanding the customer needs, ii) describing the business benefits not the technology benefits, and iii) complementing the team's skill with the right partner. In the same view, McNeil and colleagues (2007) list, in their final report for the Technology Administration agency of the United States Department of Commerce, the following barriers to commercialization in the nanotechnology industry: i) the ten-year cycle time from scientific results in a laboratory to a commercial product; ii) the difference between researchers and applied scientists; iii) the difference in funding between basic research and applied research; iv) a lack of understanding that for every dollar invested in basic research almost $100 is required for a commercially viable product; v) long timescales needed for patenting; vi) uncertainty of potential regulations, and vii) the high risk of new scientific results. In addition, Pfautsch (2007) identifies the main barriers to commercialization efforts with carbon nanotube composites: i) the high cost of equipment, ii) a lack of knowledge about environment health and safety, iii) a lack of a risk assessment or lifecycle assessment, iv) a lack of standards, v) a need for properly trained workers, and vi) cross-patenting.

Boehlje (2004) analyzed previous work on commercialization of agricultural technologies and found common challenges that included gaining customer/consumer acceptance, capital market accessibility, value capture/sharing, protecting intellectual property, and selecting innovation strategies.

In the health sector, Booz Allen Hamilton and three other organizations in the United States (2012) confirmed that the problems facing new invention commercialization are access to capital, potential limitations of traditional technology transfer, the need for entrepreneurial skills, and the difficulty of navigating the complexities of the healthcare market. Additionally, Scanlon and Lieberman (2007) analyzed historical medical breakthroughs and found that the two major challenges of commercialization in the medical field are the ability of the academic community to change the culture of the scientists to commercialize their technology and the ability of the business community to communicate successfully with the scientists.

Furthermore, O'Brien and colleagues (2004) investigated barriers to the deployment of integrated gasification combined cycle (IGCC) technology, the most successful method of producing electric power utilizing coal gasification in the US electric industry. They found that the most substantial barriers were financial, environmental, cultural, and legal. The financial barrier consisted of tax issues, credit concerns, project finance, market for emissions credits, licensing fees, and cost of operation. The environmental barrier included emission limitation, environmental permitting processes, and uncertain environmental rules and enforcement. The cultural barriers were regulator viewpoints, public perception, corporate culture of plant developers, past failures, and difficulties of IGCC plants. And, the legal barrier included plant-siting procedures, standard market design, electric industry restructuring, and uncertainty over regulatory treatment.

Although the above-mentioned scholars investigated the same topic in different fields, their findings are summarized in Table 1.

Notably, Table 1 highlights that market- and funding-related issues are the most common challenges in all aforementioned sectors. Our recent research (Al Natsheh et al., 2015) also revealed that the following

factors need to be considered during technology commercialization:

- novelty and clear added value
- technology functionality
- a non-complicated first set of products
- product certification/accreditation
- the right team
- sufficient capital
- a good business model
- a proper manufacturing plan
- ongoing updates and product maintenance

Although our recent work focused on university technology transfer, these findings may be applicable to the commercialization of any technology. To reach the source of problems facing the commercialization of high technology, we conducted the present study using QKD technology as a case study. Our goal for the QKD study was to understand how the technology could be successfully commercialized. Before presenting the results, the next section describes our research methodology.

Methodology

To maximize the efficiency and methodological self-consistency of the qualitative method, we followed the guidelines stated by Creswell (2009) and Yin (1994). We used a qualitative research method featuring six interviews with innovators (4) from metrology institutions and individuals from companies (2) engaging in QKD technology, and a survey of stakeholders. Our primary research question was:

What are the challenges that can hinder successful commercialization of QKD technology?

Based on our experience in QKD research projects and other high-technology commercialization projects, we identified five possible challenges that could hinder successful commercialization of QKD technology. They are:

1. Market size

2. Possibility of building the supply chain

3. Availability of technology validation/certification

4. Availability of infrastructure for the new technology

5. Possibility of offering after sales-sales services (especially product update and maintenance)

Table 1. Summary of commercialization challenges

Study	Challenges	Application
Pellikka et al. (2012)	Marketing, resources, business environment, and planning and management of commercialization process	General
Tahvanainen & Nikulainen (2011)	Lack of time, lack of interest, negative attitude of research environment, economic risks, conflicts of interest, bureaucratic disturbance, lack of business or commercialization knowledge, incompatibility of commercialization with the ethics of science, and ownership right problem	General
Chiesa & Frattini (2011)	Volatility, interconnectedness, and proliferation of new technologies to fit the market	General
Bulsara et al. (2010)	Patent filing processes, commercialization interest, selecting of commercialization options, commercialization supports, obsolescence of technology, educational and business background of innovator, and general business environment	General
Epting et al. (2011)	Inventor's procrastination for making a perfect product, licensing issues, insufficient funds, and insufficient time and expertise to establish distribution and supply chains	General
Rosa & Rose (2007)	Financial problems and human resource problems	General
Parker & Mainelli (2001)	Innovators' assumption, top-down market analysis, insufficient test of the technology, failure to assign specific person or team to oversee commercialization process and inability to value the new technology	General
Nassiri-Koopaei et al. (2014)	Policy, regulations, and management	Bio-pharmaceutical
Szuhaj & McCullough (2009)	Supply chain management	Bio-pharmaceutical
Kaarela (2013)	Not understanding customer needs, describing technology benefits instead of business benefits, and not complementing team's skill with the right partner	Nanotechnology
McNeil et al. (2007)	Ten-year cycle for innovation, the gap between researcher and applied scientists, the gap in funding between basic research and applied research, lack of understanding that for every dollar invested in basic research almost \$100 is required for a commercially viable product, time to patent, uncertainty of potential regulations, and the high risk of new scientific results	Nanotechnology
Pfautsch (2007)	High cost of equipment, lack of knowledge about environment health and safety, lack of a risk assessment or lifecycle assessment, lack of standards, need for properly trained workers, and the issue of cross-patenting	Nanotechnology
Boehlje (2004)	Gaining customer/consumer acceptance, capital market accessibility, value capture/sharing, protecting of intellectual property, and selection of innovation strategy	Food and Agriculture
Booz Allen Hamilton et al. (2012)	Access to capital, potential limitations of traditional technology transfer, the need for entrepreneurial skills, and the difficulty of navigating the complexities of the healthcare market	Health
Scanlon & Lieberman (2007)	Ability of the academic community to change the scientific culture to commercialize technology, and the ability of the business community to communicate successfully with the scientists	Health (Medical)
O'Brien et al. (2004)	Financial, environmental, cultural, and legal	Electricity

Interview methodology

The interview questions consisted of three parts. The first part focused on the interviewee's background, especially as it related to previous projects. The second part centralized on the commercialization of QKD technology. The last part focused on the interviewee's general opinions on the commercialization of high technology. Several weeks prior to the interviews, we sent the interview questions to the participants so that they would have prior knowledge about our goals of the study. The interviews for innovators were conducted in Italy and Finland. The average duration of their interviews was 1 hour and all interviews were recorded.

The innovators work with metrology institutions in the United Kingdom, Italy, and Finland. Three of them hold PhD degrees; the fourth holds an MSc degree. Each of them has more than 15 years' experience in the field, and they have participated in several basic and applied research studies. Three of the innovators hold patents; one has developed a few products. At the time of the interviews, they were all working on different innovation projects.

The individuals from the companies are all hold managerial roles. The first participating company was established 10 years ago. It designs and produces single-photon counting avalanche diodes and develops active-quenching integrated circuits. The company has networks in five continents and its products are applied in biomedical, industrial, and astrophysical domains. The second company was founded 11 years ago. Its products provide network encryption and photon counting.

The collected data were analyzed using the method of Miles and Huberman (1994), which includes summarization and extraction of key points. Therefore, we first transcribed the interviews and then summarized them. After that, we pinpointed the main information from the summaries. Thereafter, our qualitative results were derived.

Survey methodology

As a part of the MIQC project, the commercialization team conducted a survey on the project stakeholders' satisfaction and the team included commercialization questions designed to test the qualitative results from the interviews. In the survey, there were 22 questions but five of them were focused on commercialization.

The answers were in multiple-choice format, but respondents were allowed to state their reason for either agreeing or disagreeing. Our survey questions were:

1. Do you think that the market size of quantum cryptography can affect its commercial implementation?

2. How important is the development of standards and quality assurances related to the commercial QKD system in order to ensure the commercial success of this technology?

3. How important is the development of a metrological infrastructure for characterizing the optical components of QKD systems in relation to the development of standards for the market take-up of the QKD technology?

4. In your opinion, what do you think can hinder commercial implementation of quantum cryptography?

5. An empirical study on the commercial implementation of quantum cryptography revealed that building of supply chain, technology validation/certification, a lack of available or adequate infrastructure, and after-sales services are the most serious challenges facing successful commercialization of quantum cryptography. Do you agree?

The questions aimed to validate our findings because the intended participants of the survey are QKD professionals. Invitations to participate in the MIQC survey were sent to about 100 people who we considered the necessary stakeholders of quantum communication technology in Europe; 60 of these professionals participated in the survey, which was made available online from the 1st and 30th of September, 2014. Table 2 provides an overview of the survey participants.

Analysis

In this study, we used both qualitative methods (i.e., summarization and extraction of key points from interview data) and quantitative methods (i.e., descriptive statistics from survey data), which allowed the findings to be triangulated. Triangulation combines both qualitative and quantitative research methods to obtain various points of view as well as to validate specific claims; it enables researchers to obtain deep understanding and wide knowledge of a phenomenon (Olsen, 2004; Zawawi, 2007). Our research and triangulation process is summarized in Figure 1.

Table 2. Backgrounds and experience levels of the 60 QKD survey participants

	Categories	Number of Participants
Organization	Small and Medium Enterprise (SME)	9
	Public Liability Company (PLC)	1
	University	24
	Governmental Research Institute/Centre	23
	Private Research Institute/Centre	2
	Other: Standard Institute	1
Position	Student	6
	Researcher	35
	Professor	8
	Research and development manager	6
	Senior manager or CEO	5
Experience Level	Under 5 years	13
	5-10 years	22
	11- 15 years	14
	16-20 years	9
	Above 20 years	2

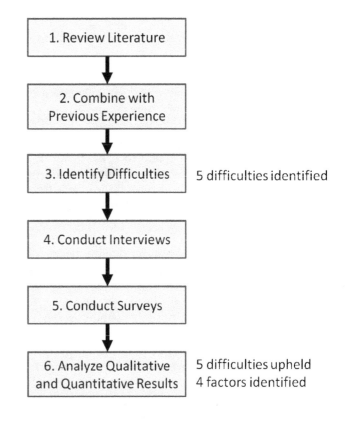

Figure 1. Research process

Findings

Our qualitative data analysis revealed that the critical challenges in commercializing QKD technologies were: i) small market size and distribution channels; ii) building a supply chain; iii) technology validation or certification; iv) a lack of available or adequate infrastructure; and v) after-sales services such as product updates and maintenance. Each of these challenges is briefly described below.

1. *Scattered and small market size:* Our interviewees said that developing an invention was not as difficult as developing a market, especially for the high-technology products. They stressed that the initial market for a new technology is often small, and it might take several years before a large market could be developed. In view of this challenge, there are other problems relating to profitability and sustainability.

Our study also revealed that the small-market challenge becomes greater if the small market is scattered geographically, particularly because of higher costs for sales and after-sales services.

2. *Building of supply chain:* Our interviewees pointed out the difficulty of building a supply chain for a new technology. One of reasons they cited was the newness of the technology to both suppliers and consumers. They explained further that the components of the new technology may not actually exist or the existing product may need modifications before they can be used as components; in either case, it can be difficult to find the right suppliers. Similarly, they stressed that finding the right distribution channel may be a serious challenge. They explained that the small market size complicates distribution in terms accessibility to customers. Nonetheless, we found that the most difficult challenge is the identification

and development of the right supply chain because the new technology might have several application areas that cannot be supported by existing supply chains.

3. *Technology validation or certification:* Our interviewees re-confirmed one of our findings in the previous studies (Al Natsheh et al., 2015). They said that validation/certification of a new technology is a challenge facing high-technology commercialization. To be certified, a technology must work properly, be of sufficient quality, and be safe to use. However, new technology usually requires new formal testing procedures, which may be expensive and may require several sub-projects. In addition, new standards will prescribe measurements that will most likely require development by the metrology community, given that existing measurements and reference artefacts will not be adequate. Thus, validation/certification appears to be a barrier to high-technology commercialization, because the standards and metrology needed to validate/certify such systems is expensive to develop.

4. *Lack of available or adequate infrastructure:* Our participants mentioned that, in some cases, there is no infrastructure to support new QKD technology. Three interview subjects quickly cited example of 3G Internet connectivity for smartphones. These participants illustrated that, if smartphone technology were developed without any Internet connectivity infrastructure to support it; then, consumers would not be able to use smartphones. One of the participants cited the example of cloud computing, which is now leading the new technologies: if cloud computing were not available, the insurgency of mobile phone applications and other related technologies would not be possible. Therefore all interviewees agreed that a lack of available or adequate infrastructure is a key challenge in the commercialization of high technology.

5. *After-sales services:* Our participants also identified after-sales services as a key challenge facing high-technology commercialization. They explained that selling high-technology products can be less challenging than providing the necessary services to maintain the technology. To confirm another finding from our earlier work (Al Natsheh et al., 2015), we asked the interviewees about the challenges of updating and maintaining products. All of them agreed that it is an important factor to be considered during the technology commercialization process because it

also serves as a bottleneck. In support of above-mentioned challenges, the case study technology (i.e., quantum key distribution) requires metrological infrastructure for optical components of quantum optical communication systems, especially for internal single optical components such as single-photon sources and single-photon detectors. A metrology system is mainly for certification and accreditation purposes. Without such a system, quality assurance is at risk. The system level needs to be validated, but validating/certifying techniques are expensive and only yield returns on investment over the long term due to the currently limited market and time-consuming development. Therefore, the aforementioned challenges are apparently evident in the commercialization of QKD technology.

In addition, our quantitative results show that 85% of the QKD professionals we surveyed agreed that market size would affect the successful commercialization of the new QKD technology and the development of standards or quality assurance is necessary for the commercial success of such technology. Forty-nine of the survey participants (82%) agreed that it is essential to have sufficient infrastructure for the new QKD technology in order to make a successful product. Likewise, 49 participants (82%) confirmed that market size, building a supply chain, technology validation/certification, a lack of available or adequate infrastructure, and after-sales services are the most serious challenges facing successful commercialization of QKD. One of the respondents emphasized that: "Customers perceive no urgent need to switch. That's the only problem."

Furthermore, the survey results also revealed that customer orientation/awareness, technical development, and government regulations could affect the commercialization. The reason why many respondents agreed that customer orientation/awareness could hinder QKD commercialization is that QKD deals with industrial systems in which many end users/final customers may not be aware of its importance in the beginning. Table 3 summarizes the quantitative results.

Discussion and Conclusion

Tanev and Frederiksen (2014), Kaarela (2013), Pellikka and colleagues (2012), Chiesa and Frattini (2011), Boehlje (2004), and Parker and Mainelli (2001) found that market-related issues were among the challenges facing technology commercialization. In the same view, our study revealed that scattered and small market size is one of the factors hinder successful commercializa-

Table 3. Summary of survey results

Research Statement	Research Question	Positive Response Percentage
1. Market size can affect QKD commercialization	Do you think that the market size of quantum cryptography can affect its commercial implementation?	85%
2. Development of standards and quality assurances are important for QKD commercialization	How important is the development of standards and quality assurances related to the commercial QKD system in order to ensure the commercial success of this technology?	93 %
3. Development of a metrological infrastructure	How important is the development of a metrological infrastructure for characterizing the optical components of QKD systems in relation to the development of standards for the market take-up of the QKD technology?	82 %
4. Market size, building a supply chain, technology validation/certification, lack of available or adequate infrastructure, and after-sales services are the main challenges.	An empirical study on the commercial implementation of quantum cryptography identified the most serious challenges facing successful commercialization of quantum cryptography. Do you agree with the challenges?	82 %

tion of QKD technology. Commercialization of QKD technology could be problematic because the technology relates to both the military and civilian markets. In particular, the military market is large, highly sensitive, bureaucratic, and structured. Thus, each of these markets needs a different approach. Market penetration and size present challenges for these markets. When a market is scattered geographically, the cost of marketing activities and after-sales services are often high; hence, it becomes a challenge for the manufacturer/entrepreneur/innovator of the high technology to have commercial success. Therefore, we argue that market size is important in the commercialization of high technologies because large investments are often involved in developing the technologies; thus, there are must be sufficient markets for such products.

Furthermore, our findings are also in agreement with Szuhaj and McCullough (2009) and Epting and colleagues (2011) in highlighting the importance of building a supply chain. Likewise, the technology validation/certification challenge is in agreement with Pfautsch (2007) because, in a field where a high degree of precision or accuracy is required, such as nanotechnology and QKD technology, technology validation/certification seems to be important. Therefore, technology validation/certification may hinder successful commercialization of QKD technology. For instance, the certification of the high-technology product can be a barrier, especially when the target customers cannot validate the system by themselves or through a third party. In the case study technology, there is no certification yet, and the technology is crucial especially where cyberse-

curity is a priority, such as in financial institutions, securities agencies, and the military. In addition, our study revealed that the lack of available or adequate infrastructure and after sales-services could hinder the successful commercialization of QKD technology. These two factors have not yet been investigated by the previous scholars.

However, this study has limitations due to its focus on particular high-technology domain and its relatively small sample size. Nonetheless, the case study is highly important to societal security and provides a starting point for further research in other sectors and with other technologies. Studies that investigate the new challenges identified here, especially technology validation/certification and lack of available or adequate infrastructure, would be particularly welcome.

In summary, based on previous studies and our new findings, we conclude that technology validation/certification, lack of available or adequate infrastructure, and after-sales services present challenges to the successful commercialization of high technology, at least in the case of QKD. Similarly, we agreed that market size or market-related issues are the challenges in technology commercialization, as previous studies have shown. In the same view, we confirmed that building a supply chain is among the high-technology commercialization challenges. Therefore, we advise the innovators, inventors, technology entrepreneurs, as well governments to consider these challenges so that their investments in research, development, and innovation are more likely to bring the desired returns.

About the Authors

Anas Al Natsheh is a Senior Business Advisor at the Centre for Measurement and Information Systems (CEMIS-Oulu) in Oulu, Finland, and he is a Principal Lecturer in Research, Development, and Innovation (RDI) at Kajaani University of Applied Sciences, also in Finland. He is an expert in empirical researches, research valorization, and technology commercialization. He holds a PhD from the University of Kuopio (now the University of Eastern Finland), where his research focused on the applications of nanotechnology.

Saheed Adebayo Gbadegeshin is a Project Researcher at the University of Oulu in Finland, and he is a Project Staff member at Kajaani University of Applied Sciences, also in Finland. He holds an MSc degree in Entrepreneurship from the University of Jyväskylä in Finland. His research interests include technology-based entrepreneurship, technology commercialization, and family-run businesses.

Antti Rimpiläinen is a Project Researcher at the University of Oulu in Finland and a Project Staff member at Kajaani University of Applied Sciences, also in Finland. He holds an MSc degree in Economics and Business Administration from the University of Oulu in Finland. His research interests include technology-based entrepreneurship, technology commercialization, networking, and international business.

Irna Imamovic-Tokalic is a Project Staff member at the Kajaani University of Applied Sciences in Finland. She holds a BSc degree in Macrofinancial Management from the University of Sarajevo, Bosnia. Her research interests include technology commercialization, digital media and marketing, graphic design, and financial management.

Andrea Zambrano is a Project Researcher at the Kajaani University of Applied Sciences in Finland. She holds a master's degree in Financial and Management Accounting from the University of Oulu in Finland, and in International Economics from the University of Antwerp in Belgium. Her research interests include financial management, research cooperation with Latin-American regions, and economic impact studies with focuses on benefit-cost analyses, financial analyses, and forecasting.

Acknowledgements

We gratefully acknowledge funding received from the European Metrology Research Programme (EMRP) for the Metrology for Industrial Quantum Communication (MIQC) project (Contract IND06). The EMRP is jointly funded by participating countries within EURAMET and the European Union. We also thank our colleagues from the University of Oulu and the Kajaani University of Applied Sciences for their support during the project.

References

Al Natsheh, A., Gbadegeshin, S. A., Rimpiläinen, A., Imamovic-Tokalic, I., & Zambrano, A. 2015. Building a Sustainable Start-Up? Factors to Be Considered During the Technology Commercialization Process. Forthcoming in the *Journal of Advanced Research in Entrepreneurship and New Venture Creation:* http://www.asers.eu/journals/jare_nvc.html

Bulsara, H. P., Gandhi, S., & Porey, P.D. 2010. Commercialization of Technology Innovations and Patents: Issues and Challenges. *Asia-Pacific Tech Monitor,* 27(6): 12–18

Boehlje, M. 2004. Business Challenges in Commercialization of Agricultural Technology. *International Food and Agribusiness Management Review,* 7(1): 91–104.

Booz Allen Hamilton, California HealthCare Foundation, Robert Wood Johnson Foundation, & von Liebig Center for Entrepreneurism and Technology Advancement. 2012. *Accelerating Commercialization of Cost-Saving Health Technologies.*

Chandler, A. D., Jr. 2005. Commercializing High-Technology Industries. *Business History Review,* 79(3): 595–604. http://dx.doi.org/10.1017/S0007680500081460

Chiesa, V., & Frattini, F. 2011. Commercializing Technological Innovation: Learning from Failures in High-Tech Markets. *Product Development & Management Association,* 28(4): 437–454. http://dx.doi.org/10.1111/j.1540-5885.2011.00818.x

Cornford, A. B. 2002. *Innovation and Commercialization in Atlantic Canada: Research Project – Final Report.* Moncton, NB: Atlantic Canada Opportunities Agency (ACOA). http://publications.gc.ca/pub?id=365765&sl=0

Creswell, J. W. 2009. *Research Design: Qualitative, Quantitative, and Mixed Methods Approaches* (3rd ed.). London: Sage Publications, Inc.

Epting, T. Gatling, K., & Zimmer, J. 2011. What Are the Most Common Obstacles to the Successful Commercialization of Research? *SML Perspectives,* 2: 9.

Fletcher, A. C., & Bourne, P. E. 2012. Ten Simple Rules to Commercialize Scientific Research. *PLoS Compututational Biology,* 8(9): e1002712. http://dx.doi.org/10.1371/journal.pcbi.1002712

Kalaitzandonakes, N. G. 1997. *Commercialization of Research and Technology.* Washington, D.C.: U.S. Agency for International Development.

Kaarela, M. 2013. *Challenges of Technology Commercialization: Lessons from Finnish-Russian Innovation Alliance on Nanotechnology.* Paper presented at the EuroNanoforum 2013 Workshop on Technology Commercialization, June 18–20, 2013, in Dublin, Ireland. http://www.euronanoforum2013.eu/presentations/presentatins-from-workshops/

Lowe, C. R. 2005. Commercialisation and Spin-Out Activities of the Institute of Biotechnology. *Journal of Commercial Biotechnology,* 11(4): 206–317. http://dx.doi.org/10.1057/palgrave.jcb.3040131

McNeil, R. D., Lowe, J., Mastroianni, T., Croni, J., & Ferk, D. 2007. *Barriers to Nanotechnology Commercialization: Final Report Prepared for U.S. Department of Commerce Technology Administration.* Springfield, IL: The University of Illinois.

Meyers, A. D. 2009. Book Review: Commercialization of Innovative Technologies: Bringing Good Ideas to the Marketplace. *Journal of Commercial Biotechnology,* 15(4): 374–375. http://dx.doi.org/10.1057/jcb.2009.18

Michael, N. T. 1990. Commercializing Technology: What the Best Companies Do. *Planning Review,* 18(6): 20–24. http://dx.doi.org/10.1108/eb054310

Miles, M. B., & Huberman, A. M. 1994. *Qualitative Data Analysis: An Expanded Sourcebook* (2nd ed.). Thousand Oaks, CA: Sage Publications, Inc.

MIQC. 2014. The Project. *Metrology for Industrial Quantum Communications.* Accessed December 1, 2014: http://projects.npl.co.uk/MIQC/project.html

Nassiri-Koopaei, N., Majdzadeh, R., Kebriaeezadeh, A., Rashidian, A., Yazdi, M. T., Nedjat, S., & Nikfar, S. 2014. Commercialization of Biopharmaceutical Knowledge in Iran: Challenges and Solutions. *DARU Journal of Pharmaceutical Sciences,* 22:29. http://dx.doi.org/10.1186/2008-2231-22-29

Nichols, S. P. 2013. *Module 1: An Introduction to Commercialization of Science and Technology.* Converting Technology to Wealth Workshop. Austin, TX: IC2 Institute, The University of Texas at Austin. Accessed December 1, 2014: http://ut.gtrade.or.kr/inc/download.asp?key=5288

O'Brien, J. N., Blau, J., & Rose, M. 2004. *An Analysis of the Institutional Challenges to Commercialization and Deployment of IGCC Technology in the U.S. Electric Industry: Recommended Policy, Regulatory, Executive and Legislative Initiatives.* New York, NY: Global Change Associates.

Olsen, W. 2004. Triangulation in Social Research: Qualitative and Quantitative Methods Can Really Be Mixed. In Holborn, M. (Ed.), *Developments in Sociology.* Ormskirk, UK: Causeway Press.

Parker, K., & Mainelli, M. 2001. Great Mistakes in Technology Commercialization. *Strategic Change,* 10(7): 383–390. http://dx.doi.org/10.1002/jsc.560

Pellikka, J., Kajanus, M., Heinonen, M., & Eskelinen, T. 2012. *Overcoming Challenges in Commercialization Process of Innovation.* Paper presented at the XXIII ISPIM Conference in Barcelona, Spain. June 17–20, 2012.

Pellikka, J., & Malinen, P. 2011. *Developing Commercialisation of Innovation in High Technology Industries – Regional Perspective.* Paper presented at the 56th International Council for Small Business (ICSB) in Stockholm, Sweden, June 15–18, 2011.

Pfautsch, E. 2007. *Challenges in Commercializing Carbon Nanotube Composites.* Washington, D.C.: Washington Internships for Students of Engineering (WISE).

Rosa, J., & Rose, A. 2007. *Report on Interviews on the Commercialization of Innovation.* Ottawa, CA: Statistics Canada.

Scanlon, K. J., & Lieberman, M. A. 2007. Commercializing Medical Technology. *Cytotechnology,* 53(1-3): 107–112. http://dx.doi.org/10.1007/s10616-007-9056-5

Slater, S. F., & Mohr, J. J. 2006. Successful Development and Commercialization of Technological Innovation: Insights Based on Strategy Type. *The Journal of Product Innovation Management,* 23(1): 26–33. http://dx.doi.org/10.1111/j.1540-5885.2005.00178.x

Speser, P. 2008. *What Every Researcher Needs to Know About Commercialization.* Providence, RI: Foresight Science & Technology Inc.

Szuhaj, M., & McCullough, P. 2009. *Supply Chain Planning and the Commercialization Dead Zone.* Deloitte Consulting LLP. Accessed September 16, 2014: http://www.deloitte.com/assets/Dcom-UnitedStates/Local%20Assets/Documents/us_lshc_Supply%20Chain%20as%20a%20Blindspot_051209.pdf

Tahvanainen, A., & Nikulainen, T. 2010. *Commercialisation at Finnish Universities: Researchers' Perspectives on the Motives and Challenges of Turning Science into Business. Discussion Paper 1234.* Helsinki: The Research Institute of the Finnish Economy.

Tanev, S., & Frederiksen, M. H. 2014. Generative Innovation Practices, Customer Creativity, and the Adoption of New Technology Products. *Technology Innovation Management Review,* 4(2): 5–10. http://timreview.ca/article/763

Valiauga, P. 2013. *Commercialization of High-tech Radical Innovations: Case Studies of X-ray Imaging Technologies.* Paper presented at the Aalto University School of Science, Finland, May 16, 2013. Accessed December 1, 2014: http://noppa.aalto.fi/noppa/kurssi/tu-22.1500/luennot/TU-22_1500_povilas__commercialisation_of_high-tech_radical_innovations.pdf

Yin, R. K. 1994. *Case Study Research: Design and Methods* (2nd ed.). Thousand Oaks, CA: Sage Publications Inc.

Zawawi, D. 2007. Quantative Versus Qualitative Methods in Social Sciences: Bridging the Gap. *Universiti Putra Malaysia.* Accessed on September 29, 2014: http://psasir.upm.edu.my/809/

Keywords: commercialization, high technology, quantum key distribution, challenges, market size, standards, certification, infrastructure, supply chains, after-sales services

16

Cybersecurity Startups: The Importance of Early and Rapid Globalization

Tony Bailetti and Erik Zijdemans

" *As the world is increasingly interconnected, everyone* **"**
shares the responsibility of securing cyberspace.

Newton Lee
Computer scientist and author

Corporations and government agencies worldwide seek to ensure that their networks are safe from cyber-attacks, and startups are being launched to take advantage of this expanded market for cybersecurity products, services, and solutions. The cybersecurity market is inherently global; therefore, cybersecurity startups must globalize to survive. With this article, we fill a gap in the literature by identifying the factors that make a technology startup valuable to specific stakeholders (e.g., investors, customers, employees) and by providing a tool and illustrating a process to describe, design, challenge, and invent the actions that should be performed to globalize a cybersecurity startup early and rapidly for the purpose of increasing its value. The development of the tool builds on recent advances in the resource-based literature, the review of the literature on born-global firms and business model discovery processes, and the experience gained operating the Lead to Win ecosystem. This article will be of interest to entrepreneurs and their venture teams, investors, business development agencies, advisors, and mentors of cybersecurity startups as well as researchers who develop tools and approaches that are relevant to technology entrepreneurs.

Introduction

Technology startups that globalize early and rapidly are more willing to change and more capable of adapting to uncertain environments (Sapienza et al., 2006), are worth more (Chetty & Campbell-Hunt, 2004), grow revenue and employment faster (Andersson et al., 2004; Gabrielsson & Manek Kirpalani, 2004; Gabrielsson et al., 2004), and bring more cash into a local economy from outside their borders (Poole, 2012). But, how can entrepreneurs discover the actions that should be carried out to make their startups valuable by globalizing early and rapidly? Although the perceived benefits from globalization are known, an approach to systematically describe, design, challenge, and invent the actions that should be performed to make a technology startup valuable by globalizing it early and rapidly is not available.

This article makes two contributions. First, it combines the ex-ante value of a resource and born-global literature streams in the development of a tool that can help

technology startups increase their value. Second, the article provides entrepreneurs with a means to identify the specific and concrete actions that should be performed to globalize their startups early and rapidly.

In the remainder of this article, we first identify what makes a technology startup valuable and what enables a technology startup to globalize early and rapidly. Then, we develop a tool, the Global Value Generator, we illustrate the process to generate the actions that can help globalize a technology startup, and we identify generic examples of the actions that 12 existing cybersecurity startups have carried out to globalize. The last section provides the conclusions.

To Make a Technology Startup Valuable

We identify the conditions that make a technology startup valuable to a stakeholder ex-ante (i.e., value of the startup is based on forecasts and not the results of the startup's performance). Traditionally, the resource-based literature posits that superior performance over other firms is a direct result of the access to and use of superior resources (Barney, 1991; Peteraf, 1993; Simon et al., 2007).

Schmidt and Keil (2012) develop a theory that identifies the ex-ante conditions under which firms attribute value to a resource. They highlight the crucial difference between the ex-ante value of a resource (i.e., value before a decision to acquire or build the resource is made) and the ex-post value of a resource (i.e., value after the performance of the resource is known). Schmidt and Keil also identify four conditions that make a resource valuable to a firm ex-ante: i) the firm's ex-ante market position; ii) its ex-ante resource base, which allows for complementarities; iii) its position in inter-organizational networks; and iv) the prior knowledge and experience of its managers.

We apply the logic that Schmidt and Keil (2012) used to examine the ex-ante value a firm allocates to a resource for the purpose of examining the ex-ante value a stakeholder allocates to a technology startup. A stakeholder is an individual or organization that can potentially make cash or in-kind contributions to the startup. In-kind contributions can include access to resources and people.

We postulate that, to increase its ex-ante value to a stakeholder, a technology startup must act to:

1. *Increase spread:* Increase the spread between customers' willingness to pay for its product and the cost of the product

2. *Increase demand:* Increase the demand for its product

3. *Increase complementarity:* Increase the demand for the stakeholder's products complemented by the startup's product

4. *Increase privileged information:* Establish a position in inter-organizational networks that improves the volume, variety, velocity, and veracity of privileged information that is accessible

5. *Increase judgment:* Attract individuals who have the requisite experience and knowledge to create value for the startup

A stakeholder, while making decisions about the value of a startup, will develop forecasts for the results from the five actions identified above. The results of carrying out these five actions will determine how much value a stakeholder attributes to a technology startup. The value of a startup is idiosyncratic to the stakeholder; even when all stakeholders have the same information they will attribute different values to the startup.

A key result of applying Schmidt and Kiel (2012) is that the ex-ante value of a technology startup is driven by forecasts of product market value creation that is made possible by the startup's existence, not just the startup's ability to generate profitable revenue. Forecasts of "increased spread" and "increased demand" express the startup's ability to increase its revenue. Forecasts of "increased complementarity", "increased privileged information", and "increased judgment" express other components of product market creation that the startup is expected to enable.

To Enable Early and Rapid Globalization in a Technology Startup

We reviewed the born-global literature to identify the factors that enable a technology startup to globalize early and rapidly. We found that startups that globalize early and rapidly tend to take the following actions:

- Use the Internet intensively (Jaw & Chen, 2006; Maltby, 2012, Tanev, 2012; Yoos, 2013)

- Partner with companies with a global footprint (Lemminger et al., 2014; Nummela et al., 2014)

- Have top managers with international experience (Hutchinson et al., 2007; Kudina et al., 2008; Poole, 2012; Sapienza et al., 2006; Spence & Crick, 2009)

- Trade control for growth (Spence & Crick, 2009)

- Develop niche products with global appeal (Spence & Crick, 2009; Chetty & Campbell-Hunt, 2004; Hutchinson et al., 2007; Kudina et al., 2008)

- Initially focus on selling in the lead market for their technology regardless of geographic location (Knight et al., 2004; Spence & Crick, 2009)

- Develop a strong brand identity (Hutchinson et al., 2007)

- Identify international opportunities (Karra et al., 2008)

- Focus on customers with overseas operations (Kudina et al., 2008)

We reduce this born-global literature into its individual constituents and postulate that the factors that enable a technology startup to globalize early and rapidly are:

1. *Niche market on 2+ continents:* address the needs of one niche market with technology development, sales channels, and online business processes on at least two continents

2. *2+ Global customers:* sell to at least two customers that have global footprints

3. *1+ global partner:* partner with at least one organization that has a global footprint

4. *Top manager experience on 2+ continents:* ensure that the top management team has work experience and networks on at least two continents

5. *Stakeholders on 2+ continents:* attract customers, partners, investors, and board of directors members who are based on at least two continents

6. *Memberships in commerce organizations on 2+ continents:* maintain active memberships in commerce organizations (e.g., chambers of commerce) on at least two continents, and publish press releases that originate from those continents

Global Value Generator and Search Process

Table 1 provides a tool in the form of a matrix that combines the five factors that enable a technology startup to be valuable and the six factors that enable a technology startup to globalize early and rapidly.

We believe that the Global Value Generator shown as Table 1 can be used by entrepreneurs to anchor the search for actions illustrated in Figure 1. The purpose of the search is to identify and test the specific and concrete actions that a technology startup should carry out to make it valuable by globalizing early and rapidly.

The discovery of the actions to increase the value of a technology startup by globalizing early and rapidly

Table 1. Global Value Generator

To Globalize Early and Rapidly	To Make a Technology Startup Valuable				
	Increase spread	Increase demand	Increase complementarity	Increase privileged information	Increase judgment
Niche market on 2+ continents					
2+ Global customers					
1+ global partner					
Top manager experience on 2+ continents					
Stakeholders on 2+ continents					
Memberships in commerce organizations on 2+ continents					

should be a disciplined process that is carried out during the early stage of a startup's lifecycle. Muegge (2012) argues that a disciplined discovery process is one that is designed to enable opportunities for learning to arise and has a work plan that results in specific deliverables.

Each cell in Table 1 identifies assertions about the actions that should be carried out. Each assertion included in one of the cells in Table 1 is a cause-effect statement about what a technology startup will do to globalize early and rapidly and what will happen to the factors that drive value as a result. The structure of the statement is as follows: If a startup does "X" to globalize early and rapidly, then "Y" will be the value result). Each statement must be clear, short, simple, and concise. The assertions build on prior knowledge, logical inference, and informed, creative imagination.

Figure 1 illustrates the search process anchored around the use of the Global Value Generator. The first step is to populate the cells in Table 1 with initial assertions. Then, in the second step, new assertions are added and existing assertions are modified, detailed, or eliminated. In the third step, a lean process is used to test the assertions. This process should be a quickly iterating cycle that continuously states and validates assertions with stakeholders and learns from the past. Assertions that stakeholders validate can be refined. Assertions that stakeholders do not validate are modified or eliminated. The fourth step is to identify a set of actions that, as a whole, will produce requisite results at an acceptable level of confidence.

The process illustrated in Figure 1 allows a technology startup to describe the actions they take in their globalization process, as well as design, challenge, and invent specific and concrete actions. Muegge (2012) provides the rationale for using a disciplined model discovery process such as the one illustrated in Figure 1. He emphasizes that discipline has two components: intent and structure. Technology entrepreneurs should deliberately identify and undertake activities to acquire new information, test assumptions, and uncover new options and organize discovery-driven activities as a project, with beginning and end points in time, specific deliverables, and a work plan to produce those deliverables.

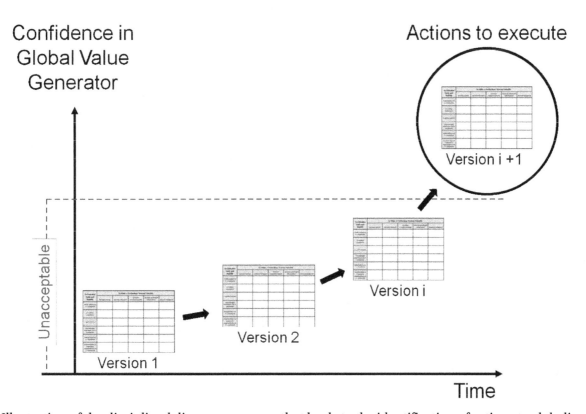

Figure 1. Illustration of the disciplined discovery process that leads to the identification of actions to globalize early and rapidly

Examples of Actions Cybersecurity Startups Carry Out to Globalize

The websites of 12 cybersecurity startups that are based in North America and have been operating for five years or less were examined for the purpose of providing generic examples of the actions that firms that operate in the cybersecurity market carry out to globalize early and rapidly. The startups were identified by two experts who work to secure the networks of the federal government of Canada and have experience with suppliers of cybersecurity products and services. We made no attempt to select startups judged to be successful because of these actions.

For each startup, we first used the information provided on its website to infer the actions undertaken to globalize and then these actions were organized into the cells included in the Global Value Generator (Table 1). This activity resulted in 12 matrices: one for each startup. Finally, we collapsed the information in the cells of the 12 matrices into the cells of one matrix.

The 12 startups examined currently operate in the following eight cybersecurity product markets:

1. Total cybersecurity solutions for specific global industries such as aerospace and defense

2. Digital identity and information security and assurance

3. Automated threat forensics and dynamic malware protection

4. Secured distribution

5. Integrated products and services

6. Password-protected login security

7. Simulation software and associated design, testing, and certification services

8. Training, consultancy, and project management

Table 2 provides the information that was collapsed from the 12 matrices (i.e., the actions we inferred that the startups carried out to globalize). The sole purpose of producing Table 2 was to provide generic examples of actions undertaken by cybersecurity startups to globalize. The decisions as to the cells where these examples are shown in Table 2 were made by the authors

solely for the purpose to illustrate what the high level results of a discovery process may look like.

The objective of an entrepreneur using the tool introduced in Table 1 as part of a disciplined discovery process is to identify a set of actions that are specific and concrete. By specific actions, we mean those that apply to a particular cybersecurity startup and are not generic like those provided as examples in Table 2. By concrete actions we mean those that are results oriented, not abstract.

Conclusion

The main motivation for writing this article was to provide a tool that can help entrepreneurs discover the actions that they should carry out to increase the exante value of their cybersecurity startups through early and rapid globalization. The tool was developed by leveraging a recent theoretical advance in resource-based theory (Schmidt & Keil, 2012), a review of the born-global literature, research on business model discovery (Muegge, 2012), and the experience gained operating the Lead to Win ecosystem (leadtowin.ca) (Bailetti & Bot, 2013).

In this article, five factors that make a technology startup valuable were identified by applying the logic that Schmidt and Kiel (2012) used to advance the resource-based theory. Moreover, six factors that enable a technology startup to globalize early and rapidly were identified from a literature review. These factors were combined into the Global Value Generator, a tool structured as a matrix that can be used to describe, design, challenge, and invent the specific and concrete actions that a cybersecurity startup should perform for the purpose of increasing its value by globalizing early and rapidly. The Global Value Generator needs to be used as part of disciplined discovery processes such as the one described by Muegge (2012). The tool can be used to complement the various business model frameworks proposed in both the management literature and consulting organizations.

We offer three questions to anchor future research efforts. The first research question is: What are the specific actions to globalize early and rapidly that have the greatest effect on the value of the cybersecurity startups? The relationship between the specific actions to globalize and the value of the startup needs to be examined empirically. This effort requires that a myriad of definitional issues be resolved and will take years to complete.

Table 2. Examples of actions a cybersecurity startup may carry out to increase its value by globalizing early and rapidly

To Globalize Early and Rapidly	To Make a Technology Startup Valuable				
	Increase spread	Increase demand	Increase complementarity	Increase privileged information	Increase judgment
Niche market on 2+ continents	Target a niche market where customers have a distinct set of cybersecurity needs and are willing to pay a premium price	Use the Internet as a global sales channel to double product demand	Develop a product that complements products offered by incumbents	Engage with members of virtual communities that attract customers and competitors	
2+ Global customers	Target customers with a global footprint that are willing to pay a premium to solve their cybersecurity problems	Target customers that are members of global supply chains and use their networks to identify the need for security solutions of their partners	Develop security solutions that add value to a customer's products or services that are sold worldwide	Establish relationships with organizations that provide information to customers	Create a network of evangelists among global customers
1+ global partner	Actively participate in the development of global standards on security requirements with global partners	Target partners with a global footprint to increase global demand for startup's product	Target partners who would benefit from the complementarity of the startup's product or service	Use connections to partners to increase access to privileged information	Seek partners with global reach
Top manager experience on 2+ continents	Use top management's intercontinental experience and networks to decrease the cost of rapid globalization	Use top management's intercontinental experience and networks to increase demand	Use top managers with experience in the market whose products/services the startup complements	Use top management's intercontinental networks to increase the access to privileged information	Attract top managers with intercontinental work experience in cybersecurity-related fields
Stakeholders on 2+ continents	Use stakeholders' intercontinental experience and networks to decrease the cost of rapid globalization	Use stakeholders' intercontinental experience and networks to increase demand	Use stakeholders on different continents to identify the geo-political differences that could shape the development of complementary products and services	Use stakeholders' intercontinental networks to increase the access to privileged information	Attract Board of Directors members with knowledge and expertise in cybersecurity-related fields on different continents
Memberships in commerce organizations on 2+ continents	Create exposure in worldwide media renowned for cybersecurity coverage to increase customers' willingness to pay	Create exposure in worldwide media renowned for cybersecurity coverage to increase global demand	Use memberships to identify partners and complementary products and services	Use memberships in commercial associations to increase access to privileged information	Attract Board of Directors members who are also active in commerce organizations

The second question is: What actions to globalize early and rapidly are unique to cybersecurity startups? The objective of this research would be to identify the specific actions that startups that depend on the existence of a global resource such as cyberspace need to do that other born-global firms do not. For example, cybersecurity startups can and perhaps should issue specific "threat-scapes" for the global markets they target. This action would be unique to cybersecurity firms. Managerial judgment and imagination about how a cybersecurity startup can help create value for customers worldwide may be key factors that drive its value.

The third research question is: How can business development agencies improve the support they provide to cybersecurity ventures? Hundreds of incubators and accelerators for startups operate worldwide. They address the needs of startups that operate in many different product markets. The objective of this research would be to identify the tools, processes, simulations, and so on required to better support the startups that operate in the cybersecurity domain. For example, what can business development agencies do to support startups that wish to issue threat-scapes for global markets, improve their managerial judgment, and imagine solutions to specific cybersecurity problems of customers worldwide?

About the Authors

Tony Bailetti is the Director of Carleton University's Technology Innovation Management (TIM) program in Ottawa, Canada. His research, teaching, and community contributions support technology entrepreneurship, regional economic development, and the early and rapid globalization of technology ventures.

Erik Alexander Zijdemans is a Master's degree candidate in Product Development and Innovation with a focus on Global Supply Chain Development at the University of Southern Denmark in Odense. He holds a BEng in Business Engineering from Hogeschool Utrecht, The Netherlands. Currently, he is conducting his research on the role of business development agencies in the support of early globalization in technology startups at Carleton University in Ottawa, Canada.

References

Andersson, S., Gabrielsson, J., & Wictor, I. 2004. International Activities in Small Firms: Examining Factors Influencing the Internationalization and Export Growth of Small Firms. *Canadian Journal of Administrative Sciences/Revue Canadienne des Sciences de l'Administration*, 21(1): 22-34.
http://dx.doi.org/10.1111/j.1936-4490.2004.tb00320.x

Bailetti, T., & Bot, S. D. 2013. An Ecosystem-Based Job-Creation Engine Fuelled by Technology Entrepreneurs. *Technology Innovation Management Review*, 3(2): 31-40.
http://timreview.ca/article/658

Barney, J. B. 1991. Firm Resources and Sustained Competitive Advantage. *Journal of Management*, 17(1): 99-120.
http://dx.doi.org/10.1177/014920639101700108

Chetty, S., & Campbell-Hunt, C. 2004. A Strategic Approach to Internationalization: A Traditional versus a "Born-Global" Approach. *Journal of International Marketing*, 12(1): 57-81.
http://dx.doi.org/10.1509/jimk.12.1.57.25651

Gabrielsson, M., & Manek Kirpalani, V. H. 2004. Born Globals: How to Reach New Business Space Rapidly. *International Business Review*, 13(5): 555-571.
http://dx.doi.org/10.1016/j.ibusrev.2004.03.005

Gabrielsson, M., Sasi, V., & Darling, J. 2004. Finance Strategies of Rapidly-growing Finnish SMEs: Born Internationals and Born Globals. *European Business Review*, 16(6): 590-604.
http://dx.doi.org/10.1108/09555340410565413

Hutchinson, K., Alexander, N., Quinn, B., & Doherty, A. M. 2007. Internationalization Motives and Facilitating Factors: Qualitative Evidence from Smaller Specialist Retailers. *Journal of International Marketing*, 15(3): 96-122.
http://dx.doi.org/10.1509/jimk.15.3.96

Jaw, Y.-L., & Chen, C.-L. 2006. The Influence of the Internet in the Internationalization of SMEs in Taiwan. *Human Systems Management*, 25(3): 167-183.
http://iospress.metapress.com/content/18x6y4kt4e414m20/

Karra, N., Phillips, N., & Tracey, P. 2008. Building the Born Global Firm: Developing Entrepreneurial Capabilities for International New Venture Success. *Long Range Planning*, 41(4): 440-458.
http://dx.doi.org/10.1016/j.lrp.2008.05.002

Knight, G., Madsen, T. K., & Servais, P. 2004. An Inquiry into Born-Global Firms in Europe and the USA. *International Marketing Review*, 21(6): 645-665.
http://dx.doi.org/10.1108/02651330410568060

Kudina, A., Yip, G. S., & Barkema, H. G. 2008. Born Global. *Business Strategy Review*, 19(4): 38-44.
http://dx.doi.org/10.1111/j.1467-8616.2008.00562.x

Lemminger, R., Svendsen, L., Zijdemans, E., Rasmussen, E., & Tanev, S. 2014. Lean and Global Technology Start-ups: Linking the Two Research Streams. The ISPIM Americas Innovation Forum 2014. Montreal, Canada.
Maltby, T. 2012. Using Social Media to Accelerate the Internationalization of Startups from Inception. *Technology Innovation Management Review*, 2(10): 22-26.
http://timreview.ca/article/616

Muegge, S. 2012. Business Model Discovery by Technology Entrepreneurs. *Technology Innovation Management Review*, 2(4): 5-16.
http://timreview.ca/article/545

Nummela, N., Saarenketo, S., Jokela, P., & Loane, S. 2014. Strategic Decision-Making of a Born Global: A Comparative Study From Three Small Open Economies. *Management International Review*, 54(4): 527-550.
http://dx.doi.org/10.1007/s11575-014-0211-x

Peteraf, M. A. 1993. The Cornerstone of Competitive Advantage: A Resource-Based View. *Strategic Management Journal*, 14(3): 179-191.
http://dx.doi.org/10.1002/smj.4250140303

Poole, R. 2012. Global Mindset: An Entrepreneur's Perspective on the Born-Global Approach. *Technology Innovation Management Review*, 2(10): 27-31.
http://timreview.ca/article/617

Sapienza, H. J., Autio, E., George, G., & Zahra, S. A. 2006. A Capabilities Perspective on the Effects of Early Internationalization on Firm Survival and Growth. *Academy of Management Review*, 31(4): 914-933.
http://dx.doi.org/10.5465/AMR.2006.22527465

Schmidt, J., & Keil, T. 2012. What Makes a Resource Valuable? Identifying the Drivers of Firm-idiosyncratic Resource Value. *Academy of Management Review*, 38(2): 206-228.
http://dx.doi.org/10.5465/amr.10.0404

Sirmon, D. G., Hitt, M. A., & Ireland, R. D. 2007. Managing Firm Resources in Dynamic Environments to Create Value: Looking Inside the Black Box. *Academy of Management Review*, 32(1): 273-292.
http://dx.doi.org/10.5465/AMR.2007.23466005

Spence, M., & Crick, D. 2009. An Exploratory Study of Canadian International New Venture Firms' Development in Overseas Markets. *Qualitative Market Research: An International Journal*, 12(2): 208-233.
http://dx.doi.org/10.1108/13522750910948798

Tanev, S. 2012. Global from the Start: The Characteristics of Born-Global Firms in the Technology Sector. *Technology Innovation Management Review*, 2(3): 5-8.
http://timreview.ca/article/532

Yoos, S. 2013. Market Channels of Technology Startups that Internationalize Rapidly from Inception. *Technology Innovation Management Review*, 3(10): 32-37.
http://timreview.ca/article/618

Keywords: cybersecurity, born global, startups, globalization

17

Assessing Scientific Contributions: A Proposed Framework and Its Application to Cybersecurity

Dan Craigen

“ *The philosophy of science is about as useful to scientists* **”** *as ornithology is to birds.*

Attributed to Richard P. Feynman (1918–1988)
Theoretical physicist

Through a synthesis of existing work on evaluating scientific theories and contributions, a framework for assessing scientific contributions is presented. By way of example, the framework is then applied to two contributions to the science of cybersecurity. The science of cybersecurity is slowly emerging. As the science and its theories emerge, it is important to extract the key contributions that characterize actual progress in our understanding of cybersecurity. Researchers and funding agencies will be interested in the assessment framework as a means of assessing scientific contributions to cybersecurity. In a nascent research area such as the science of cybersecurity, this article may contribute to a focused research program to accelerate the growth of the science.

Introduction

Hardly a day goes by without yet another report of significant information security vulnerabilities. Some of the most recent attacks, such as the heartbleed bug (MITRE, 2014a) and the shellshock bug (MITRE, 2014b), have focused on core functionalities. The former vulnerability is in an implementation of an Internet-wide protocol (SSL) and the latter vulnerability is in a widely used UNIX command-line interpreter (bash).

After decades of substantial investment into cybersecurity, it is almost unfathomable that such vulnerabilities continue to expose societies to potentially significant exploitation. In the author's view, the existence of these vulnerabilities reflects the complexity of the cybersecurity space and suggests that the existing paradigms for identifying, responding to, or mitigating vulnerabilities and their potential exploitation are failing. Given the perceived ad hoc nature of cybersecurity, which is usually exemplified by patching systems in response to identified vulnerabilities, there is an emerging belief that the foundations of cybersecurity need to be revisited with a sound theoretical/scientific perspective.

It is through a sound theoretical/scientific perspective that we can evolve cybersecurity from its current (largely) ad hoc nature, to a foundation that is well-principled and informed by scientifically-based tenets (Schneider, 2012). Such a theoretical foundation then informs a rigorous engineering discipline, which, it is hoped, will positively impact cybersecurity postures.

However, a difficulty facing researchers, funding agencies, government, and industry is how to assess putative contributions to such a theory. In this article, we synthesize a framework for assessing scientific contributions to cybersecurity. The framework was motivated by the author's involvement with various initiatives in the science of cybersecurity and the need to ascertain whether contributions were truly progressing and contributing to such a nascent science. Particularly, given that development of such a science will be a multi-decade exercise, being able to measure progress and contributions, at least incrementally, would provide important objective input into both research and funding decisions.

First, we introduce the concept of theory and an approach to building theory. We then review the literature on measuring progress in science and assessing theories. The key concepts arising from the literature are then synthesized into a framework for assessing scientific contributions to cybersecurity. Finally, we demonstrate the use of the framework by applying it to two scientific contributions in cybersecurity.

Building Theories

Theory refers to "a well-confirmed type of explanation of nature, made in a way consistent with the scientific method and fulfilling the criteria required by modern science" (Wikipedia, 2014). Weber (2012) notes that "theories provide a representation of someone's perceptions of how a subset of real-world phenomena should be described" and defines theory as "a particular kind of model that is intended to account for some subset of phenomena in the real world". However, Weber also offered a slightly different definition of theory in an earlier article: "an account that is intended to explain or predict some phenomena that we perceive in the world" (Weber, 2003).

Weber's work builds upon an ontology described by Bunge (1977, 1979), which is used to define theory-related concepts. The key assumptions, as described by Weber (2003), can be summarized as follows:

- The world is perceived as a collection of "things" and "properties of things".

- A state is the values associated with the various properties at a particular time and space.

- Events occur that can result in a change of state.

- Phenomena are defined as states of things or events that occur to things.

Weber (2003) takes the view that "the choice and articulation of the phenomena we are seeking to explain or predict via our theories are the two most-critical tasks we undertake as researchers." A role of a theory is to express "laws" that relate various values of a state. Weber (2003) defines the "account of the phenomena" as "the explanation of the laws that are hypothesized to relate them" and normally uses "constructs," a property of a thing, and association among constructs (a law).

Weber (2012) then introduces the following parts of a theory:

- *Constructs:* represent an attribute (the way we perceive a property)

- *Associations:* for static phenomena, relate construct values; for dynamic phenomena, relate histories of values between constructs

- *States:* identification of state space that is the object of the theory – the range of legal values

- *Events:* identification of the events that are the object of the theory – the range of legal state transitions.

Using these terms, Weber (2012) then discusses how to build a theory:

1. Articulate the constructs of a theory.

2. Articulate the laws of interaction (relationships) among the constructs of a theory.

3. Articulate the lawful state space of a theory.

4. Articulate the lawful event space of a theory.

Although the process is presented linearly, it is important to recognize that theory building is iterative. The process starts with good observations and descriptions, and it improves through inductive/deductive cycles, with anomalies resulting in evolution of the theories. In the early stages of understanding phenomena, it may be necessary to use the theories of other disciplines to first articulate our understandings. As we better comprehend our phenomena, new theories or adapted theories may be developed.

In a similar manner, Sjøberg and colleagues (2008) describe the theory-building enterprise as:

1. Defining the constructs of the theory

2. Defining the propositions of the theory

3. Providing explanations to justify the theory

4. Determining the scope of the theory

5. Testing the theory through empirical research

Measuring Progress in Science

For researchers and funding agencies, it is pertinent to ascertain whether we are making scientific progress: are the scientific contributions meaningful? One key input into such considerations was written by the Committee on Assessing Behavioral and Social Science Research on Aging (Feller & Stern, 2007). Though motivated by research into aging, their characterization of progress transcends the discipline to other scientific endeavours. The committee identified two kinds of progress: i) internally defined (i.e., characterized as intellectual progress and contributions to science), and ii) externally defined (i.e., characterized by contributions to society).

For internally defined progress in science, the committee identified five types of progress:

1. *Discovery:* demonstration of the existence of previously unknown phenomena or relationships among phenomena, or when the discovery that widely shared understandings of phenomena is wrong or incomplete

2. *Analysis:* development of concepts, typologies, frameworks of understanding, methods, techniques, or data that make it possible to uncover phenomena or test explanations of them

3. *Explanation:* discovery of regularities in the ways phenomena change over time or evidence that supports, rules out, or leads to qualifications of possible explanations of these regularities

4. *Integration:* linking theories or explanations across different domains or levels of organization

5. *Development:* stimulation of additional research in a field or discipline, including research critical of past conclusions, and when it stimulates research outside the original field, including interdisciplinary research and research on previously under-researched questions. It also develops when it attracts new people to work on an important research problem.

For externally defined progress in science, the committee identified four types of progress:

1. *Identifying issues:* identifying problems that require societal action or showing that a problem is less serious than previously believed

2. *Finding solutions:* developing ways to address issues or solve problems

3. *Informing choices:* providing accurate and compelling information, thus promoting better informed choices

4. *Educating society:* producing fundamental knowledge and developing frameworks of understanding that are useful for making decisions in the private sector, and participating as citizens in public policy decisions. Science can also contribute by educating the next generation of scientists.

Assessing Theories

Prior to discussing our criteria for assessing contributions to science, we note various criteria that are used to assess theories (Berg, 2009; Cramer, 2013; Sjøberg et al., 2008):

• Testibility; refutability

• Precision

• Empirical validity/support

• Explanatory power; predictability; quantifiable

• Parsimony; consilience; simplicity; self-consistent; rational; inductive

• Generality; comprehensiveness

• Utility; heuristic and applied value

• Repeatability

Weber (2012) uses the ontological structure, briefly discussed above, to evaluate a theory from two perspectives: evaluating the components of a theory and evaluating the whole theory. Weber notes that the components of the theory must be described precisely because they essentially define the domain of the theory. From his perspective, a key advantage of precision is that tests can be better designed.

Weber (2012) evaluates the components of a theory using the following key concepts:

1. *Constructs:* Should be defined precisely; underlying variables clearly identified

2. *Associations:* Described to various levels of precision. With static phenomena, there is a relationship, but no sign; the sign of association between constructs identified; and a functional relationship is described. With dynamic phenomena, there is a relationship, but no sign or direction; the sign of association between constructs identified but not the direction; the direction of association known (implying causality) or time relationship; and a functional relationship identified.

3. *States:* How clear and precise is the description of the state space?

4. *Events:* How clear and precise are the events?

Weber (2012) evaluates a whole theory using the following key concepts:

1. *Importance:* Does the theory address important phenomena from either a practice or research perspective?

2. *Novelty:* Does it resolve anomalies? Does it change research paradigms?

3. *Parsimony:* Is the theory sufficiently simple?

4. *Level:* Is the theory sufficiently abstract? Weber discusses micro-level and macro-level theories, both of which have associated pros and cons.

5. *Falsifiability:* Can the theory be refuted?

Assessing Scientific Contributions

From the above literature review, we synthesize our framework for assessing scientific contributions. There are two aspects to assessing a scientific theory: *Evaluation* and *Contribution.* These two aspects and their components are summarized in Table 1.

Evaluation has two constituents: i) *Well-formedness* and ii) *Testing and Analysis.* Broadly speaking, *Evaluation* refers to expectations of how a theory should be expressed and the means through which the scientific and philosophical communities test and analyze theories for acceptance. In large part, evaluation focuses on technical attributes of the theory.

Contribution has three constituents: i) *Contribution to Science,* ii) *Contribution to Society,* and iii) *Depth of the Contribution.* The first two constituents align directly with the work by the Committee on Assessing Behavioral and Social Science Research on Aging (Feller & Stern, 2007) in that the *Contribution to Science* aligns to a subset of internally defined progress, while *Contribution to Society* aligns to a modified subset of externally defined progress. In large part, contribution focuses on social attributes of the theory – its role within scientific and societal communities.

Evaluation: Well-formedness
In the framework illustrated in Table 1, we identify six attributes to determine if a theory is well-formed:

1. *Components:* Evaluation was discussed by (Weber,

Table 1. Proposed framework for assessing a scientific theory

Evaluation		Contribution		
Well-formedness	**Testing and Analysis**	**Contribution to Science**	**Contribution to Society**	**Depth of the Contribution**
• Components	• Falsifiability	• Discovery	• Identifying issues	• Generality
• Precision (Formalism)	• Accuracy	• Analysis	• Finding solutions	• Comprehensiveness
• Consistency	• Repeatability	• Explanation	• Making educated choices	• Non-obvious results/observations
• Completeness	• Consilience			• Novelty
• Measurability	• Parsimony			
• Testability				

2012), as summarized earlier in this article. We expect each of these components to be present.

2. *Precision (Formalism):* Consistent with Weber, we argue that the components of a theory should be described as precisely as possible. Although natural languages are often used in stylized manners to describe concepts "precisely", the "gold standard" is to describe the components formally using mathematical concepts.

3. *Consistency:* The expression of the theory should be internally consistent; that is, there are no contradictions.

4. *Completeness:* In our context, we view completeness from an "expressively complete" perspective in which the theory can describe all of the properties for which it has been developed.

5. *Measurability:* It should be possible to objectively measure the theory components, particularly the constructs. Key concepts must be quantifiable and the measurements must be objective.

6. *Testability:* The theory components should be amenable to scientific experimentation. This attribute is closely related to both the measurable attribute above and the falsifiable attribute described below.

Evaluation: Testing and Analysis
In Table 1, we identify five attributes for the evaluation of testing and analysis:

1. *Falsifiability:* A key attribute/principle of science – it must be possible to show that the theory is incompatible with possible empirical observations.

2. *Accuracy:* The empirical observations should be in line with the expectations of the theory.

3. Repeatability: The empirical observations should be reproducible.

4. *Consilience:* Evidence from independent, unrelated sources can "converge" to strong conclusions.

5. *Parsimony:* Measures the number of kinds of entities postulated by a theory; theories should be as simple as possible for the phenomena being modelled.

Each of these attributes is testing or analyzing the theory and mostly relate to empirical validation. The first four specifically speak to experiments: Can we fail? Are the experimental results being accurately described or predicted by the theory? Can we repeat the experiment and obtain the same results? Can we obtain the same results by different experimental means? If all of these conditions hold, it then makes sense to ask ourselves whether we have elegance in our theory. Have we truly identified the core relationships and constructs?

Contributions to Science and to Society
The elements *Contribution to Science* and *Contribution to Society* are largely those identified by the Committee on Assessing Behavioral and Social Science Research on Aging (Feller & Stern, 2007). *Contribution to Society* merges their "Informing Choices" and "Education" into *Making Educated Choices* within the proposed framework. Further, for *Contribution to Science,* only the first three attributes are included; development and integration can be viewed as attributes of an *Evaluation of the Contribution.*

As depicted in Table 1, the importance and utility of contributions to science and society are captured in *Evaluation of the Contribution:*

1. *Generality:* Is the scientific contribution of specific or general validity?

2. *Comprehensiveness:* Is the scientific contribution inclusive and of broad scope? Is the scientific contribution inclusive and broadly applicable to societal challenges?

3. *Non-obvious results:* Are there interesting challenges for scientists to explore? Are there unexpected consequences suggested by the theory when contextualized societally?

4. *Novelty:* Does the theory provide new insights otherwise not explored by science? Is it normal science or paradigm changing? Does the theory provide new insights otherwise not explored by society?

Measuring Evaluation

Having defined the various evaluation attributes, we posit some potential values for each of the attributes. For simplicity, we define only three values per attribute:

• Well-formedness

  · Components: all components present; some components present; no components

· Precision (Formalism): formal/mathematical; semi-formal; informal

· Consistency: provable consistency; unclear; inconsistent

· Completeness: provable completeness; unclear; incomplete

· Measurability: measurable; unclear; not measurable

· Testability: testable; unclear; not testable

• Testing and analysis

· Falsifiability: falsifiable; unclear; not-falsifiable

· Accuracy: accurate; unclear; not-accurate

· Repeatability: repeatable; unclear; not-repeatable

· Consilience: consilient; unclear; not-consilient

· Parsimony: parsimonious; unclear; complex

• Depth of the contributions

· Generality: general; generalized; specific

· Comprehensiveness: comprehensive; moderately comprehensive; narrow

· Non-obvious results/observations: non-obvious; unclear; uninteresting

· Novelty: paradigm/society shifting; substantive normal progress; not substantive

Applying the Framework

Having defined the framework, we now apply it to two contributions from the science of cybersecurity. These assessments are preliminary, but are intended to illustrate how the framework could be applied.

Phishing in International Waters

At the 2014 Symposium and Bootcamp on the Science of Security (hot-sos.org/2014/), Tembe and colleagues (2014) presented the paper "Phishing in International Waters", in which they reported on a survey of American, Chinese, and Indian Internet users and explored the role of culture in the three nationalities responses to phishing attacks. The authors performed various statistical

analyses based on responses to questionnaires and found that there were *cross-national differences in agreement* regarding the characteristics of phishing, the media of phishing, and the consequences of phishing. Conclusions were drawn in part from the individualistic culture represented by Americans and the collectivist cultures represented by China and India.

The statistical analyses included multivariate analysis of covariance and logistic regression analysis. According to the paper, a logistic regression was used to compare nationality with phishing and the characteristics of the risk profile. Further, the authors reported that a multivariate analysis of covariance was used to compare nationality with characteristics of phishing, types of media, and the consequences of phishing. Notably, neither age nor education had any influence on the likelihood of being phished.

Table 2 summarizes our analysis of "Phishing in International Waters" using our framework for assessing scientific contributions.

Selective Interleaving Functions

McLean (2014) presented one of the keynote presentations at the Science of Security conference (HOTSoS, 2014), His presentation, "The Science of Security: Perspectives and Prospects", provided two case studies: one on access control models and the second on information flow models. Here, we assess the scientific contribution of the second case study using our proposed framework. In this second case, McLean examined the evolution of information-flow models and how our understanding in this area has improved over time and has resulted in a compelling framework that could be used to explain information flow models. Table 3 summarizes our analysis of portion of his paper on "Selective Interleaving Functions" and his related earlier paper (McLean, 1994).

Contribution

In this article, we have presented a framework for assessing scientific contributions to cybersecurity and then applied the framework to two contributions to the Science of Cybersecurity. Our assessment framework consists of two parts: Evaluation and Contribution. Through these two parts, we have synthesized and structured a number of approaches cited in the literature for assessing scientific contributions. Prior work, such as that of Weber and the Committee on Assessing Behavioral and Social Science Research on Aging has focused on one part solely (either evaluation or contribu-

Table 2. Assessing the scientific contribution of "Phishing in International Waters" (Tembe et al., 2014) using the proposed framework

Well-formedness		
Components	Some components present	Statistical variables identified
Precision (Formalism)	Semi-formal	Questionnaire used natural language descriptions; statistical analysis is formal
Consistency	Unclear	Further analysis required
Completeness	Incomplete	Probably very difficult to characterize completeness in this case
Measurability	Measurable	The paper identifies measurable criteria through the questionnaire and definition of variables. There are potential biases introduced (as noted by the authors).
Testability	Testable	Variables were identified, a questionnaire defined, responses obtained. In principle, similar surveys could be performed on the same cultures or other cultures (such as European or African cultures – as suggested by the authors).
Testing and Analysis		
Falsifiability	Falsifiable	Hypotheses were not specifically identified, except for the collective/individualistic aspect of the societies.
Accuracy	Unclear	Hypotheses were not specifically identified, except for the collective/individualistic aspect of the societies.
Repeatability	Unclear	While the experiment could be rerun, there has been no demonstration of repeatability.
Consilience	Unclear	No other means of studying the cultural aspects were posited.
Parsimony	Unclear	No comment; insufficient information.
Contributions to Science and Society		
To Science	Explanation	Though an argument could be made that the contribution is analytical, the paper largely explains why Americans, Chinese, and Indians respond differently to phishing attacks.
To Society	Making educated choices	By understanding the cultural nuances of phishing and, as suggested in the paper, by modifying training programs and considering different approaches to security mechanism, the role of culture impacts phishing mitigations.
Depth of the Contributions		
Generality	Specific	The analysis focused on cultural responses to a particular form of attack: phishing.
Comprehensiveness	Narrow	The sample set was small; potential admitted biases from Mechanical Turk
Non-obvious results/observations	Unclear	No relevant comments were provided in the paper
Novelty	Not substantive	While characterized as not substantive, it still demonstrates a multi-disciplinary approach to cybersecurity. It is an early step in understanding cultural attributes of cybersecurity.

Table 3. Assessing the scientific contribution of "Selective Interleaving Functions" (McLean, 2014) using the proposed framework

Well-formedness		
Components	All components present	Not evaluated here
Precision (Formalism)	Formal/mathematical	Not evaluated here
Consistency	Consistent	See McLean (1994) for mathematical presentation
Completeness	Unclear	Not evaluated here
Measurability	Measurable	Systems could be implemented to demonstrate whether, for example, composition claims hold.
Testability	Testable	Systems could be implemented to demonstrate whether, for example, composition claims hold.
Testing and Analysis		
Falsifiability	Falsifiable	Systems could be implemented to demonstrate whether, for example, composition claims hold.
Accuracy	Unclear	Papers cited within are theoretical contributions. While testable and measurable, it is unclear whether any experiments have been performed.
Repeatability	Unclear	Papers cited within are theoretical contributions. While testable and measurable it is unclear whether any experiments have been performed.
Consilience	Unclear	Papers cited within are theoretical contributions. While testable and measurable it is unclear whether any experiments have been performed.
Parsimony	Parsimonious	Selective interleaving functions are effective in unifying information flow models.
Contributions to Science and Society		
To Science	Discovery	McLean argued that selective interleaving functions provided a common framework for an otherwise incomparable collection of information-flow security models. Further benefits arose because they explained why certain types of compositions were harder on security than others.
To Society	Finding solutions	Selective interleaving functions provided an overall characterization of information-flow models and explained difficulties in composability, hence providing information on how systems could be developed with composition in mind.
Evaluation of the Contributions		
Generality	General	Subsumed prior existing work and a miscellaneous collection of information-flow security models. Provided a common framework.
Comprehensiveness	Comprehensive	Within the context of information-flow security models, this approach covers "possibilistic" security properties.
Non-obvious results/observations	Non-obvious	While setting a general framework, it appears this framework also can be used to explore other composition properties.
Novelty	Substantive normal progress	Built upon prior work on understanding safety/liveness, composition theories, etc.

tion). Weber provides a significant assessment of an Information Systems paper that can usefully inform how to proceed with theory evaluations. We expand upon Weber's evaluation by discussing both well-formedness and testing/analyzing criteria a theory more comprehensively.

Particularly, given that development of a Science of Cybersecurity will be a multi-decade exercise, being able to measure progress and contributions, at least incrementally, will provide important objective input into both research and funding decisions and is expected to contribute to a focused research program and accelerate the growth of the science.

Conclusion

The assessment framework presented in this article is preliminary. Specifically, whether the values for each criterion are sensible and whether there should be additional criteria is open for refinement. Weber (2003, 2012) uses an ontological framework to motivate his analysis; future work should build upon these ontological considerations.

Moreover, this type of work can be used to assess "scientific progress". For example, the science of cybersecurity is in its early stages, and it would be beneficial to measure the progress made in the field. Assessing contributions provides potentially rational inputs into the determination of scientific progress and thereby potentially contribute to a focused research program to accelerate the growth of the science.

About the Author

Dan Craigen is a Science Advisor at the Communications Security Establishment in Canada. Previously, he was President of ORA Canada, a company that focused on High Assurance/Formal Methods and distributed its technology to over 60 countries. His research interests include formal methods, the science of cybersecurity, and technology transfer. He was the chair of two NATO research task groups pertaining to validation, verification, and certification of embedded systems and high-assurance technologies. He received his BScH and MSc degrees in Mathematics from Carleton University in Ottawa, Canada.

References

Berg, R. 2009. Evaluating Scientific Theories. *Philosophy Now*, 74: 14-17.

Bunge, M. 1977. *Treatise on Basic Philosophy, Volume 3: Ontology I: The Furniture of the World*. Dordrecht, Holland: D. Reidel Publishing Company.

Bunge, M. 1979. *Treatise on Basic Philosophy, Volume 3: Ontology II: A World of Systems*. Dordrecht, Holland: D. Reidel Publishing Company.

Cramer, K. 2013. Six Criteria of a Viable Theory: Putting Reversal Theory to the Test. *Journal of Motivation, Emotion, and Personality*, 1(1): 9-16. http://dx.doi.org/10.12689/jmep.2013.102

Feller, I., & Stern, P. C. (Eds.) 2007. *A Strategy for Assessing Science: Behavioral and Social Research on Aging*. Washington, DC: National Academies Press (US).

McLean, J. 1994. A General Theory of Composition for Trace Sets Closed Under Selective Interleaving Functions. *Proceedings of the 1994 IEEE Symposium on Research in Security and Privacy:* 79.

McLean, J. 2014. The Science of Computer Security Perspectives and Prospects. Keynote presentation at the 2014 Symposium and Bootcamp on the Science of Security, April 8-9, Raleigh, NC, United States.

MITRE. 2014a. CVE-2014-0160. *Common Vulnerabilities and Exposures*. November 1, 2014: http://cve.mitre.org/cgi-bin/cvename.cgi?name=CVE-2014-0160

MITRE. 2014b. CVE-2014-7169. *Common Vulnerabilities and Exposures*. November 1, 2014: http://cve.mitre.org/cgi-bin/cvename.cgi?name=CVE-2014-7169

Sjøberg, D., Dybå, T., Anda, B. C. D., & Hannay, J. E. 2008. *Building Theories in Software Engineering*. In F. Shull, J. Singer, & D. I. K. Sjøberg (Eds.), Guide to Advanced Empirical Software Engineering: 312-336. London: Springer-Verlag. http://dx.doi.org/10.1007/978-1-84800-044-5_12

Tembe, R., Zielinksa, O., Liu, Y., Hong, K. W., Murphy-Hill, E., Mayhorn, C., & Ge, X. 2014. Phishing in International Waters: Exploring Cross-National Differences in Phishing Conceptualizations between Chinese, Indian and American Samples. *Proceedings of the 2014 Symposium and Bootcamp on the Science of Security*. http://dx.doi.org/10.1145/2600176.2600178

Schneider, F. B. 2012. Blueprint for a Science of Cybersecurity. *The Next Wave*, 19(2): 47-57.

Weber, R. 2003. Editor's Comment: Theoretically Speaking. *MIS Quarterly*, 27(3): iii-xii.

Weber, R. 2012. Evaluating and Developing Theories in the Information Systems Discipline. *Journal of the Association for Information Systems*, 13(1): 1-30.

Wikipedia. 2014. Theory. *Wikipedia*. October 1, 2014: http://en.wikipedia.org/wiki/Theory

Keywords: cybersecurity, science of cybersecurity, scientific progress, scientific contributions, societal contributions, assessing science

18

The Business of Cybersecurity

David Grau and Charles Kennedy

" Fundamentally, the key problem in cybersecurity isn't "
the technology – it's a people problem.

David Grau
Head of Threat Response, TD Bank Group

Overview

The TIM Lecture Series is hosted by the Technology Innovation Management program (carleton.ca/tim) at Carleton University in Ottawa, Canada. The lectures provide a forum to promote the transfer of knowledge between university research to technology company executives and entrepreneurs as well as research and development personnel. Readers are encouraged to share related insights or provide feedback on the presentation or the TIM Lecture Series, including recommendations of future speakers.

The third TIM lecture of 2014 was held at Carleton University on March 26th, and was presented by David Grau, Vice President and Head of Threat Response, Intelligence, and Defensive Technologies at TD Bank Group (td.com), and Charles Kennedy, VP Credit Card Technology. Kennedy and Grau discussed the state of the information security industry and current trends in threat management and focused their lecture on the banking industry and the TD Bank Group's experience with cybersecurity within it. However, many of the messages are applicable to broader and multidisciplinary domains.

Summary

The lecture began with an overview of the state of the industry, including types of common threats faced today, such as malware, physical attacks, social engineering, social media, misuse, errors, and environmental effects. Kennedy highlighted that hacking is a particular priority that disproportionately introduces risk to the bank and its customers. Hacking can take the form of system hacking (e.g., operating systems), infrastructure hacking (e.g., wireless, hardware, network devices), or application and data hacking (e.g., ports, code, users). Typically, events that occur as a result of these types of activities are not a case of one individual criminal targeting an individual user; more common and significant threats come from automated systems.

These threats are not perceived in the same way by all people or organizations. Kennedy explained that the degree and nature of concerns – or posture – in relation cybersecurity threats varies between citizens, governments, and infrastructure organizations:

1. **Citizens** are typically worried about identity protection and identity theft, social networks, convenience, privacy, confidentiality, and issues relating to mobile (e.g., payments, reservations, location, retail applications). In this group, the typical demographics point to high rates of use and adoption of the Internet and mobile technologies among young adults.

2. **Governments** are typically worried about data protection and theft, as well as the reliability of both the public and private sectors. The concerns of individual governments may be unique, and there is a wide range of postures around the globe. Initial steps are being taken to define the international rules of engagement for governments combating cyberterrorism and cyberwarfare. Examples include *The Talinn Manual on the International Law Applicable to Cyber Warfare* (NATO, 2013; ccdcoe.org/249.html)

3. **Banks and key infrastructure** are typically worried about maintaining financial services (e.g., payments and exchanges), utilities, and commercial activities. Innovation, research, and response all depend upon co-operation between industries and between gov-

ernment and industry. The increasing complexity of the threats necessitates increasing co-operation in the future.

Threat actors and motivations

Grau highlighted the natural tendency of information security staff – as technologists – to look at problems from a technology perspective. When evaluating a security threat or incident, this tendency leads to a focus on the tangibles – the what, the when, and the where – that can be analyzed and processed. Often, this analysis comes at the expense of considering the human element – the who and the why – and leads to the creation of tools that reinforce the technology bias, and leaves staff overwhelmed with a massive and increasing volume of unmanageable data. In response to the current state of affairs in information security, much greater attention must be paid to the factors that motivate actors. Unless efforts are focused on indentifying and understanding the who and the why, there is insufficient context to detect the important patterns in large volumes of event data and to make intelligent decisions based on that data.

Broadly speaking, the threats facing citizens, governments, and infrastructure organizations come from three types of actor:

1. **The Criminal:** motivated by profit; focused on fraud; the "top of the food chain"

2. **The Hactivist:** motivated by sociopolitical causes; focused on drawing attention through disruption and shaming; adopts tools and methods from criminal actors; examples: Anonymous, AntiSec.

3. **The Nation-State:** motivated by political or economic advantage; focused on espionage; late adopters that learn from criminal actors and hactivists

Of these three types of actors, criminal actors are the greatest concern in the banking industry, and so the greater part of the lecture focused on describing the threats posed by criminal actors and the bank's strategies to not only defend against them, but take proactive steps to reduce the risk they pose. The threat levels from the other two types of actor are increasing; however, criminal actors remain the greatest threat to the banking industry, in part because of their profit motive, but also because most of the innovation tends to come from this group – the hactivist and nation-state actors typically adopt the techniques and technologies that were first developed by the criminal actors.

Compared to just 15 years ago, the criminal landscape has changed considerably. Whereas criminal activity in cyberspace was typically initiated by "one-man shows", there are now complex criminal ecosystems that are both stratified and service oriented. For example, the tiers of actors in an ecosystem might include the following:

1. funders (e.g., organized crime)
2. malware writers
3. botnet operators
4. botnet users
5. money mules (i.e., those who transfer money out of the ecosystem)
6. mule herders (i.e., those who line up the connections to money mules)
7. state-funded "skunkworks"

In the past, security efforts might have targeted the individual who writes the malicious code, who likely also would have played all or most of the roles listed above. Now, the servitization of the criminal ecosystem means that actors wishing to commit fraud do not require advanced technical skills; the required tools and services are readily available and easy to use. However, once the fraud has been committed, it remains a challenge for the criminal actors to retrieve the money. As the people who take the money out of the ecosystem, the money mules are the weakest link in the chain – the most likely to be detected and the most likely starting point for further investigation of the ecosystem. To illustrate the sophistication and stratification of the criminal ecosystems, Grau provided examples of services offered within such networks, such as fraud aggregators, which are websites that collect and organize stolen data (e.g., credit card numbers), which can then be queried by criminal actors.

Current and emerging trends

Grau examined some of the current and emerging trends in techniques used by threat actors, including:

1. **Man-in-the-browser attacks:** a method of using malware to create a false, but truly convincing, browser experience to a victim and to harvest credentials and other valuable data in the background. This type of malware is fully automated, easy to use, and very powerful. Because it is so convincing – even the URLs in the browser address bar appear correct – this type of approach is much more effective than traditional phishing techniques. It is also very difficult to detect with anti-virus and anti-spyware applications, and so there is an urgent need for innovation in this area.

2. **Ransomware:** malware that installs itself on a computer and pretends to be anti-virus or other well-intentioned software. For example, it may present the user with a choice of whether or not to allow the software to "clean" the computer, but if the user declines, it either permanently damages the victim's hard drive or demands online ransom payments.

3. **Polymorphism:** malware that is customized to each user, meaning that each version of the malware is unique to that user even if it may be functionally identical to another version. This approach can overcome the types of general rules and definition databases that traditional anti-virus software depend upon.

4. **Packaged exploit kits:** malware frameworks that deliver tailored packages of malware components that correspond to a victim's particular vulnerabilities. If a user can be tricked into visiting a website where a packaged exploit kit is installed, the framework tests the victim's computer and then packages a set of exploits designed specifically to suit the victim's vulnerabilities. This customized approach also means that the criminal actors do not need to "show all of their cards" in terms of the full complement of exploits they have available. This approach can also take advantage of polymorphism to obfuscate the new, customized package.

5. **Distributed denial-of-service attacks (DDoS):** an approach that effectively creates a massive digital traffic jam in the target organization's infrastructure, usually by amplifying and redirecting traffic to the target's network. Although in the past, DDoS attacks were typically "nuisance" attacks, this approach is now often used as a diversionary tactic to facilitate fraud.

6. **New-generation botnets:** networks of computers under an outside actor's control for the purposes of sending spam or participating in DDoS attacks. In the past, botnets primarily recruited thousands of individual home computers; however, the scale of the botnet approach has grown massively not by increased recruitment of additional computers, but by focusing on servers, which provide much greater power per infection, resulting in smaller but more powerful botnets that can have enormous disruptive potential.

In describing current and emerging threats, Grau cautioned that the term "advanced persistent threat", or APT, is often misused and overused, because all modern malware is advanced, is persistent, and is a threat, in addition to being sophisticated, stealthy, and evasive. A true APT shares all of these characteristics, but it is also rare, targeted, customized, and attributable (i.e., not opportunistic).

Unfortunately, traditional anti-virus software is largely ineffective against the current and emerging techniques used by criminal actors. Verizon (2011; tinyurl.com/lvdpsnl) reported a 37% success rate for anti-virus applications in its study of data breaches; other datasets report even lower numbers. The key reason is the growing complexity of the problem: as additional devices and features appear, the attack surface grows. As more and more ways appear for criminal actors to infiltrate a system, it becomes increasingly difficult to protect the entire attack surface. Grau provided several industry examples, including the Zeus Trojan horse and Cryptolocker ransomware, and the 2013 Target data breach, to reinforce the sophistication of current and emerging threats.

Innovation opportunities
Based on their experiences, Grau and Kennedy identified the following areas where innovation is needed in the cybersecurity domain:

1. **Skilled workers and innovators:** there is a shortage of talent in the information security domain.

2. **Borderless networks:** organizations no longer have a well-defined perimeter – this paradigm has become outdated. Today, organizations are more porous and no longer have clearly defined "doors" that simply need to be locked down by security staff. There is now a need for ubiquitous security (e.g., a portable security stack) that does not just assume a defensive posture, but is nimble, pervasive, and dynamic.

3. **Avoiding fragmentation of the Internet:** changes to the Internet over time in response to the cybersecurity threats provides incentive for nations to fragment the Internet (e.g., the Great Firewall of China). The underlying problem is that efforts to enhance cybersecurity are often at odds with the ideals upon which the Internet is based and requires to function effectively.

4. **Security as big data analytics:** there is a need for real-time detection of events with in-line correlation and decision making based on scores derived from analytics.

5. **Wetware versus software:** there is a mismatch between the data experts, who do not understand the threat scenarios, and the security professionals, who do not understand the data analyses.

6. **Intelligence gap**: threat intelligence is extremely valuable – it helps focus efforts and greatly increases the speed of response. There is a need for tools and processes that allow more mature intelligence analyses; however, tools will never replace analysis and interpretation by humans, and increasingly, the availability of threat intelligence skills is falling short of demand.

Lessons Learned

In the discussions that followed each portion of the presentation, audience members shared the lessons they learned from the presentation and injected their own knowledge and experience into the conversation.

The audience identified the following key takeaways from the presentation:

1. Security is expensive, but insecurity is more expensive.

2. Cybersecurity is now a global issue with global players.

3. Available automated tools and processes make it easy enough to catch the unsophisticated criminals; determined, sophisticated actors do not make it easy.

4. Understanding the motivations of threat actors is vitally important: the who and the why.

5. In terms of innovation, the "bad guys" (criminal actors) are leading the industry. And, we should try to learn from them.

6. Anti-virus software gives users a false sense of security.

7. Big data analytics is growing in importance as we try to make sense of large volumes of data and detect patterns of interest, because individual malicious events or fraudulent behaviour may look similar or even identical to normal, everyday transactions.

8. The problem is acute in the banking industry, but it is not unique to it. However, the real issue stems from the software industry that underpins these other commercial industries.

9. Small and medium-sized businesses are particularly vulnerable and should practice ensure they have good Internet "hygiene".

10. There is a skillset shortage: we need more intelligence experts and data scientists.

11. Our current approaches are not working – there is a need for innovation, which will likely come through a paradigm shift.

12. The industry is too fragmented. There is a need for greater collaboration between governments, technologists, and industry: a holistic approach to security.

About the Speakers

David Grau is Vice President and Head of Threat Response, Intelligence, and Defensive Technologies at TD Bank Group. David has more than 20 years of professional information security experience and leads a multi-national team of information security specialists, with a global responsibility for providing TD Bank Group's Security Incident Response, Threat Intelligence, and Defensive Technologies programs.

Chuck Kennedy is the VP for Credit Card Technology for North American Credit Card for TD Bank Group. He is responsible for technology service delivery, project management, and technology innovation for the credit card businesses for TD. Chuck has been a member of the CIO Association of Canada and has served on the Canadian Banker's Association's (CBA), Canadian Financial Institution – Computer Incident Response Team (CFI-CIRT). Chuck holds the CRISC designation (Certified In Risk and Systems Control) and was educated in the United States, Europe, and Canada. He holds a BA in Political Science (Business minor) from the University of Calgary and an MSc in Information Technology (Information Assurance) from the University of Maryland – University College. His graduate work involved the study of geo-spatial intrusion detection and its integration with complex event processing.

This report was written by Chris McPhee

Keywords: cybersecurity, information security, banking, threats, targets, hacking, incident response, intelligence, analytics

19

Defining Cybersecurity

Dan Craigen, Nadia Diakun-Thibault, and Randy Purse

" To choose a definition is to plead a cause. "

Charles Leslie Stevenson (1908–1979)
Analytic philosopher

Cybersecurity is a broadly used term, whose definitions are highly variable, often subjective, and at times, uninformative. The absence of a concise, broadly acceptable definition that captures the multidimensionality of cybersecurity impedes technological and scientific advances by reinforcing the predominantly technical view of cybersecurity while separating disciplines that should be acting in concert to resolve complex cybersecurity challenges. In conjunction with an in-depth literature review, we led multiple discussions on cybersecurity with a diverse group of practitioners, academics, and graduate students to examine multiple perspectives of what should be included in a definition of cybersecurity. In this article, we propose a resulting new definition: "Cybersecurity is the organization and collection of resources, processes, and structures used to protect cyberspace and cyberspace-enabled systems from occurrences that misalign de jure from de facto property rights." Articulating a concise, inclusive, meaningful, and unifying definition will enable an enhanced and enriched focus on interdisciplinary cybersecurity dialectics and thereby will influence the approaches of academia, industry, and government and non-governmental organizations to cybersecurity challenges.

Introduction

The term "cybersecurity" has been the subject of academic and popular literature that has largely viewed the topic from a particular perspective. Based on the literature review described in this article, we found that the term is used broadly and its definitions are highly variable, context-bound, often subjective, and, at times, uninformative. There is a paucity of literature on what the term actually means and how it is situated within various contexts. The absence of a concise, broadly acceptable definition that captures the multidimensionality of cybersecurity potentially impedes technological and scientific advances by reinforcing the predominantly technical view of cybersecurity while separating disciplines that should be acting in concert to resolve complex cybersecurity challenges. For example, there is a spectrum of technical solutions that support cybersecurity. However, these solutions alone do not solve the problem; there are numerous examples and considerable scholarly work that demonstrate the challenges related to organizational, economic, social, political, and other human dimensions that are inextricably tied to cybersecurity efforts (e.g., Goodall et al., 2009; Buckland et al., 2010; Deibert, 2012). Fredrick Chang (2012), former Director of Research at the National Security Agency in the United States discusses the interdisciplinary nature of cybersecurity:

"A science of cybersecurity offers many opportunities for advances based on a multidisciplinary approach, because, after all, cybersecurity is fundamentally about an adversarial engagement. Humans must defend machines that are attacked by other humans using machines. So, in addition to the critical traditional fields of computer science, electrical engineering, and mathematics, perspectives from other fields are needed."

In attempting to arrive at a more broadly acceptable definition aligned with the true interdisciplinary nature of cybersecurity, we reviewed relevant literature to identify the range of definitions, to discern dominant themes, and to distinguish aspects of cybersecurity. This research was augmented by multiple engagements with a multidisciplinary group of cybersecurity practitioners, academics, and graduate students. Together, these two activities resulted in a new, more inclusive, and unifying definition of cybersecurity that will hopefully enable an enhanced and enriched focus on interdisciplinary cybersecurity dialectics and thereby influence the approaches of academia, industry, and government and non-government organizations to cybersecurity challenges. This article reflects the process used to develop a more holistic definition that better situates cybersecurity as an interdisciplinary activity, consciously stepping back from the predominant technical view by integrating multiple perspectives.

Literature Review

Our literature review spanned a wide scope of sources, including a broad range of academic disciplines including: computer science, engineering, political studies, psychology, security studies, management, education, and sociology. The most common disciplines covered in our literature review are engineering, technology, computer science, and security and defence. But, to a much lesser extent, there was also evidence of the topic of cybersecurity in journals related to policy development, law, healthcare, public administration, accounting, management, sociology, psychology, and education.

Cavelty (2010) notes there are multiple interlocking discourses around the field of cybersecurity. Deconstructing the term cybersecurity helps to situate the discussion within both domains of "cyber" and "security" and reveals some of the legacy issues. "Cyber" is a prefix connoting cyberspace and refers to electronic communication networks and virtual reality (Oxford, 2014). It evolved from the term "cybernetics", which referred to the "field of control and communication theory, whether in machine or in the animal" (Wiener, 1948). The term "cyberspace" was popularized by William Gibson's 1984 novel, *Neuromancer*, in which he describes his vision of a three-dimensional space of pure information, moving between computer and computer clusters where people are generators and users of the information (Kizza, 2011). What we now know as cyberspace was intended and designed as an information environment (Singer & Friedman, 2013), and there is an expanded appreciation of cyberspace today. For example, Public Safety Canada (2010) defines cyberspace as "the electronic world created by interconnected networks of information technology and the information on those networks. It is a global commons where... people are linked together to exchange ideas, services and friendship." Cyberspace is not static; it is a dynamic, evolving, multilevel ecosystem of physical infrastructure, software, regulations, ideas, innovations, and interactions influenced by an expanding population of contributors (Deibert & Rohozinski, 2010), who represent the range of human intentions.

As for the term "security", in the literature we reviewed, there appeared to be no broadly accepted concept, and the term has been notoriously hard to define in the general sense (Friedman & West, 2010; Cavelty, 2008). According to Buzan, Wæver, and Wilde (1998), discourses in security necessarily include and seek to understand who securitizes, on what issues (threats), for whom (the referent object), why, with what results, and under what conditions (the structure). Although there are more concrete forms of security (e.g., the physical properties, human properties, information system properties, or mathematical definitions for various kinds of security), the term takes on meaning based on one's perspective and what one values. It remains a contested term, but a central tenet of security is being free from danger or threat (Oxford, 2014). Further, although we have indicated that security is a contested topic, Baldwin (1997) states that one cannot use this designation as "an excuse for not formulating one's own conception of security as clearly and precisely as possible".

As a result of our literature review, we selected nine definitions of cybersecurity that we felt provided the material perspectives of cybersecurity:

1. "Cybersecurity consists largely of defensive methods used to detect and thwart would-be intruders." (Kemmerer, 2003)

2. "Cybersecurity entails the safeguarding of computer networks and the information they contain from penetration and from malicious damage or disruption." (Lewis, 2006)

3. "Cyber Security involves reducing the risk of malicious attack to software, computers and networks. This includes tools used to detect break-ins, stop viruses, block malicious access, enforce authentication, enable encrypted communications, and on and on." (Amoroso, 2006)

4. "Cybersecurity is the collection of tools, policies, security concepts, security safeguards, guidelines, risk management approaches, actions, training, best practices, assurance and technologies that can be used to protect the cyber environment and organization and user's assets." (ITU, 2009)

5. "The ability to protect or defend the use of cyber-space from cyber-attacks." (CNSS, 2010)

6. "The body of technologies, processes, practices and response and mitigation measures designed to protect networks, computers, programs and data from attack, damage or unauthorized access so as to ensure confidentiality, integrity and availability." (Public Safety Canada, 2014)

7. "The art of ensuring the existence and continuity of the information society of a nation, guaranteeing and protecting, in Cyberspace, its information, assets and critical infrastructure." (Canongia & Mandarino, 2014)

8. "The state of being protected against the criminal or unauthorized use of electronic data, or the measures taken to achieve this." (Oxford University Press, 2014)

9. "The activity or process, ability or capability, or state whereby information and communications systems and the information contained therein are protected from and/or defended against damage, unauthorized use or modification, or exploitation." (DHS, 2014)

Although some of these definitions include references to non-technical activities and human interactions, they demonstrate the predominance of the technical perspective within the literature. As stated by Cavelty (2010), the discourse and research in cybersecurity "necessarily shifts to contexts and conditions that determine the process by which key actors subjectively arrive at a shared understanding of how to conceptualize and ultimately respond to a security threat". Accordingly, within their particular context, the definitions above are helpful but do not necessarily provide a holistic view that supports interdisciplinarity. Referring back to Buzan, Wæver, and Wilde's (1998) discussion of securitization studies, any definition should be able to capture an understanding of the actor, subject, the referent object, the intentions and purposes, the outcomes, and structure. In our review of the literature, we did not find a definition that is inclusive, impactful, and unifying. Cybersecurity is a complex challenge requiring interdisciplinary reasoning; hence, any resulting definition must attract currently disparate cybersecurity stakeholders, while being unbiased, meaningful, and fundamentally useful.

Towards a New Definition

Faced with many definitions of cybersecurity from the literature, we opted for a pragmatic qualitative research approach to support the definitional process, which melds objective qualitative research with subjective qualitative research (Cooper, 2013). In effect, the result is a notional definition that is grounded in objectivity (e.g., an intrusion-detection system) versus supposition (e.g., the intentions of a hacker). This definitional process included: a review of the literature, the identification of dominant themes and distinguishing aspects, and the development of a working definition. This definition was in turn introduced to the multidisciplinary group discussions for further exploration, expansion, and refinement to arrive at the posited definition.

Dominant themes

In our literature review, we identified five dominant themes of cybersecurity: i) technological solutions; ii) events; iii) strategies, processes, and methods; iv) human engagement; and v) referent objects (of security). Not only do these themes support the interdisciplinary nature of cybersecurity, but, in our view, help to provide critical context to the definitional process.

Distinguishing aspects

In conjunction with the emergence of the themes, we formulated distinguishing aspects of cybersecurity, initially through discussion amongst the authors to be refined later through the multidisciplinary group discussions. In the end, we identified that cybersecurity is distinguished by:

- its interdisciplinary socio-technical character

- being a scale-free network, in which the capabilities of network actors are potentially broadly similar

- high degrees of change, connectedness, and speed of interaction

Through the process, there was consensus within the multidisciplinary group to adopt the view that the Internet is a scale-free network (e.g., Barabási & Albert, 1999), meaning it is a network whose degree distribution follows a power law, at least asymptotically. Even though this characterization of the Internet is a subject of debate (e.g., Wallinger et al., 2009), we argue that there are cyber-attack scenarios, and especially the evolution of malware markets, where the capabilities for launching attacks has been largely commoditized, hence flattening the space of network actors.

Throughout the initial part of the process that resulted in a working paper, we intentionally attempted to redress the technical bias of extant definitions in the cybersecurity literature by ensuring that scholars and practitioners contributed to the discussion and were provided an opportunity to review and comment on our initial definition, themes, and distinguishing aspects. To expand the discussion and create additional scholarly dialogue, we posited an original "seed" definition for discussion and further refinement during two three-hour engagements with a multidisciplinary group of cybersecurity practitioners, academics, industry experts from the VENUS Cybersecurity Institute (venus

cyber.com), and graduate students in the Technology Innovation Management program (timprogram.ca) at Carleton University in Ottawa, Canada.

Emergent definitions of cybersecurity

Our engagement with the multidisciplinary group primarily consisted of providing selected readings from the literature, an initial presentation and discussion of our own work to date, followed by a syndicate activity related to distinguishing aspects and defining cybersecurity. Three syndicates were formed from the group and they were asked to develop their own definitions. These definitions, along with the authors' brief critiques, are presented in Table 1. The first two definitions were developed by the authors, whereas the next three definitions arose from group participants.

Table 1. Emergent cybersecurity definitions and critiques

	Participant Working Definitions	**Critique(s)**
1	"Cybersecurity is the protection of information/data, assets, services, and systems of value to reduce the probability of loss, damage/corruption, compromise, or misuse to a level commensurate with the value assigned."	In the main, the feedback suggested that the inclusion of value introduced the human concepts related to security, but that the definition was too prescriptive and suffered the problem of a restrictive "listing" of what is being protected.
2	"Cybersecurity is a collection of interacting processes intended to protect cyberspace and cyberspace-enabled systems (collectively resources) from intentional actions designed to misalign actual resource property rights from the resource owner perceived property rights."	This definition introduced the emerging cyber-physical environment and included the important concept of control over property rights. However, the definition's focus on "human intentional actions" was viewed as being overly restrictive.
3	"Cybersecurity is a collection of interacting processes intended to make cyberspace safe and secure."	Specifically intended to be broader than the seed definition, this definition introduced more problems than it solved because it was unnecessarily broad and introduced the contested notion of safety with security.
4	"Cybersecurity is a domain dedicated to the study and practice of the protection of systems or digital assets from any action taken to impose authorization on those systems or digital assets that do not align with the property rights of the resource facility as understood by its owner."	In this definition, the concepts of property rights and control were introduced. However, there were concerns about the potential implications of "action taken" to mean limiting cybersecurity to human actors. Also there were concerns regarding the terms, which imposed limits on the scope of the definition such as "study" and "practice", thereby situating the issues largely within the academic domain.
5	"Cybersecurity is the state in which power over the execution of computers (sensu lato) and over information in the control of computers is where it should be."	This definition reinforced the notions of control over information and systems. The main criticism was defining cybersecurity as a state.

A New Definition of Cybersecurity

We propose the following definition, which integrates key concepts drawn from the literature and engagement with the multidisciplinary group:

Cybersecurity is the organization and collection of resources, processes, and structures used to protect cyberspace and cyberspace-enabled systems from occurrences that misalign de jure *from* de facto *property rights.*

We deconstruct this definition as follows:

• ...*the organization and collection of resources, processes, and structures*...: This aspect captures the multiple, interwoven dimensions and inherent complexity of cybersecurity, which ostensibly involve interactions between humans, between systems, and between humans and systems. By avoiding discussion of which resources, processes, or structures, the definition becomes non-prescriptive and recognizes the dynamic nature of cybersecurity.

• ...*used to protect cyberspace and cyberspace-enabled systems*...: This aspect includes protection, in the broadest sense, from all threats, including intentional, accidental, and natural hazards. This aspect also incorporates the traditional view of cyberspace but includes those systems that are not traditionally viewed as part of cyberspace, such as computer control systems and cyber-physical systems. By extension, the protection applies to assets and information of concern within cyberspace and connected systems.

• ...*from occurrences*...: This aspect recognizes that "protections" are intended to address the full range of intentional events, accidental events, and natural hazards. It also suggests that some of the occurrences are unpredictable.

• ...*that misalign* de jure *from* de facto *property rights*...: This aspect incorporates the two separate notions of ownership and control that dominate discussion of cybersecurity and digital assets introduced in the property rights framework of Ostrom and Hess (2007), which include access, extraction, contribution, removal, management, exclusion, and alienation. Any event or activity that misaligns actual (*de facto*) property rights from perceived (*de jure*) property rights, whether by intention or accident, whether known or unknown, is a cybersecurity incident.

Substantiating Our Definition

As discussed earlier, our definition should engender greater interdisciplinary and collaborative efforts on cybersecurity. Our goal is to "bring together" not to "push apart" or "isolate". Our success (or failure) can be partly validated if we can demonstrate that:

1. We can map other definitions of cybersecurity into our definition.

2. Our definition is unifying and inclusive in that it supports interdisciplinarity.

To assist in the analysis and mapping of the definitions to our new definition, we identified conceptual categories from definitions drawn from the literature as well as our own definition (Table 2). Unless otherwise cited, the category definitions are drawn largely from the Oxford (2014) online dictionary. The exact wordings of the definitions are meant to be as encompassing as possible.

A number of definitions of cybersecurity were presented in this article. Some of the definitions are from the literature and drive the perspectives of certain communities. Other definitions arose through our group discussions and related activities. Table 3 provides examples of how our analysis was applied to sample definitions from the literature and group discussions.

The above analysis helps to demonstrate that our new definition is inclusive of key components from a sample of extant and participant definitions. Furthermore, three of the dominant themes – technological solutions; strategies, processes, and methods; and human engagement – are all refinements of the "the organization and collection of resources, processes, and structures used to protect..." component of our definition. The dominant theme of "events" is a refinement of "occurrences." We also view "referent objects (of security)" as a refinement of "cyberspace and cyberspace-enabled systems." Retrospectively, we therefore show how our definition is consistent with the dominant themes of cybersecurity and reflects the previously identified distinguishing aspects. Therefore, this mapping illustrates how our definition supports interdisciplinarity.

Conclusion

We have provided a new, more inclusive, and unifying definition of cybersecurity that we believe will enable an enhanced and enriched focus on interdisciplinary cybersecurity dialectics and, thereby, will influence the approaches of researchers, funding agencies, and organizations to cybersecurity challenges. For example, the new definition and associated perspectives could lead to changes in public policy and inform legislative actions.

The definition resulting from the work reported herein has a number of potentially salutary features, including:

1. Contributing a major unifying theme by positioning cybersecurity as an interdisciplinary domain, not a technical domain.

2. Supporting inclusiveness demonstrated through the relationship to the five dominant cybersecurity themes and mapping to previous definitions.

3. Incorporating the evolution towards a more interconnected world through inclusion of both cyberspace and cyberspace-enabled systems. The latter includes cyber-physical systems and control systems.

4. Using protection – as a fundamental concept within security – in a broad sense within the definition, including protection from intentional events, accidental events, and natural hazards.

5. Incorporating the "property rights" framework of Ostrom and Hess (2007), which includes access, extraction, contribution, removal, management, exclusion, and alienation. Thus, the discussion moves beyond traditional assets and information terms to broadly include that which has meaning or value.

The absence of a concise, universally acceptable definition that captures the multidimensionality of cybersecurity impedes technological and scientific advances by reinforcing the predominantly technical view of cybersecurity while separating disciplines that should be acting in concert to resolve complex cybersecurity challenges. It has become increasingly apparent that cybersecurity is interdisciplinary. The more inclusive, unifying definition presented in this article aims to facilitate interdisciplinary approaches to cybersecurity. We hope that the definition will be embraced by the multiple disciplines engaged in cybersecurity efforts, thereby opening the door to greater understanding and collaboration needed to address the growing and complex threats to cyberspace and cyberspace-enabled systems.

Table 2. Conceptual categories and their definitions

Category	Definition
Asset	In general, defined as "a useful or valuable thing or person". Here, we refine the definition to refer to "cyberspace and cyberspace-enabled systems".
Capability	An abbreviation for the organization and combination of resources, processes, and structures.
Misalign	Align is defined as "put (things) into correct appropriate relative positions"; hence, misalign results in incorrect or inappropriate positions.
Occurrence	An incident or event.
Organization	"A firm's policies and procedures 'organized to exploit the full competitive potential of its resources and capabilities'" (Kozlenkova et al., 2013). We generalize "firms" to "institutions".
Process	The fact of going on or being carried on, as an action or series of actions; progress, course. *in (the) process of (doing something):* in the course of; in the act of carrying out (a particular task, etc.). *in process:* going on, being done; in progress.
Property right	An enforceable authority to undertake particular actions in specific domains. Includes the rights of access, withdrawal, management, exclusion, and alienation (Ostrom & Hess, 2007).
Protect	Keep safe from harm or injury.
Resource	"Tangible and intangible assets ['firms'] use to conceive of and implement [their] strategies" (Kozlenkova et al., 2013). We generalize "firms" to "institutions".

Table 3. Examples of cybersecurity definitions and related analysis of the proposed definition

Definitions of Cybersecurity	Analysis (Key Terms → Corresponding Terms in Proposed Definition)
"The state of being protected against the criminal or unauthorized use of electronic data, or the measures taken to achieve this." (Oxford University Press, 2014)	"protected" → PROTECT "criminal or unauthorized use" → MISALIGN "electronic data" → ASSETS and PROPERTY RIGHTS "measures taken..."→ CAPABILITY
"The activity or process, ability or capability, or state whereby information and communications systems and the information contained therein are protected from and/or defended against damage, unauthorized use or modification, or exploitation." (DHS, 2014)	"activity or process, ability or capability, or state" → CAPABILITY " information and communications systems and the information contained therein" → ASSETS and PROPERTY RIGHTS "protected from and/or defended" → PROTECT "damage, unauthorized use or modification, or exploitation" → MISALIGN
"Cybersecurity entails the safeguarding of computer networks and the information they contain from penetration and from malicious damage or disruption." (Lewis, 2006)	"safeguarding" → CAPABILITY "computer networks and information" → ASSETS and PROPERTY RIGHTS "penetration and from malicious damage or disruption" → OCCURRENCES or MISALIGN
"Cybersecurity involves reducing the risk of malicious attack to software, computers and networks. This includes tools used to detect break-ins, stop viruses, block malicious access, enforce authentication, enable encrypted communications, and on and on." (Amoroso, 2006).	"involves reducing the risk" → CAPABILITY "of malicious attack" → OCCURRENCES or MISALIGN "software, computers and networks" → ASSETS and PROPERTY RIGHTS "includes tools used to detect break-ins, stop viruses, block malicious access, enforce authentication, enable encrypted communications, and on and on" → CAPABILITY
"Cybersecurity is the collection of tools, policies, security concepts, security safeguards, guidelines, risk management approaches, actions, training, best practices, assurance and technologies that can be used to protect the cyber environment and organization and user's assets." (ITU, 2009)	"the collection of tools, policies, security concepts, security safeguards, guidelines, risk management approaches, actions, training, best practices, assurance and technologies" → CAPABILITY "to protect" → PROTECT "cyber environment and organization and user's assets" → ASSETS and PROPERTY RIGHTS
"Cybersecurity is a collection of interacting processes intended to make cyberspace safe and secure." (Definition from group discussions)	"interacting processes" → PROCESS and CAPABILITY "safe and secure" → PROTECT
"Cybersecurity is the state in which power over the execution of computers (sensu lato) and over information in the control of computers is where it should be." (Definition from group discussions)	"power over the execution of computers and over information in the controls of computers is where it should be"→ ASSETS and PROPERTY RIGHTS

About the Authors

Dan Craigen is a Science Advisor at the Communications Security Establishment in Canada. Previously, he was President of ORA Canada, a company that focused on High Assurance/Formal Methods and distributed its technology to over 60 countries. His research interests include formal methods, the science of cybersecurity, and technology transfer. He was the chair of two NATO research task groups pertaining to validation, verification, and certification of embedded systems and high-assurance technologies. He received his BScH and MSc degrees in Mathematics from Carleton University in Ottawa, Canada.

Nadia Diakun-Thibault is Senior Science and Analytics Advisor at the Communications Security Establishment in Canada. She holds a Master's degree in Public Administration from Queen's University in Kingston, Canada, and an ABD (PhD) degree in Slavic Languages and Literatures from the University of Toronto, Canada. She has served as Parliamentary Advisor to Members of Parliament and held an Order-in-Council appointment to the Province of Ontario's Advocacy Commission. Her research interests include neurophilosophy, semiotics, linguistics, and public policy. She is also an adjunct faculty member in the Department of Computer Science and Engineering at North Carolina State University in the United States.

Randy Purse is the Senior Learning Advisor at the Information Technology Security Learning Centre at the Communications Security Establishment in Canada. A former officer in the Canadian Forces, he is an experienced security practitioner and learning specialist. His research interests include the human dimensions of security and collective and transformative learning in the workplace. He has a Master's of Education in Information Technology from Memorial University of Newfoundland in St. John's, Canada, and he is a PhD candidate specializing in Adult and Workplace Learning in the Faculty of Education at the University of Ottawa, Canada.

Acknowledgements

The authors wish to thank Tony Bailetti, George Cybenko, George Dinolt, Risto Rajala, and Mika Westerlund for reviewing and commenting on an earlier draft of this article. We also wish to thank the participants in the multidisciplinary group for their informed engagement.

References

Amoroso, E. 2006. *Cyber Security.* New Jersey: Silicon Press.

Baldwin, D. A. 1997. The Concept of Security. *Review of International Studies,* 23(1): 5-26.

Barabási, A. L., & Albert, R. 1999. Emergence of Scaling in Random Networks. *Science,* 286(5439): 509-512.
http://dx.doi.org/10.1126/science.286.5439.509

Buzan, B., Wæver, O., & De Wilde, J. 1998. *Security: A New Framework for Analysis.* Boulder, CO: Lynne Rienner Publishers.

Canongia, C., & Mandarino, R. 2014. Cybersecurity: The New Challenge of the Information Society. In *Crisis Management: Concepts, Methodologies, Tools and Applications:* 60-80. Hershey, PA: IGI Global.
http://dx.doi.org/10.4018/978-1-4666-4707-7.ch003

Cavelty, M. D. 2008. Cyber-Terror—Looming Threat or Phantom Menace? The Framing of the US Cyber-Threat Debate. *Journal of Information Technology & Politics,* 4(1): 19-36.
http://dx.doi.org/10.1300/J516v04n01_03

Cavelty, M. D. 2010. Cyber-Security. In J. P. Burgess (Ed.), *The Routledge Handbook of New Security Studies:* 154-162. London: Routledge.

Chang, F. R. 2012. Guest Editor's Column. *The Next Wave,* 19(4): 1–2.

CNSS. 2010. National Information Assurance Glossary. Committee on National Security Systems (CNSS) Instruction No. 4009:
http://www.ncix.gov/publications/policy/docs/CNSSI_4009.pdf

Cooper, S. 2013. Pragmatic Qualitative Research. In M. Savin-Baden & C. H. Major (Eds.), *Qualitative Research: The Essential Guide to Theory and Practice:* 170-181. London: Routledge.

Deibert, R., & Rohozinski, R. 2010. Liberation vs. Control: The Future of Cyberspace. *Journal of Democracy,* 21(4): 43-57.
http://dx.doi.org/10.1353/jod.2010.0010

DHS. 2014. A Glossary of Common Cybersecurity Terminology. National Initiative for Cybersecurity Careers and Studies: Department of Homeland Security. October 1, 2014:
http://niccs.us-cert.gov/glossary#letter_c

Friedman, A. A., & West, D. M. 2010. Privacy and Security in Cloud Computing. *Issues in Technology Innovation,* 3: 1-13.

Goodall, J. R., Lutters, W. G., & Komlodi, A. 2009. Developing Expertise for Network Intrusion Detection. *Information Technology & People,* 22(2): 92-108.
http://dx.doi.org/10.1108/09593840910962186

ITU. 2009. Overview of Cybersecurity. Recommendation ITU-T X.1205. Geneva: International Telecommunication Union (ITU).
http://www.itu.int/rec/T-REC-X.1205-200804-I/en

Kozlenkova, I. V., Samaha, S. A., & Palmatier, R. W. 2014. Resource-Based Theory in Marketing. *Journal of Academic Marketing Science,* 42(1): 1-21.
http://dx.doi.org/10.1007/s11747-013-0336-7

Kemmerer, R. A. 2003. *Cybersecurity. Proceedings of the 25th IEEE International Conference on Software Engineering:* 705-715.
http://dx.doi.org/10.1109/ICSE.2003.1201257

Lewis, J. A. 2006. *Cybersecurity and Critical Infrastructure Protection.* Washington, DC: Center for Strategic and International Studies.
http://csis.org/publication/cybersecurity-and-critical-infrastructure-protection

Ostrom, E., & Hess, C. 2007. Private and Common Property Rights. In B. Bouckaert (Ed.), *Encyclopedia of Law & Economics*. Northampton, MA: Edward Elgar.

Oxford University Press. 2014. *Oxford Online Dictionary*. Oxford: Oxford University Press. October 1, 2014: http://www.oxforddictionaries.com/definition/english/Cybersecurity

Public Safety Canada. 2010. *Canada's Cyber Security Strategy*. Ottawa: Public Safety Canada, Government of Canada. http://www.publicsafety.gc.ca/cnt/rsrcs/pblctns/cbr-scrt-strtgy/index-eng.aspx

Singer, P. W., & Friedman, A. 2013. *Cybersecurity and Cyberwar: What Everyone Needs to Know*. New York: Oxford University Press.

Public Safety Canada. 2014. *Terminology Bulletin 281: Emergency Management Vocabulary*. Ottawa: Translation Bureau, Government of Canada. http://www.bt-tb.tpsgc-pwgsc.gc.ca/publications/documents/urgence-emergency.pdf

Wallinger, W., Alderson, D., & Doyle, J. 2009. Mathematics and the Internet: A Source of Enormous Confusion and Great Potential. *Notices of the American Mathematical Society*, 56(5): 586-599.

Keywords: cybersecurity, definition, interdisciplinary, cyberspace, security

20

The Businesses of Open Data and Open Source: Some Key Similarities and Differences

Juho Lindman and Linus Nyman

" *It's difficult to imagine the power that you're going to have* **"** *when so many different sorts of data are available.*

Tim Berners-Lee
Inventor of the World Wide Web

Open data and open source are phenomena that are often automatically grouped together, perhaps because they share the word "open". A careful analysis of what open means in each of these cases is a stepping stone towards building viable businesses around both open source applications and on open data. Although there are, indeed, elements they share through their openness, the ways in which they differ are significant. In this conceptual paper, we aim to outline the differences and similarities of the two phenomena from a commercial perspective.

Introduction

Open source and open data both have a focus on "openness", and most developers and researchers could easily identify similarities between the two phenomena. For example, both open source and open data are enabled – or at the very least greatly helped – by the Internet, which provides a backbone for collaborative development efforts, communication infrastructure, as well as a means to support the sharing of both application and data. However, open source and open data are distinct phenomena with significant differences, and these differences clearly impact how commercial success can be achieved in each domain.

Given that TIM Review readers tend to be more familiar with open source than open data, our goal is to explore the concept of open data through a comparison with open source and with an emphasis on the similarities and differences that are relevant to technology businesses. We focus on three key questions:

1. Are the phenomena similar?

2. Are the licenses of software and data similar?

3. Are the businesses and revenue models similar?

Understanding these two phenomena is useful to managers and entrepreneurs interested in the business potential of the released data sets. This understanding is also useful for open data proponents who are interested in the business aspects of open source and the lessons that the business of open source offers. Designers of related services may be interested what potential open data and open source have to offer in terms of novel and better service opportunities.

The structure of the article is as follows. We first describe key characteristics of open source and open data. We then compare these two phenomena from three business-oriented perspectives: licensing, commercial aspects, and relevant actors. Finally, we provide some takeaways for managers and entrepreneurs.

Comparing Open Source and Open Data

In computer science, in theory as well as in practice, the distinction between data and application is critical. Therefore, the most obvious and fundamental difference between open data and open source is that the former focuses on the data and the latter focuses on applications.

Data has multiple meanings, including any end-product of measurement, but in this investigation, we use a slightly more technical definition of data: data refers to stored symbols. Data is considered a resource – raw material for the application. Open data means data that is technically and legally made available for reuse and republication. The underlying idea is that the increased transparency will help to create trust in users and developers, as well as offer a way to create new services based on the collected data. In many cases, the data is collected by government entities for various purposes and thus additional economic value would be created when the published data is put to use. However, open data includes open government-collected data as well as data released by private actors.

An application, on the other hand, is compiled source code that operates on data. Open source refers to a legal and technical arrangement related to software production that results in open source code that is accepted under an license that complies with the Open Source Definition (opensource.org/definition). These licenses are based on the copyright protection of the code; thus, the "open" of open source refers to the source code.

To summarize: the first significant difference between open data and open source is that of data versus application. Data can be numbers, locations, names, etc. In and of itself, data does nothing. Source code, or rather an application, is something that uses or produces data. These two aspects, although they rely on one another for their significance, are different in both essence and purpose. Indeed, it is some of these differences that this article seeks to point out and clarify.

Comparing Licensing Aspects

The key similarity between open data and open source lies in the prerequisite of openness. But what, exactly, is it that is open, and are there degrees, or types, of openness? For open source software, the openness primarily means a guaranteed access to the application's source code as well as an arrangement that makes sure that the code can be forked, modified, and redistributed. (For more on the significance of the right to fork, see Nyman and Lindman [2013; timreview.ca/article/644].)

For open data, a similar "access principle" provides access to the data (and metadata) and it provides the opportunity to reuse it in applications. Data also needs to be maintained and updated. The actor that collects or mashes up the data from different sources usually has the option to stop providing access or maintenance to the data (i.e., to "close" the data).

Source code can be copyrighted (or copylefted: tinyurl.com/qygb2) but, in some cases, data falls outside copyright protection. Whether particular data can be copyrighted is subject to national legislation. However, copyright is not the only law that applies to data; depending on its content, other laws may also regulate its use. Laws may govern the collection, storage, maintenance, access, use, and representation of data. For example, laws relating to sensitivity, privacy concerns, or national security may apply to different datasets.

Table 1 compares different licensing aspects of open source versus open data. The legal arrangements (i.e., copyright, licenses, original publisher, and role of contracts) for the two phenomena are different. For a more thorough discussion on data licensing, see the "Guide to Open Data Licensing" (tinyurl.com/lkhg6df), which is published by the Open Definition project.

Table 1. Licensing of open data versus open source

	Open Source (Application)	**Open Data (Data)**
Copyright	Applies to all source code	May apply
Licensing	Licenses must comply with the Open Source Definition (opensource.org/osd-annotated)	Relevant if protected by copyright. Possible licensing options include the Wikimedia commons (commons.wikimedia.org) and the Creative Commons (creativecommons.org)
Original publisher	Several versions (distributions) of application and forking are possible	Data often collected, maintained, and controlled by data publisher
Contracts	Normally not required; the license agreement defines the rights of the developers and users	Data publisher may have an incentive to monitor data use or to create feedback loops to reusers of their data

Comparing Commercial Aspects

The business of open source is in itself a diverse field, with companies generating income from various sources related to open source products. The two main categories of income are those from support and services related to a program (e.g., training, consulting, feature development) and from selling closed source versions of an open source program, a practice called "dual licensing". For a primer on the business of open source, see Widenius and Nyman (2014) in this issue of the TIM Review.

In contrast, the business of open data is a young field, but it holds promise for service innovation. Discussion on the viable revenue sources is still ongoing. The data publisher or the user of the application pays the costs related to the collection, maintenance, and enrichment of data, but customers normally do not pay subscription fees for accessing data.

In the following subsections, we compare the expense-related and income-related considerations of businesses that rely on open data or open source .

Who pays the bill, and why?
Open source can save firms money if they are able to attract free community participation. However, companies may also be willing to support open source development, for example by paying a developing group or foundation, or by assigning its own developers to an open source project. Even though anyone, even the firm's competitors, can then benefit from any improvements to the code, this approach is common in open source development. Typically, firms use this strategy to develop aspects of their product offering that would be considered "table stakes" (tinyurl.com/5u4aut). By collaborating – even with competitors in the same or similar markets – to develop non-unique

foundational aspects of an application, companies save time and development effort, which can then be redirected into developing the aspects of their offering that will differentiate them from their competitors.

In addition to the costs of collecting data, open data providers must often spend money and effort both to clean up the data for publishing as well as for keeping it open. With such tasks, providers may benefit from community participation, just as in the case of open source software. Issues related to "community management" are therefore similar in both cases.

Who makes money, and how?
Openness usually means that an application or dataset can be acquired free of charge. In the case of open data, the publishers are normally considered to have given permission for others to build services on top of their released dataset. The services provided by these other parties may add value above and beyond just the provision of data, and the costs of designing the applications, collecting the data, and maintaining the services are covered by various different arrangements depending on the motivations of the other parties, their possible business models, and the nature of the value created.

Value can stand for both economic value (i.e., money) or a wider benefit. The openness of both open source and open data can potentially offer either one of these two types of value. However, it is notable that the dynamics that produce value are different. In Table 2, we list some of the benefits perceived by the key actors in each case. The table is not exhaustive list, but it provides an illustration of topical issues.

One of the main differences in the business aspects of open data and open source is that, at least currently, it is rare for the data provider to make money on open

Table 2. Examples of key value sources in open source versus open data

	Actor	Economic value	Other value
Open Source	Companies	Dual licensing, support and services	Product innovation, platform innovation
	Customers	Cost savings	Evade vendor lock-in
	Actor	Economic value	Other value
Open Data	Data owner	Sales of premium access	Public service, receive additional developmental resources
	3rd party	Sell applications	Increased transparency, novel services

data. The main perceived sources of benefits are related to public service or to situations where the data needs to be collected and maintained anyway. Releasing the datasets would then enable others to benefit from them and may result in new and useful services. Typically, the funding for the collection and maintenance of the data in such situations also comes from public sources. Normally, a company waives the possibility of data sales when it decides to release a dataset. However, we speculate that open data could also be accompanied by a "premium access" option, meaning access to more real-time data, faster access, or access to datasets that contain both open and closed data.

For open source, the commercial actors have established business models that rely on, for example, dual-licensing. Open source has tried and true ways to cut costs and evade lock-in situations. However, many open source contributions are driven not solely by commercial interests, but by the desire for useful software that addresses specific needs, among other motives.

Open data can offer opportunities for downstream service provision. In such situations, some actors that provide open data might be keen to share their costs with the downstream actors that make a profit. It is possible to sell downstream applications, such as closed source software subscriptions. Developers might also have other motivations in writing software that uses open data, such as increased transparency, new visualizations, service provision, etc.

Comparing Elements and Actors

In comparing the elements and actors involved in open data versus open source, we limit our investigation to the four questions illustrated in Figure 1:

1. Who are the main actors?
2. How is the output developed?
3. What is the output of the development?
4. Who is interested in the output?

In an open source project, both a corporate community and an open source community can participate in the software development. When data is being developed for release, data consultants as well as those who clean data participate to the process. Output of the processes are released as open source programs and as published open data.

As shown in Figure 1, the main difference concerning the processes is that the open source process is more open than the open data process. The developers are able to participate in open source software development with varying motivations. For community driven projects in particular, motivations commonly are not financial. In open data, the data publisher is usually expected to carry costs related to releasing the data, such as the costs of collection, aggregation, and anonymization. If these services are outsourced, there is new business opportunity for companies that provide them.

The output is also different: in open data, the data ultimately remains the same through the process, whereas the open source development process aims to change the software. The software is an end in itself, whereas the released open dataset is just the first step in providing the service to the customer.

Conclusions

Although open source licensing has established its value for developers in enabling a viable development model, the business of open data needs further study. Nonetheless, both open source and open data hold potential for business. Their main difference as phenomena is that of data versus application.

Proponents of both phenomena promote the openness of the output, which offers transparency but also changes the competition dynamic. The open source alternative hampers traditional software subscription sales. Open datasets can be easily copied, but the original data collector still has a prominent role in the maintenance of the said dataset: a copied dataset, if not maintained properly, may soon become obsolete.

The commercial potential of open source has been tested and proven over the years, and several business models have emerged. However, the business of open data is still in a pioneering phase. The publisher's role is critical in any open data business, but the publisher might not be the actor that benefits most from data publication; the greater opportunity for entrepreneurship may lie downstream, where value may be captured from services built upon the open data.

Despite their differences, both open source and open data aim to attract development efforts far beyond the originator of the project. Contributors may be driven by a variety of motivations, not excluding economic gain. Economic gains are feasible and attainable, but capturing them requires entrepreneurs and managers to understand the differences in the development process and economic value capture.

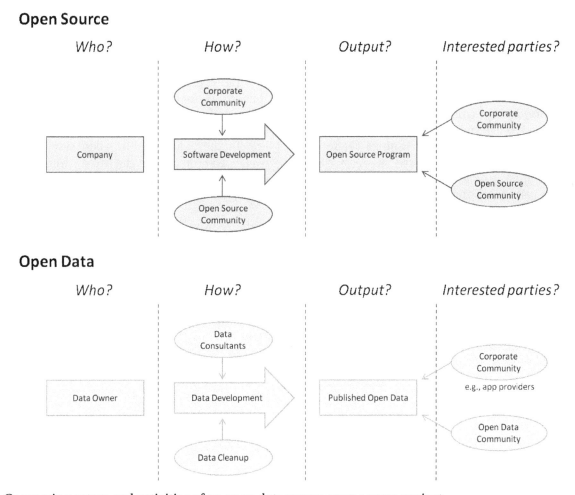

Figure 1. Comparing actors and activities of an open data versus open source project

Insights for managers and entrepreneurs

When evaluating business models based on open data, managers and entrepreneurs should consider the following key questions:

1. Do you have sufficient familiarity about the dynamics of open data ecosystems and the required technical capabilities? Open data is a significantly different field from open source; in-depth knowledge of one does not automatically guarantee sufficient knowledge of the other, although open source experts will easily find similarities.

2. If the data is not yours, how certain are you that it will continue to be provided openly in the future? How can you safeguard the relationship between the data collector/maintainer?

3. What is the legal status of the data? Does it allow fees, and what would happen if fees were introduced?

4. What is the license of the software application? Is it possible to gain software subscription revenue from a proprietary application built on the open data stack?

5. What national and international legislation poses obstacles to the service? Whereas software is relatively free of these concerns, many datasets may contain sensitive information. Open datasets can also be combined with other (also private) datasets, and this combination may raise new legal issues.

6. How will you attract developers? What are the dynamics of the development community? How will you support a relationship that takes into account different motivations to participate and benefits the different actors?

In conclusion, a final similarity we can note regarding open source and open data is that open data is now in a position not dissimilar to that of open source some two decades ago: a new, interesting phenomenon with promise, but also skepticism and challenges regarding an entrepreneurial potential for revenue creation and value capture.

The business models and strategies surrounding open source did not evolve overnight. Open data is an emerging field that may have many opportunities yet to be discovered. We believe that the world of open data holds great untapped potential for knowledgeable entrepreneurs that can identify opportunities for its use.

About the Authors

Juho Lindman is an Assistant Professor of Information Systems Science at the Hanken School of Economics in Helsinki, Finland. Juho's doctoral dissertation from the Aalto University School of Economics in Helsinki focused on open source software development organization In the field of information systems, his current research is focused in the areas of open source software development, open data, and organizational change.

Linus Nyman is a doctoral researcher at the Hanken School of Economics in Helsinki, Finland, where he is researching code forking in open source software. A further research interest of his is free-to-play gaming. He also lectures on corporate strategy, open source software, and the new business models of the Internet age. Linus has a Master's degree in economics from the Hanken School of Economics.

Keywords: open source, open data, business models, licensing, entrepreneurship

21

Cyber-Attack Attributes

Mehdi Kadivar

" *The bottom line of security is survival, but it* " *also reasonably includes a substantial range of concerns about the conditions of existence.*

Barry Gordon Buzan
Professor of International Relations
Central figure of the Copenhagen School

Cyber-attacks threaten our ability to use the Internet safely, productively, and creatively worldwide and are at the core of many security concerns. The concept of cyber-attacks, however, remains underdeveloped in the academic literature. To advance theory, design and operate databases to support scholarly research, perform empirical observations, and compare different types of cyber-attacks, it is necessary to first clarify the attributes of the "concept of cyber-attack". In this article, attributes of cyber-attacks are identified by examining definitions of cyber-attacks from the literature and information on ten high-profile attacks. Although the article will be of interest to a broad community, it will be of particular interest to senior executives, government contractors, and researchers interested in contributing to the development of an interdisciplinary and global theory of cybersecurity.

Introduction

Senior corporate executives, government officials, and academics have become aware that there are: i) serious financial and regulatory costs arising from cyber-attacks (Pearson, 2014; Sugarman, 2014; US Securities and Exchange Commission, 2014); ii) vulnerabilities in high-value assets such as supervisory-control and data-acquisition systems (Ashford, 2013; Crawford, 2014; Kovacs, 2014; Nicholson et al., 2012; Weiss, 2014); iii) concerns about the upcoming deployment of the "Internet of Things" (IoT) (NSTAC, 2014); and iv) few constraining mechanisms to inhibit malicious behaviours of threat actors (Castel, 2012; Jowitt, 2014, Scully, 2013; Sugarman, 2014; Weiss, 2014).

The urgency of research and development is underlined by the US National Security Telecommunications Security Advisory Committee (NSTAC, 2014): "There is a small – and rapidly closing – window to ensure that IoT is adopted in a way that maximizes security and minimizes risk. If the country fails to do so, it will be coping with the consequences for generations." This state-of-affairs has parallels to the experience with supervisory control and data acquisition systems, though in that case the threat space evolved over time. With the Internet of Things, the NSTAC believes that the window of time in which we can take action will only be open for another three to five years.

Although the word "cyber-attack" is used frequently, its meaning remains obscure (Hathaway et al., 2012, Roscini, 2014). In this article, the approach to clarify what is meant by cyber-attack is similar to the approach researchers followed to clarify what was meant by "security" in the late 1990s (e.g., Baldwin, 1997; Buzan, 1998; Huysmans, 1998). Security researchers identified essential attributes to make explicit what was meant by security. They eliminated ambiguities and inconsistencies in the different uses of the security concept. Their objective was not to produce another one-sentence definition of security; they set out to identify the essential attributes of security.

This article contributes a set of attributes of the cyber-attack concept. It does so by examining various definitions published in the literature and information on ten high-profile cyber-attacks. The main motivation for identifying the attributes of cyber-attacks is to enable building the theory of cyber-attacks as a unity of intellectual frameworks beyond the disciplinary perspectives (i.e., a transdisciplinary theory).

The remainder of this article infers the essential attributes of the cyber-attack concept from definitions of cyber-attacks found in the literature, synthesizes information on ten high-profile cyber-attacks, and uses it to provide concrete examples of the attributes of cyber-attacks.

Attributes from Definitions of Cyber-Attacks

The journal articles published in the English language by organizations in North America and Europe were reviewed for the purpose of identifying definitions of "cyber-attack". The following six definitions of cyber-attack were identified:

1. "Any action taken to undermine the functions of a computer network for a political or national security purpose." (Hathaway et al., 2012: p. 821)

2. "Use of deliberate actions – perhaps over an extended period of time – to alter, disrupt, deceive, degrade, or destroy adversary computer systems or networks or the information and/or programs resident in or transiting these systems or networks." (Owens et al., 2009: p. 10)

3. "Operations, whether in offence or defence, intended to alter, delete, corrupt, or deny access to computer data or software for the purposes of (a) propaganda or deception; and/or (b) partly or totally disrupting the functioning of the targeted computer, computer system or network, and related computer-operated physical infrastructure (if any); and/or (c) producing physical damage extrinsic to the computer, computer system or network." (Roscini, 2014: p. 17)

4. "An exploitation of cyberspace for the purpose of accessing unauthorized or secure information, spying, disabling of networks, and stealing both data and money." (Uma & Padmavathi, 2013: p. 390)

5. "A hostile act using computer or related networks or systems, and intended to disrupt and/or destroy an adversary's critical cyber systems, assets, or functions." (US Joint Chiefs of Staff, 2010: p.5).

6. "Efforts to alter, disrupt, or destroy computer systems or networks or the information or programs on them." (Waxman, 2011: p. 422)

Each definition shown above addresses one or more of the following five questions: i) What types of assets do cyber-attacks target?; ii) What effect do cyber-attacks have on assets targeted?; iii) What motivates cyber-attacks?; iv) Which actors are involved in cyber-attacks?; and v) What are the durations of cyber-attacks?

The six definitions identified suggest that the concept of cybersecurity has at least five attributes.

1. *Actors:* At least two actors are involved in each cyber-attack: the owner of the asset that is targeted and an adversary (US Joint Chiefs of Staff, 2010). The definitions of cyber-attack are not concerned with the nature of the adversaries. The offensive and defensive operations can be carried out by nation states, companies, groups, collectives, or individuals.

2. *Assets targeted:* Five of the six definitions provided above identify the assets cyber-attacks target. These assets include: computer systems and networks (Hathaway et al., 2012; Owens et al., 2009; US Joint Chiefs of Staff, 2010; Waxman, 2011); information, programs, or functions resident in or transiting systems or networks (Hathaway et al., 2012; Owens et al., 2009, Roscini, 2014; Waxman, 2011); computer-operated physical infrastructure (Roscini, 2014); and physical objects extrinsic to a computer, computer system, or network (Roscini, 2014).

3. *Motivation:* The motivations for cyber-attacks include accessing unauthorized or secure information, spying, and stealing both data and money (Uma & Padmavathi, 2013); national security and political causes (Hathaway et al., 2012); and propaganda or deception (Roscini, 2014).

4. *Effect on targeted assets:* Cyber-attacks result in the alteration, deletion, corruption, deception, degradation, disablement, disruption, or destruction of assets (Owens, et al., 2009; Roscini, 2014; Uma & Padmavathi, 2013; Waxman, 2011) as well as denying access to assets (Roscini, 2014). Definitions of cyber-attacks identify logical, physical, and cognitive effects on assets. Denial of access to assets is an example of logical effects. Cognitive effects include deception, meaning the use of false information to convince an adversary that something is true. Destruction of capital assets is an example of physical effects.

5. *Duration:* Only one definition of cyber-attacks mentions its intended duration. The definition by Owens, Dam, and Lin (2009) includes the possibility of a cyber-attack over an extended duration.

Examination of High-Profile Cyber-Attacks

Information on 10 high-profile cyber-attacks was examined for the purpose of i) collecting data for the five attributes identified from the definitions of cyber-attacks and ii) identifying additional attributes. A security expert who provided advice throughout this research helped select the 10 high-profile cyber-attacks that would result in the highest possible diversity of industries in which the target organizations operated. He also helped identify reliable online sources of information about these cyber-attacks.

The use of high-profile attacks was purposeful. The intent was to gather as much information as possible about an attack from reliable sources. Upfront, it was clear that the selection of high-profile cyber-attacks would prevent overgeneralizing findings to attacks that were not high profile.

For each high-profile cyber-attack, a scenario was developed. A cyber-attack scenario is a description of the sequence of events that results from the interactions among the individuals and organizations involved in a cybersecurity breach as well as their stakeholders. A cybersecurity breach refers to an event where an individual has obtained information on a protected computer that the individual lacks authorization to obtain by knowingly circumventing one or more technological or physical measures that are designed to exclude or prevent unauthorized individuals from obtaining that information. The main actors in a cyber-attack scenario are the "known target" and the "alleged attacker."

Attributes of High-Profile Cyber-Attacks

For each of the 10 cyber-attacks examined, Table 1 provides the information collected for the five attributes identified from the examination of the definitions of cyber-attacks.

Eight of the 10 cyber-attacks shown in Table 1 meet Damballa's (2010) definition of an advanced persistent threat: a cyber-attack that requires a high degree of stealthiness over a prolonged duration of operation in order to be successful. The two cyber-attacks in Table 1 that are not advanced persistent threats are (5) Cyber-Bunker's distributed denial-of-service attack on The Spamhaus Project and (9) Criminals who encrypt and decrypt data in users' computers. An advanced persistent threat attack is sophisticated and seeks to achieve ongoing access without discovery (Hashimoto et al.,

2013). The duration of the advanced persistent threats ranged from 8 to 32 weeks. Four of the advanced persistent threats contained customized code specifically developed for the attack: the attacks that targeted (1) Google, (2) Iran, (6) Target Corporation, and (7) TJX Companies.

The examination of these 10 cyber-attacks suggested that at least six additional cyber-attack attributes exist:

1. *Attack vector:* The path or means by which an attacker can gain access to a computer or network server in order to deliver a payload or malicious outcome. An attack vector enables the exploitation of system vulnerabilities. Seven of the 10 cyber-attacks examined started with phishing or spear phishing (i.e., an email that appears to be from an individual or business that the user knows, but it is not). The cyber-attacks that started with phishing include those that targeted: (6) Target Corporation, (8) Bank customers, and (9) Computer owners. Those that started with spear phishing include: (1) Google, (3) New York Times, (4) Chemical and defence firms in United States, and (10) Gaming companies.

2. *Vulnerability:* Any form of weakness in a computing system or environment that can let attackers compromise a system's or environment's confidentiality, integrity, and availability (Foreman, 2009). A vulnerability is a weakness or gap in the efforts to protect an asset. A total of 18 vulnerabilities were exploited in the 10 cyber-attacks examined, and they can be organized into the five types specified in the United Kingdom's implementation of "ISO/IEC 27005: 2008: Hardware, Software, Network, Site and Personnel/Users (ISO, 2008). In our small sample, people and software account for 14 of the 18 vulnerabilities that attackers exploited.

3. *Malicious software:* Refers to software programs designed to damage or do other unwanted actions on a computer system. A variety of malicious software programs were used in the cyber-attacks examined. They include: Hydraq, Stuxnet, Poison Ivy, Botnet malware, Citadel, BlackPOS, Blabla sniffing, SpyEye, Nitro, and PlugX.

4. *Botnet reliance:* Refers to the cyber-attacks dependence on botnets (i.e., networks of computers infected with malicious software and controlled as a group without the owners' knowledge). Eight cyber-attacks relied on botnets: (1) Google, (3) New York Times, (4)

Table 1. Five attributes of high-profile cyber-attacks

Attack	1. Actor: Known Target	1. Actor: Alleged Attacker	2. Asset Targeted	3. Motivation	4. Effect on Targeted Asset	5. Attack Duration
1	Google (multinational specializing in Internet-related services and products)	Elderwood Gang (large Chinese cyberespionage organization)	Source code repositories that support supply chain functions	Collect valuable proprietary information of businesses	Gmail database was modified to allow extraction of information without detection	28 weeks (Jun to Dec '09)
2	Iran	Israel & US	Nuclear centrifuges controlled by computers at Natanz, Iran	Delay Iran's nuclear R&D program	1,000 centrifuges destroyed	32 weeks (Nov '07 to Jun '10)
3	New York Times: publisher of American daily newspaper	Hackers who used methods of the Chinese military	Passwords and data of reporters and other employees	Obtain names of people who provided information about relatives of China's prime minister accumulating billions through business dealings	Data of 50 employees copied and uploaded to external server without detection	28 weeks (Oct '12 to Jan '13)
4	Chemical & defence firms in US	Covert Grove (group located in Hebei region in China)	Domain administrator credentials and networks of computers that store information	Collect valuable proprietary information of businesses	Data from 48 companies copied and uploaded to external server without detection	12 weeks (Jul to Sep '11)
5	The Spamhaus Project (not-for-profit that tracks spammers)	CyberBunker (an Internet service provider)	The Spamhaus Project website	Retaliate against Spamhaus for identifying CyberBunker as hosting spammers and asking its upstream service provider to cancel service	Website not available to users	2 weeks (Mar '13)
6	Target Corporation (American discount retailer)	Criminal group	Confidential customer information	Obtain confidential information	Data from 110 million customers copied and uploaded to external server without detected	8 weeks (Nov to Dec '13)
7	TJX Companies (American apparel and home goods company)	Criminal group	Credit and debit card numbers	Obtain confidential information to sell	Data from 94 million customers copied and uploaded to external server without detection	32 weeks (May '06 to Jan '07)
8	Bank customers	Aleksandr Andreevich Panin, a.k.a. "Gribodemon" and "Harderman" (Hacker)	1.4 million computers that store online banking credentials, credit card data, user names, PINs, and other sensitive information	Obtain confidential information to sell	Sensitive information in 30,000 bank accounts was copied and uploaded to external server without detection	In progress
9	Computer owners	Criminals	Users' data or systems	Demand ransom to restore access	250,000 computers encrypted	In progress
10	Gaming companies	Criminals	Digital certificates for the secure exchange of information over the Internet using the public key infrastructure	Obtain confidential information to sell	Data from up to 30 gaming companies copied and uploaded to external server without detection	In progress

Chemical and defence firms, (5) The Spamhaus Project, (6) Target Corporation, (8) Bank customers, (9) Computer owners, and (10) Gaming companies.

5. *Origin:* Refers to the geographical origin of the cyber-attack. Four of the 10 cyber-attacks in the sample were alleged to have originated from China: (1) Google, (3) New York Times, (4) Chemical and defence firms, and (10) Gaming companies; four were from Eastern Europe (6) Target Corporation, (7) TJX Companies, (8) Bank customers, and (9) Computer owners: one originated from the United Kingdom and Spain; and one was from Israel and the United States.

6. *Destination:* Refers to the region affected by the cyber-attack in the near term. Eight of the 10 high-profile cyber-attacks targeted organizations in the United States. The two cyber-attacks that did not target organizations in the United States were (2) Iran and (5) The Spamhaus Project. However, seven of the eight attacks that targeted organizations in the United States also targeted organizations in other parts of the world (i.e., Australia, Bahrain, Bangladesh, Brazil, Canada, China, Eastern Europe, France, India, Ireland, Mexico, Oman, Puerto Rico, Russia, Saudi Arabia, South East Asia, and the United Kingdom).

Conclusion

Through the analysis of six definitions of the term cyber-attack and ten high-profile cases of cyber-attack, this article identified 11 important attributes of cyber-attacks following an approach similar to the one that was used in the late 1990s to clarify what is meant by "security". In summary, these attributes are:

1. Actors
2. Assets targeted
3. Motivation
4. Effect on targeted assets
5. Duration
6. Attack vector
7. Vulnerability
8. Malicious software
9. Botnet reliance
10. Origin
11. Destination

These attributes could be further categorized as Attack Intent (Actors, Origin, Destination, Motivation), Attack Impact (Assets targeted, Effect on targeted assets, Duration) and Attack Path (Initiation approach, Vulnerability, Malicious software, Botnet reliance).

Cyber-attack studies are at the core of cybersecurity studies. However, what is meant by "cyber-attack" is not clear and the field is underdeveloped. Definitions of cyberattack vary (Hathaway et al., 2012; Owens et al., 2009), and some are ambiguous. Ambiguous definitions of cyber-attacks hamper the prosecution of criminals (Whitehouse, 2014).

The analysis carried out opens up interesting areas for future research. For example, this study examined 10 instances of *successful* cyber-attacks; future studies can examine the attributes of cyber-attacks that failed or were only partially successful. The purpose of studying failed cyber-attacks or those that were partially successful is to identify missteps, symptoms, causes, and the reasons that attackers came and went.

About the Author

Mehdi Kadivar is completing his MASc in Technology Innovation Management at Carleton University in Ottawa, Canada. He holds a Bachelor of Science degree in Business Administration from the American University of Sharjah, Iran. Previously, he worked as a system maintenance expert at the Petrochemical Industries Design and Engineering company and as an intern at the Emirates National Bank of Dubai.

References

Ashford, W. 2013. US Researchers Find 25 Security Vulnerabilities in SCADA Systems. *ComputerWeekly.com*, October 18. http://www.computerweekly.com/news/2240207488/US-researchers-find-25-security-vulnerabilities-in-SCADA-systems

Blank, L.R. 2013. International Law and Cyber Threats from Non-Sate Actors, *International Law Studies*, 89:157-197. http://ssrn.com/abstract=2194180

Buzan, B. 1991. *People, States and Fear: An Agenda for Security Analysis in the Post-Cold War Era*. Brighton: Wheatsheaf.

Buzan, B., Waever, O., & De Wilde, J. 1998. *Security: A New Framework for Analysis*. Boulder, CO: Lynne Rienner Publishers.

Castel, M. E. 2012. International and Canadian Law Rules Applicable to Cyber Attacks by State and Non-State Actors. *Canadian Journal of Law & Technology*, 10(1): 89-120. https://ojs.library.dal.ca/CJLT/article/view/4833/4353

Crawford, J. 2014. The U.S. Government Thinks China Could Take Down the Power Grid. *CNN*, November 20. http://www.cnn.com/2014/11/20/politics/nsa-china-power-grid/

Damballa. 2010. Advanced Persistent Threats: A Brief Description. *Damballa, Inc.* Accessed November 1, 2014: http://www.damballa.com/advanced-persistent-threats-a-brief-description/

Foreman, P. 2009. *Vulnerability Management.* Boca Raton, FL: Auerbach Publications.

Hathaway, O. A., Crootof, R., Levitz, P., Nix, H., Nowlan, A., Perdue, W., & Spiegel, J. 2012. The Law of Cyber-Attack. *California Law Review.* 100(4): 817-885. http://www.californialawreview.org/articles/the-law-of-cyber-attack

Huysmans, J. 1998. Security! What Do You Mean? From Concept to Thick Signifier. *European Journal of International Relations,* 4(2): 226-255. http://dx.doi.org/10.1177/1354066198004002004

ISO. 2008. ISO/IEC 27005:2008: Information Technology - Security Techniques - Information Security Risk Management. *International Organization for Standardization.* Accessed November 1, 2014: http://www.iso.org/iso/catalogue_detail?csnumber=42107

Jowitt, T. 2014. White House Advisory Group: Governments Have Five Years To Secure IoT. *TechWeek Europe*, November 20. http://www.techweekeurope.co.uk/e-regulation/governments-secure-iot-156149

Kaspersky Lab. 2014. Malware Classifications. *Kaspersky Lab.* Accessed November 1, 2014: http://www.kaspersky.com/internet-security-center/threats/malware-classifications

Kovacs, E. 2014. U.K. Invests Heavily in ICS Cyber Security Research. *Security Week*, October 3. http://www.securityweek.com/uk-invests-heavily-ics-cyber-security-research

National Security Telecommunications Security Advisory Committee. 2014. *Draft Report to the President on the Internet of Things,* November. Washington, DC: Department of Homeland Security.

Nicholson, A., Webber, S., Dyer, S., Patel, T., & Janicke, H. 2012. SCADA Security in the Light of Cyber-Warfare. *Computers & Security*, 31(4):418-436. http://dx.doi.org/10.1016/j.cose.2012.02.009

O'Connell, M.E. 2012. Cyber Security without Cyber War. *Journal of Conflict and Security Law*, 17(2): 187-209. http://dx.doi.org/10.1093/jcsl/krs017

Owens, W. A., Dam, K., & Lin, H. S. 2009. *Technology, Policy, Law, and Ethics Regarding U.S. Acquisition and Use of Cyber-attack Capabilities.* Washington, DC: National Academies Press.

Pearson, N. 2014. A Larger Problem: Financial and Reputational Risks. *Computer Fraud & Security*, 2014(4): 11-13. http://dx.doi.org/10.1016/S1361-3723(14)70480-4

Rattray, G., & Healey, J. 2010. *Categorizing and Understanding Offensive Cyber Capabilities and Their Use. Proceedings of a Workshop on Deterring Cyber-attacks: Informing Strategies and Developing Options for U.S. Policy.* Washington, DC: National Academies Press.

Roscini, M. 2014. *Cyber Operations and the Use of Force in International Law.* Oxford: Oxford University Press.

Scully, T. 2013. The Cyber Security Threat Stops in the Boardroom. *Journal of Business Continuity & Emergency Planning*, 7(2):139-147. http://www.ncbi.nlm.nih.gov/pubmed/24457325

Sugarman, E. 2014. Cybersecurity is a Severe and Growing Challenge for Government Contractors. *Forbes*, August 24. http://www.forbes.com/sites/elisugarman/2014/08/26/cybersecurity-is-a-severe-and-growing-challenge-for-government-contractors/

Šulović, V. 2010. *Meaning of Security and the Theory of Securitization.* Belgrade: Belgrade Center of Security Policy.

Uma, M., & Padmavathi, G. 2013. A Survey on Various Cyber Attacks and their Classification. *International Journal of Network Security*, 15(5): 390-396.

US Securities and Exchange Commission. 2014. Form 8-K (001-15935): Community Health Systems, Inc. *United States Securities and Exchange Commission*, August 18. http://www.sec.gov/Archives/edgar/data/1108109/0001193125143 12504/d776541d8k.htm

United States Joint Chiefs of Staff. 2010. Memorandum: Joint Terminology for Cyberspace Operations. Washington, DC: United States Department of Defense.

Weiss, M. 2014. Do We Need a CDC for Cybersecurity? *CIO Insight*, October 30. http://www.cioinsight.com/security/do-we-need-a-cdc-for-cybersecurity.html

Whitehouse, S. 2014. Opening Statement: Judiciary Subcommittee on Crime and Terrorism Hearing on Taking Down Botnets: Public and Private Efforts to Disrupt and Dismantle Cybercriminal Networks, July 15. Washington, DC: U.S. Senate Committee on the Judiciary, Subcommittee on Crime and Terrorism. http://www.hsdl.org/?view&did=756247

Keywords: cyber-attack, attributes, cybersecurity, attack characteristics

22

The Expanding Cybersecurity Threat

Cheri F. McGuire

" *It used to be that not a month would go by without some new data* "
breach being reported. Then it seemed not a week would go by. Today,
we see daily reports about some new attack vector, some new cyber-
espionage group, some new kind of cyber-attack occurring against our
critical networks and our critical data.

Cheri F. McGuire
Vice President of Global Government Affairs & Cybersecurity Policy
Symantec

Overview

The TIM Lecture Series is hosted by the Technology Innovation Management program (carleton.ca/tim) at Carleton University in Ottawa, Canada. The lectures provide a forum to promote the transfer of knowledge between university research to technology company executives and entrepreneurs as well as research and development personnel. Readers are encouraged to share related insights or provide feedback on the presentation or the TIM Lecture Series, including recommendations of future speakers.

The first TIM lecture of 2015 was held at Carleton University on February 19th, and was presented by Cheri F. McGuire, Vice President of Global Government Affairs & Cybersecurity Policy at Symantec (symantec.com). McGuire provided an overview of Symantec's view of the expanding cybersecurity threat and the measures the company is employing to mitigate the risk for companies and individuals. The slides from her presentation are available here (tinyurl.com/m63vk7t).

Summary

To begin, McGuire provided background on Symantec's systems for identifying and evaluating cyberthreats around the world, which it uses as a basis for developing protection measures. In particular, she described Symantec's Global Intelligence Network (GIN), a massive array of monitoring systems, attack sensors, and decoy accounts, combined with the world's largest vulnerability database and capability for big data analytics, which together provide real-time insights on what is happening on a global scale.

Globally, a wide range of threats are being detected across many platforms and devices. There is also wide range of attackers, from highly-organized criminal enterprises to individual cyber-criminals to "hacktivists" (i.e., politically motivated actors) to state-sponsored groups. The variety of threats and motivations make Symantec's task of identifying threats and developing protections an increasing challenge and drives its focus on the attackers' tactics, techniques, and procedures (TTP). A detailed understanding of the attackers is essential in building effective defenses against them.

Today, the key categories of threats raised by attackers are:

1. Data breaches: more than 550 million identities were exposed due to data breaches in 2013, and Symantec expects this number to soon exceed 1 billion, which is equivalent to nearly 1 out of every 7 people on the planet, or about 1 in 3 Internet users. And, data breaches are becoming increasingly broad: intellectual property, trade agreements, and business agreements, are often now the target, not just credit card data, etc.

2. Mobile and social: a key area where threats are proliferating and where social engineering is carried out (i.e., attackers gather personal data about persons of interest via social networks and then use it to make targeted emails more convincing).

3. Ransomware: malware that locks a computer and encrypts the data, then demands payment for decryption. Ransomware is becoming increasingly prevalent: Symantec observed a 500% month-on-month increase in ransomware in 2013.

4. Cyber-espionage: the identity of malicious intruders is not always known, and the distinctions between categories of attackers is not clear-cut: one group may pose as another to obscure their identities and intentions, particularly when the attacks are initiated by nation-states.

5. Internet of Things: innovation in this area is happening very quickly, but the security is a step behind. Symantec believes that, to be effective, security must be built into products as they are being developed, not "bolted on" later.

In terms of targets, McGuire highlighted critical infrastructure (e.g., power grids, transportation networks, manufacturing sectors, financial systems) as an important area of concern.

McGuire also highlighted the increase in web-based attacks: in 2013, Symantec blocked 23% more web attacks than in 2012. However, targeted attacks are of particular concern, such as emails targeted at persons of interest using personal data gathered to increase the apparent authenticity of the communication. Such targeted emails are designed to trick people into taking actions that they would not otherwise take if they understood the consequences. Examples include spearphishing (i.e., sending an email to a person of interest) and watering holes (i.e., drawing targets to infected websites, where the malware lies waiting to infect visitors).

Beyond Symantec's efforts to develop its products and services, the company has also been actively pursuing public–private partnerships to help counter the expanding cybersecurity threat. These partnerships are both private-to-private and private-to-public; Symantec is working with other companies and with many government agencies that span policy, operations, law enforcement, as well as education and awareness. Such partnerships are motivated by the desire to cooperate and share high-level information, support prosecutions of cyber-crimes, and develop an ecosystem approach to cybersecurity. This approach also reflects the shift towards a defense that is not solely founded on signature-based technologies (i.e., antivirus software), but reflects an increasingly sophisticated, layered approach to cybersecurity.

Finally, McGuire provided a list of best practices for businesses to help protect against cyber-threats:

1. Employ defence-in-depth strategies

2. Monitor for network incursion attempts and vulnerabilities

3. Antivirus on endpoints is not enough

4. Secure websites against man-in-the-middle attacks

5. Protect private keys

6. Use encryption to protect sensitive data

7. Ensure all devices on company networks have security protections

8. Implement a removable media policy

9. Be aggressive with updating and patching

10. Enforce an effective password policy

11. Ensure regular backups are available

12. Restrict email attachments

13. Ensure an infection and incident response procedure is in place

14. Educate users on basic security protocols

About the Speaker

Cheri McGuire is Vice President for Global Government Affairs and Cybersecurity Policy at Symantec, where she is responsible for the global public policy agenda and government engagement strategy, which includes cybersecurity, data integrity, critical infrastructure protection, and privacy. She currently serves on the World Economic Forum Global Agenda Council on Cybersecurity, and on the boards of the Information Technology Industry Council, the US Information Technology Office in China, and the National Cyber Security Alliance. She also is a past board member of the IT Information Sharing and Analysis Center, a former member of the Industry Executive Subcommittee of the President's National Security Telecommunications Advisory Committee, and a former Chair of the US IT Sector Coordinating Council. Ms. McGuire is a frequent presenter on technology policy issues, including testifying five times before the US Congress on cybersecurity, privacy, and cybercrime. Prior to joining Symantec, she served as Director for Critical Infrastructure and Cybersecurity in Microsoft's Trustworthy Computing Group, and she has held numerous positions in the Department of Homeland Security, Booz Allen Hamilton, and a telecom engineering firm that was acquired by Exelon Infrastructure Services. She was also a Congressional staffer for seven years. Ms. McGuire holds an MBA from The George Washington University and a BA from the University of California, Riverside.

This report was written by Chris McPhee.

Keywords: cybersecurity, cyber-attacks, cyber-threats, data breaches, cyber-espionage, social engineering, malware, ransomware, scareware, antivirus, private-public partnerships, Symantec

23

The Internet of Everything:
Fridgebots, Smart Sneakers, and Connected Cars

Jeff Greene

" *Cybersecurity considerations need to be at the forefront of our minds as* "
the Internet of Things moves from expectation to reality.

Jeff Greene
Director of NAM Government Affairs & Senior Policy Counsel
Symantec

Overview

The TIM Lecture Series is hosted by the Technology Innovation Management program (carleton.ca/tim) at Carleton University in Ottawa, Canada. The lectures provide a forum to promote the transfer of knowledge between university research to technology company executives and entrepreneurs as well as research and development personnel. Readers are encouraged to share related insights or provide feedback on the presentation or the TIM Lecture Series, including recommendations of future speakers.

The second TIM lecture of 2015 was held at Carleton University on March 18th, and was presented by Jeff Greene, Director of NAM Government Affairs & Senior Policy Counsel at Symantec (symantec.com). Greene provided an overview of the Internet of Things to compare the hype versus reality and to examine the security implications of connecting myriad physical devices to the Internet and to each other.

Summary

Greene began by sharing examples of new technologies in which privacy concerns, vulnerabilities, and even intrusions that increasingly come from unexpected places, such as trash cans that track pedestrians via smartphones (Satter, 2013), Smart TVs with security gaps through which hackers could view and record users through their webcams (Fink & Segall, 2013), and camera-enabled baby monitors that hackers have been able to control remotely (Hill, 2013). Technologies such as these will become familiar components of the

Internet of Things (IoT), or the Internet of Everything, although Greene cautions against defining these terms too closely:

> *"There is no hard and fast definition of the Internet of Things, in part, because it is so new and continues to evolve. Even five or ten years from now, we will likely be calling the IoT something different."*

In the context of the lecture, Greene's view of the Internet of Things is quite broad, and it includes "a whole host of connected endpoints that in some way interact with the physical world, whether sensing, acting, or reacting". This view extends beyond computers and handheld devices – it includes factories, water treatment plants, fitness devices, toys, and so on. And, generally, he finds that it can be helpful to distinguish between the industrial Internet of Things (e.g., heavy machinery, manufacturing, critical infrastructure) and the consumer Internet of things (e.g., appliances, toys, home devices).

Greene argued that, although we see current technologies that will likely contribute to the Internet of Things, we are likely still five to ten years a from realizing it, meaning that we still have a window of opportunity to shape it and ensure that it is as secure as possible. In particular, we must recognize the clash of cultures between the physical world and the IT world that the Internet of Things brings about. For example, manufacturers and critical infrastructure utilities depend on having their systems up and running 24 hours per day, whereas the IT culture assumes systems will be taken down on a regular basis for patching and other maintenance.

Greene's presentation included examples of the intersections between vulnerabilities in the physical and IT worlds and the poor practices that are increasing creating cyber-risks as the Internet of Things evolves. Notably, many of the underlying vulnerabilities do not represent a shortcoming in technical development, but rather point to poor security practices that can be remedied, such as re-using or sharing passwords, hard-coding passwords, and having (or not changing) default passwords. Thus, there are basic steps that can be taken to improve security through behavioural changes, without requiring innovative technological solutions. Equally, there can be greater consideration paid to human behaviour when designing and implementing technical solutions. For greater cybersecurity, this human-behaviour element should also factor into our expectations of how devices will be used. Increasingly, devices are being used in ways or for purposes not intended by their designers. As users, Greene encourages us to focus less on the question "can it be connected?" and ask instead "should it be connected?"

In closing, Greene examined what is being done to assess the risks of the Internet of Things and to develop appropriate policies for its cybersecurity so that we can all enjoy the tremendous benefits that it may bring. As identified by the National Security Telecommunications Security Advisory Committee (NSTAC, 2014) in the United States, there is "a small – and rapidly closing – window to ensure that IoT is adopted in a way that maximizes security and minimizes risk. If the country fails to do so, it will be coping with the consequences for generations." Greene reports that this small and rapidly closing window is likely on the scale of two to four years:

> *"Based on our experience with the Internet itself, and its key lesson that security should be part of design, we have only a short time to avoid making the same mistake with the Internet of Things. Cybersecurity considerations need to be at the forefront of our minds as the Internet of Things moves from expectation to reality."*

About the Speaker

Jeff Greene is the Director of Government Affairs for North America and Senior Policy Counsel at Symantec, where he focuses on issues including cybersecurity, the Internet of Things, and privacy. In this role, he monitors executive and legislative branch activity and works extensively with industry and government organizations. Prior to joining Symantec, Jeff was Senior Counsel with the U.S. Senate Homeland Security and Governmental Affairs Committee, where he focused on cybersecurity and Homeland Defense issues. He has also worked in the House of Representatives, where he was a subcommittee staff director on the House Committee on Homeland Security. Previously, he was an attorney with a Washington, D.C. law firm, where his practice focused on government contracts and contract fraud, as well as general civil and criminal investigations. Jeff recently served as the staff co-chair of the "Internet of Things" research subcommittee of the President's National Security Telecommunications Advisory Committee. He is also a Senior Advisor at the Truman National Security Project, where he is on the Steering Committee for the Cyberspace and Security Program. He is co-chair of the Homeland Security Committee of the American Bar Association's Section of Science & Technology Law and is on the Executive Committee of the Information Technology Sector Coordinating Council. He has a BA in International Relations from Boston University in the United States and a JD with Honors from the University of Maryland, also in the United States, where he has taught classes in Homeland Security law and policy.

This report was written by Chris McPhee.

References

Fink, E., & Segall, L. 2013. Your TV Might Be Watching You. *CNN Money*. August 1, 2013. Accessed March 1, 2015:
http://money.cnn.com/2013/08/01/technology/security/tv-hack/

Hill, K. 2013. How a Creep Hacked a Baby Monitor to Say Lewd Things to A 2-Year-Old. *Forbes*. August 13, 2013. Accessed March 1, 2015:
http://www.forbes.com/sites/kashmirhill/2013/08/13/how-a-creep-hacked-a-baby-monitor-to-say-lewd-things-to-a-2-year-old/

NSTAC. 2014. *Draft Report to the President on the Internet of Things*, November. Washington, DC: Department of Homeland Security, National Security Telecommunications Security Advisory Committee.

Satter, R. 2013. London's Creepiest Startup' Forced to Pull 'Spy' Trash Cans that Could Track London Pedestrians via Smartphones. *National Post*. August 12, 2013. Accessed March 1, 2015:
http://news.nationalpost.com/2013/08/12/londons-creepiest-startup-forced-to-pull-spy-trash-cans-that-could-track-london-pedestrians-via-smartphones/

Keywords: cybersecurity, Internet of Things, IoT, Internet of Everything, Industrial Internet, Consumer Internet of Things, hackers, cyber-attacks

24

Assessing the Intentions and Timing of Malware

Brent Maheux

" Bien mal acquis ne profite jamais. "

(Ill-gotten gains seldom prosper.)

French proverb

Malware has become a significant, complex, and widespread problem within the computer industry. It represents one of the most prevalent threats to cybersecurity and is increasingly able to circumvent current detection and mitigation techniques. To help better understand when a malware attack might happen, this article proposes an intention-based classification of malware and merges it with an optimal timing model to help predict the timing of malware based on its classification. The classification model is based on an examination of eight malware samples, and it identifies four malware classifications and commonalities based on the dimensions of persistence and stealth. The goal of the article is to provide a better understanding of when cyber-conflict will happen, and to help defenders better mitigate the potential damage.

Introduction

In today's online environment, computer systems now dominate our personal, business, and financial lives. However, our dependency on these systems also makes us vulnerable to cybercriminals. The cost of cybercrime now exceeds $110 billion USD and affects 566 million victims annually, which equates to 1.5 million victims per day or 18 victims per second (Semantec, 2012). Malware, which is short for "malicious software" and includes computer viruses, worms, trojan horses, and spyware (TechTerms, 2014), which are used for a range of illicit activities such as distributing spam email and stealing sensitive information.

Although there has been a lot of research on detecting malware (e.g., Baecher et al., 2006; Gu et al., 2007; Invernizzi et al., 2014; Jain & Bajaj, 2014; Jiang et al., 2007; Peng et al., 2013) and analyzing it from a technical perspective (e.g., Dinaburg et al., 2008; Jain & Bajaj, 2014; Moser et al., 2007; Willems et al., 2007; Yin et al., 2007), there is a lack of research on timing and categorizing malware based on its intentions. A greater understanding of the intentions of attackers will increase the defender's knowledge on how to mitigate attacks.

This article examines an evolutionary timeline of malware based on eight examples of malware dating from the first computer virus in 1971 (Gatto, 2011) through to a recent example from 2012. These examples are used

to develop an intention-based classification of malware, which is then combined with Axelrod and Iliev's (2013) optimal timing model. The optimal timing model deals with the question of when the malware should be used given that its use today may well prevent it from being available for use later. The optimal timing model is presented from the perspective of the offense – helping predict the best time to use a resource. However, the results are equally relevant to a defender who wants to estimate how high the stakes have to be in order for the offense to use their resource. When the optimal timing model is combined with the intention-based classification, the new model helps clarify how the timing of malware can depend on the stakes involved in the present situation, as well as the characteristics of the resource for exploitation. Even further, the model helps predict the level of sophistication one could be facing, increasing the chances of mitigating the malware (Galarneau, 2002; Mell et al., 2005; Symantec, 2014).

Axelrod and Iliev test their optimal timing model on four individual case study examples. Combining the model on a broader class of malware samples will further test their model or allow new perspectives and theories to evolve. Because both models use the same definitions for a malware's stealth and persistence capabilities, they can be easily combined to provide a better understanding of the intentions and timing of the attacker's malware.

This article is structured as follows. The first section describes and analyzes eight examples of malware, from the first computer virus in 1971 to a case of cyberwarfare in 2012. Next, Axelrod and Iliev's (2013) optimal timing model is introduced and applied to the context of malware. Then, drawing upon the examples of malware analyzed earlier, an intention-based classification of malware is proposed and combined with the optimal timing model to illustrate how the optimal timing of malware can be determined depending on the attacker's intentions. The final section provides conclusions.

Examples of Malware

In this section, eight examples illustrate the evolution of malware, ranging from the first experimental computer virus from 1971 to a cyberespionage application that was discovered in 2012. These eight cases were selected as being noteworthy examples of malware based on a combination of timelines (Hansen, 2013; Infoplease, 2012; Khanse, 2014; Larsen, 2012; Malware Database, 2014; PC History, 2003; Standler, 2008). The eight examples are spread out over the history of malware and are generally representative of contemporary malware examples.

1. *Creeper:* The first virus. In 1971, the Creeper system, now considered to be the first computer virus, was an experimental self-replicating program that infected DEC PDP-10 computers running the TENEX operating system (Gatto, 2011). Creeper gained access via the ARPANET by searching for a machine within the network, transferring itself, displaying a message, then starting over, thereby hopping from system to system. It was developed for experimental purposes, as a proof of concept within an academic research context.

2. *Elk Cloner:* The first outbreak. Elk Cloner was created in 1982 as a prank by a 15-year-old high school student. The virus attached itself to the operating system of Apple II computers and then spread itself via floppy disk to other computers, on which it would display a poem instead of loading a game. Elk Cloner is one of the first known viruses that spread beyond the computer system or laboratory in which it was written (Rouse, 2005).

3. *Happy99:* The happy worm. As the name suggests, this worm was developed 1999 and usually arrived as an email attachment or new post that was named Happy99.exe. Once executed, Happy99 would display fireworks, then copy itself to the windows system folder and then email itself to all contacts listed on the system. Lacking any destructive payload, Happy99 would not cause damage to the actual affected computer; it was simply a prank (Elnitiarta, 2007).

4. *Code Red:* Vulnerable web servers. In 2001, Code Red infected web servers, where it automatically spread by exploiting a known vulnerability in Microsoft IIS servers. In less than one week, nearly 400,000 servers were infected, and the homepage of their hosted websites was replaced with the message "Hacked By Chinese!" Code Red had a distinguishing feature designed to flood the White House website with traffic from the infected servers, which likely makes it the first case of documented political "hacktivism" on a large scale (Lovet, 2011).

5. *Blaster:* A large prank. In 2003, the Blaster worm spread on computers running the Microsoft operating systems Windows XP and Windows 2000, with damage totaling in the hundreds of millions (Dougherty et al, 2003). It was notable for the two hidden text strings, the first of which said "I just want to say LOVE YOU SAN!" and the second of which was a message to Microsoft CEO Bill Gates.

6. *Zeus:* Malware as a service. Over $70 million USD was stolen from users who were infected with the Zeus malware. It was one of the first major botnet malware applications that would go undetected by updated antivirus and go unnoticed by people who were using infected computers. Zeus was capable of being used to carry out malicious and criminal tasks, often being used to steal banking information. Zeus initially started to infect computers in 2007, and by 2009, security company Prevx discovered that Zeus had compromised over 74,000 FTP accounts on websites of such companies as Bank of America, NASA, Monster.com, ABC, Oracle, Cisco, Amazon, and BusinessWeek (Ragan, 2009).

7. *Stuxnet:* The stealthy one. Discovered in 2010, the Stuxnet virus would propagate across a network, scanning for unique Programmable Logic Controllers (PLCs) and certain software. Once it found the correct machine to reside on, it would infect the machine with a rootkit and start modifying the code, giving unexpected commands to the PLC while returning a loop of normal operating system values to the users. Multiple zero-day exploits were used on an estimated 16,000 computers that were infected by the Stuxnet virus, including Iran's nuclear enrichment plant at Natanz (Emerson, 2012).

8. *Flame:* Cyberespionage. Flame is a modular computer malware application discovered in 2012 that attacks computers running the Microsoft Windows operating system. The program is being used for targeted cyberespionage in Middle Eastern countries. Flame can spread over systems through the local area network (LAN) or via USB device and has the ability to record audio, screenshots, keyboard activity, and network traffic. According to estimates by Kaspersky in May 2012, Flame had initially infected approximately 1,000 machines with victims including governmental organizations, educational institutions, and private individuals. In total, Kaspersky estimates more than 5,000 computers were infected (Kaspersky Lab, 2013).

As shown in Table 1, the eight examples of malware can be summarized along the following six dimensions:

1. *Year:* date of first discovery.

2. *Intention:* the reason the malware was created. Types of intentions include experimental (including research, entertainment, demonstrations of skill), financial (including theft and fraud), political (including "hacktivists"), and cyberwarfare (including state-sponsored attacks).

3. *Initial access:* how the malware gained access to the system or network. Means of initial access include social engineering (i.e., psychological manipulation), a zero-day vulnerability (i.e., a previously unknown vulnerability in a computer application), and a known vulnerability.

4. *Stealth:* the probability that, if you use a resource now, it will still be available to use later (Axlerod & Iliev, 2013).

5. *Persistence:* the probability that, if you refrain from using a resource now, it will still be available to use in the future (Axlerod & Iliev, 2013).

6. *Extent:* the number of computers affected.

As Table 1 shows, the number of computers affected by the malware increases over time, except in the recent case of Flame, which is malware for targeted espionage, not widespread impact. Early examples of malware were readily detected and did not persist for long, and tended to rely on known vulnerabilities and social engineering for initial access. Later examples, particularly in malware for cyberwarfare, show a trend toward more targeted attacks with increased stealth and persistence.

Modelling Malware Based on Intentions and Timing

The design and features of a particular malware application will depends on the creator's intentions, and its users must also take into account the optimal timing of its desired impact. In the general context of cybersecur-

Table 1. Examples of malware

Name	Year	Intention	Initial access	Stealth	Persistence	Extent
Creeper	1971	Experimental	Known vulnerability	Low	Low	< 1k
Elk Cloner	1982	Experimental	Social engineering	Low	Low	< 1k
Happy99	1999	Experimental	Social engineering	Low	Low	10k
Code Red	2001	Political	Known vulnerability	Medium	High	400k
Blaster	2003	Experimental	Known vulnerability	Low	Low	8M
Zeus	2007	Financial	Social engineering	Medium	Low	3.6M
Stuxnet	2010	Cyberwarfare	Zero-day	High	High	16k
Flame	2013	Cyberwarfare	Zero-day	High	High	1k

ity, Axelrod and Iliev (2013) developed an optimal timing model to help understand when a given attacker should exploit its capacity to do harm. Their model considers important assumptions about the stakes at hand and the resource characteristics in terms of stealth and persistence:

1. *Stakes:* their model assumes that the attacker knows the current stakes of how important the target currently is but does not know what the stakes will be at any future point – although they do know the distribution of stakes over time.

2. *Stealth:* the probability that, if you use a resource now, it will still be available to use later.

3. *Persistence:* the probability that, if you refrain from using a resource now, it will still be available to use in the future.

Thus, Axelrod and Iliev's (2013) optimal timing model can be used to predict the optimal time to maximize the value of a particular malware application if an attacker knows the current stakes and the application's capabilities in terms stealth and persistence. An attack-value threshold can be calculated based on the malware's stealth and persistence and the capacity and vigilance of the intended target. For instance, the stealth of malware used against a well-protected target is likely to be less than the stealth of the same malware against a target that is not particularly attentive to security. Likewise, malware will typically have less persistence against a target that keeps its systems up-to-date with security patches than against a target that does not.

Thus, stealth and persistence depend on both the characteristics of the malware itself and the context of its use. Ideally, the attacker would have security knowledge of the systems they are trying to compromise. In the real world, and in Axelrod and Iliev's (2013) optimal timing model, the characteristics of stealth, persistence, and stakes can be weighted differently. However, for simplicity in this preliminary proposal, the model weighs each of the characteristics the same.

Overall, the optimal timing model predicts the three factors that favour attacker patience: low stealth, high persistence, and low stakes. However, when the stakes are high, the model favours high stealth and low persistence. Indeed, based on the analysis of the cases shown in Table 1, the attacker's intentions can be mapped along the two dimensions of stealth and persistence, as shown in Figure 1.

The political malware examples would be found in the top left corner of Figure 1, which is characterized by high persistence and low stealth. For example, "hacktivist" malware often has high persistence and goes undetected until the group wants to raise awareness of a particular situation (Tarzey & Fernandes, 2013). Cyberwarfare malware uses high stealth and high persistence to stay undetected for as long as possible. Financial malware has high stealth, enabling its creators to steal information through social engineering or misleading users; however, it has low persistence because cases of social engineering often have a limited lifespan because they are often based on current events (Conheady, 2012). The final classification is experimental, with low stealth and low persistence, experimental malware does not persist on computers nor does have a potential lifespan because they are often based off of publicly known weaknesses in a system and are created simply to show how an attacker can take advantage of the weakness. Within the set of malware samples studied in this article, all experimental malware displayed messages indicating that it was on the computer and then it would be deleted by users or the vulnerability would be patched.

The classification shown in Figure 1 can be enhanced by introducing variable stakes, as described in Axelrod and Iliev's (2013) model. Table 2 shows three scenarios of low, constant, and high stakes and the optimal timing for the use of malware depending on its intention. When the stakes are low, the optimal timing model determines that the current time is not the optimal time to use the malware for any malware classification, except, potentially financial malware.

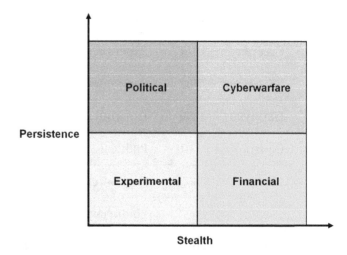

Figure 1. An intention-based classification of malware

Under constant stakes, the results in Table 2 show that financial malware should be used immediately. The model suggests the use of financial malware because, as defined by the intention-based classification, financial malware has low persistence and high stealth, making it the exact candidate to use under the optimal timing model. For example, a setting where the stakes are constant over time is the exploitation of stolen credit card information.

Under high stakes, the results in Table 2 show that it is optimal to use the resource immediately, except perhaps when the intention is political. The famous political, or "hacktivist" group, Anonymous, continues to use their resources, but only to send a message relating to a particular event. There is likelihood that they believe their message should be voiced on a particular world event so their stakes are so large that they are willing to sacrifice their resources to do so.

It is important to note the limitations of these results using the same weight for each of the three variables: persistence, stealth, and stakes. In real world examples, and in Axelrod and Iliev's optimal timing model, these values can be weighted differently.

Conclusion

It has been more than 40 years since our first example of malware. Malware evolved, but some of the principles have remained the same. The purposes and motives for malware have changed from educational, protests, and pranks to profit then finally to espionage and sabotage. Intention is an important part of understanding malware; originally, antivirus companies were looking for malware that had financial profit, so many systems were being skipped. Knowing that malware is also being used by governments and military, the search for potential malware activities can be broadened to other poten-

Table 2. The optimal timing of malware use depending on intentions, persistence, stealth, and stakes

Low Stakes	Intention	Persistence	Stealth	Timing
	Political	High	Low	Wait
	Cyberwarfare	High	High	Wait
	Experimental	Low	Low	Wait
	Financial	Low	High	---
Constant Stakes	Intention	Persistence	Stealth	Timing
	Political	High	Low	Wait
	Cyberwarfare	High	High	---
	Experimental	Low	Low	---
	Financial	Low	High	Use now
High Stakes	Intention	Persistence	Stealth	Timing
	Political	High	Low	---
	Cyberwarfare	High	High	Use now
	Experimental	Low	Low	Use now
	Financial	Low	High	Use now

tial systems. Understanding the intentions of malware enables the evaluation of the effectiveness of malware defenses.

The concept of initial access has changed slightly over the years. Many of the early examples of malware discussed here needed to be distributed, for instance through email, floppy disk, or USB device, or through a vulnerability in a web service that has an open port. However, the more recent examples – Stuxnet and Flame – were using zero-day exploits. This pattern may be a relatively new trend, because organizations are no longer telling the public or the vulnerable vendors about vulnerabilities; instead they are keeping or selling the techniques (Radianti & Gonzalex, 2007). Again, understanding the purpose of the malware helps in determining how many systems might be affected and how they originally became compromised. If the purpose is financial gain, then it seems likely that many systems will be infected. However, for cyberwarfare, or government-related instances, the examples studied show that only a small, unique set of systems will be infected.

Presented in this article is a model that represents the majority of malware today. The model was created to help understand the potential effectiveness of a malware application's stealth and persistence techniques based on their intentions. And, by combing the optimal timing model by Axelrod and Iliev (2013) with the results of studying the eight malware samples, Table 2 can help predict when an initial attack would likely happen.

About the Author

Brent Maheux is a Senior Software Specialist for the Canadian Government. He holds an MEng degree in Technology Innovation Management from Carleton University in Ottawa, Canada, and a BCS degree in Computer Science from Dalhousie University in Halifax, Canada. He has over 7 years working experience within the public and private sector specializing in product design and implementation.

References

Axelrod, R., & Iliev, R. 2013. Timing of Cyber Conflict. *Proceedings of the National Academy of Sciences of the United States of America*, 111(4): 1298-1303.
http://dx.doi.org/10.1073/pnas.1322638111

Baecher, P., Koetter, M., Holz, T., Dornseif, M., & Freiling, F. 2006. The Nepenthes Platform: An Efficient Approach to Collect Malware. *Recent Advances in Intrusion Detection*, 4219: 165-184.
http://dx.doi.org/10.1007/11856214_9

Conheady, S. 2012. The Future of Social Engineering. *Privacy PC*. July 17, 2012.
http://privacy-pc.com/articles/the-future-of-social-engineering.html

Dinaburg, A., Royal, P., Sharif, M., & Lee, W. 2008. Ether: Malware Analysis Via Hardware Virtualization Extensions. *Proceedings of the 15th ACM Conference on Computer and Communications Security:* 51-62.
http://dx.doi.org/10.1145/1455770.1455779

Dougherty, C., Havrilla, J., Hernan, S., & Lindner, M. 2003. W32/Blaster Worm. Historical Advisory CA-2003-20, CERT Division of the Software Engineering Institute. October 1, 2014:
http://www.cert.org/historical/advisories/CA-2003-20.cfm

Elnitiarta, R. 2007. Security Response: Happy99.Worm. *Symantec*. October 1, 2014:
http://www.symantec.com/security_response/writeup.jsp?docid=2000-121812-3151-99

Emerson, R. 2012. Stuxnet Virus Infected 16,000 Computers, Iran Says. *Huffington Post*, February 18, 2012:
http://www.huffingtonpost.com/2012/02/18/stuxnet-virus-iran_n_1286281.html

Galarneau, L. 2002. Anti-virus Software: The Challenge of Being Prepared for Tomorrow's MalWare Today. SANS Institute 2002.

Gatto, K. 2011. The Virus Turns 40. *Phys Org*. November 1, 2014:
http://phys.org/news/2011-03-virus.html

Gruener, W. 2012. Kaspersky: Flame Has Three Unidentified Malware Siblings. *Tom's Hardware*. November 1, 2014:
http://www.tomshardware.com/news/virus-flame-stuxnet,17644.html

Gu, G., Porras, P., Yegneswaran, V., Fong, M., & Lee, W. 2007. BotHunter: Detecting Malware Infection Through IDS-Driven Dialog Correlation. *Proceedings of the 16th USENIX Security Symposium:* 167-182.

Hansen, P. 2013. History of Malware. *Technology Bell*. November 1, 2014:
http://www.technologybell.com/history-of-malware/

Infoplease. 2012. Computer Virus Timeline. *Information Please*. November 1, 2014:
http://www.infoplease.com/ipa/A0872842.html

Invernizzi, L., Miskovic, S., Torres, R., Saha, S., Lee, S., Mellia, M. Kruegel, C., & Vigna, G. 2014. Nazca: Detecting Malware Distribution in Large-Scale Networks. Network and Distributed System Security (NDSS) Symposium 2014. February 23, 2014.

Jain, M., & Bajaj, P. 2014. Techniques in Detection and Analyzing Malware Executables: A Review. *International Journal of Computer Science and Mobile Computing,* May, 2014 (5): 930–935.

Jiang, X., Wang, X., & Xu, D. 2007. Stealthy Malware Detection through VMM-Based "Out-of-the-Box" Semantic View Reconstruction. *Proceedings of the 14th ACM Conference on Computer and Communications Security:* 128-138. http://dx.doi.org/10.1145/1315245.1315262

Khanse, A. 2014. Evolution of Malware – How It All Began! *The Windows Club.* November 1, 2014: http://www.thewindowsclub.com/evolution-of-malware-virus

Kaspersky Lab, 2013. Who's Spying on You? *Kaspersky Lab.* November 1, 2014: http://media.kaspersky.com/en/business-security/kaspersky-cyber-espionage-whitepaper.pdf

Larsen, C. 2012. A Malware Hall of Fame. *Blue Coat.* November 1, 2014: http://www.bluecoat.com/security/security-archive/2012-10-31/malware-hall-fame

Lovet, G. 2011. 40th Anniversary of the Computer Virus. *Help Net Security.* October 1, 2014: http://www.net-security.org/malware_news.php?id=1668

Malware Database. 2014. Timeline of Noteworthy Computer Viruses, Worms and Trojan Horses. *The Malware Database.* November 1, 2014. http://malware.wikia.com/wiki/Timeline_of_noteworthy_computer_viruses,_worms_and_Trojan_horses.

McDowell, M. 2013. Security Tip (ST04-014): Avoiding Social Engineering and Phishing Attacks. *United States Computer Emergency Readiness Team.* November 1, 2014: https://www.us-cert.gov/ncas/tips/ST04-014

Mell, P., Kent, K., & Nusbaum, J. 2005. *Special Publication 800-83: Guide to Malware Incident Prevention and Handling.* Gaithersburg, MD: Nation Institute of Standards and Technology.

Moser, A., Kruegel, C., & Kirda, E. 2007. Exploring Multiple Execution Paths for Malware Analysis. *Proceedings of 2007 IEEE Symposium on Security and Privacy:* 231-245. http://dx.doi.org/10.1109/SP.2007.17

PC History. 2003. The History of the PC Virus. *PC History.* November 1, 2014: http://www.pc-history.org/pc-virus.htm

Peng, W., Li, F., Zou, X., & Wu, J. 2013. Behavioral Malware Detection in Delay Tolerant Networks. *IEEE Transactions on Parallel and Distributed Systems,* 25(1): 53–63. http://dx.doi.org/10.1109/TPDS.2013.27

Ragan, S. 2009. ZBot Data Dump Discovered with over 74,000 FTP Credentials. *The Tech Herald.* November 1, 2014: http://www.thetechherald.com/articles/ZBot-data-dump-discovered-with-over-74-000-FTP-credentials/6514/

Rouse, M. 2005. Elk Cloner. *SearchSecurity.com.* October 1, 2014: http://searchsecurity.techtarget.com/definition/Elk-Cloner

Semantec. 2012. 2012 Norton Cybercrime Report. Mountain View, CA: Symantec Corporation.

Semantec. 2014. *Preparing for Future Attacks.* Mountain View, CA: Symantec Corporation.

Standler, R. 2008. Examples of Malicious Computer Programs. *Website of Dr. Ronald B. Standler.* November 1, 2014: http://www.rbs2.com/cvirus.htm

Tarzey, B., & Fernandes, L. 2013. The Trouble Heading for Your Business. *Quocirca,* February 2013

TechTerms. 2014. Malware. *TechTerms.com.* November 1, 2014: http://www.techterms.com/definition/malware

Willems, C., Holz, T., & Freiling, F. 2007. Toward Automated Dynamic Malware Analysis Using CWSandbox. *IEEE Security & Privacy,* 5(2): 32-39. http://dx.doi.org/10.1109/MSP.2007.45

Yin, H., Song, D., Egele, M., Kruegel, C., & Kirda, E. 2007. Panorama: Capturing System-Wide Information Flow for Malware Detection and Analysis. *Proceedings of the 14th ACM Conference on Computer and Communications Security:* 116-127. http://dx.doi.org/10.1145/1315245.1315261

Keywords: malware, cybersecurity, optimal timing, stealth, persistence

25

Supply Chain Cyber-Resilience: Creating an Agenda for Future Research

Omera Khan and Daniel A. Sepúlveda Estay

*" Resilience is all about being able to overcome the "
unexpected. Sustainability is about survival. The goal
of resilience is to thrive.*

Jamais Cascio
Writer and futurist specializing in design strategies

Supply chains have become more vulnerable in recent years, and high-profile cyber-attacks that have crippled the supply chains of well-known companies reveal that the point of entry for hackers is often through the weakest link in the chain. Exacerbated by growing complexity and the need to be visible, these supply chains share vital streams of information every minute of the day, thereby becoming an easy and highly lucrative target for talented criminals, causing financial losses as well as damaging brand reputation and value. Companies must therefore invest in supply chain capabilities to withstand cyber-attacks (i.e., cyber-resilience) in order to guard against potential threats. They must also embrace the reality that this often-unknown dimension of risk is the "new normal". Although interest on this topic has grown in the business world, less has been reported by the academic community. One reason for this could be due to the convergence of two different disciplines, information technology and supply chains, where supply chain cyber-risk and cyber-resilience appear to have a natural fit. The topic of cyber-resilience in supply chains is still in early stages of development, and this is one of the first journals to focus a special issue on it. Currently, the closest academic literature is within the realms of supply chain risk and resilience, where numerous models and frameworks exist. In this article, this literature is explored to identify whether these models can incorporate the dimension of cyber-risk and cyber-resilience. In doing so, we create a research agenda for supply chain cyber-resilience and provide recommendations for both academia and practice.

Introduction

Supply chain management has become dependent on electronic systems; since the 2000s, we have seen the emergence of information technology solutions to support business operations, to share information, to connect businesses, and to generate greater visibility along supply chains in order to gain knowledge and control of processes. On the other hand, although supply chains have pursued aspects such as the standardization of business processes, increased communication, connectivity, and data exchange, the vulnerability of these systems to cyber-attacks is nevertheless increasing. Why is this? In modern supply chains, information is shared digitally more than any other way, and supply chains are so reliant on good quality information that, without it, supply chain managers cannot make decisions on forecasts, production, distribution, etc. Equally importantly, poor data leads to poor decisions and performance. So, even with the most efficient and responsive supply chain, performance will be greatly compromised without good quality information.

For supply chains to thrive, managers must recognize that cyber-attacks are becoming common occurrences and that the "new normal" operating environment is one that is increasingly impacted by unknown risks. A key lesson for supply chain managers is that cyber-attacks do not always "come through the front door"; a business can be greatly impacted by an attack on the weakest link in their supply chain. A key difficulty with cyber-attacks is that often a business will not know the types of cyber-risks to which it has exposure, until it realizes that it is being attacked. Therefore, businesses must develop cyber-resilience to protect their supply chains.

Cyber-attacks can cause considerable economic costs to the companies that suffer these breaches, although the costs may not be noticed until after the damage is done. Estimates of the annual costs from cyber-crimes range from $375 billion to $575 billion (USD) (Intel Security, 2014), with significant effects on supply chains and resulting business performance with customers. Missing or erroneous data and information in supply chains, as a result of cyber-attacks, can lead to undesirable effects as diverse as intellectual property breaches, sub-standard or interrupted operations, sensitive data custody breaches, and decreases in service level to final customers. For example, some estimates indicate annual losses of £9.2bn from the theft of intellectual property and a further £7.6bn from industrial espionage.

Businesses that are able to understand what data is critical, where it is, who has access to it, and who is responsible for it, as well as where potential risks are in terms of information and data in the supply chain, are those that will be able to correctly communicate these risks to the supply chain in order to implement actions to mitigate them.

However, there has been a lack of managerial action to acknowledge the relevance and impact of cyber-crime (Burnson, 2013; Deloitte, 2012, 2013). It has been stated that "only a few CEOs realize that the real cost of cyber-crime stems from delayed or lost technological innovation" (Bailey et al., 2014) and companies have likely underestimated their risk (Intel Security, 2014). This is, either by delayed decision making or by a lack of awareness, the resulting inaction is leading to higher organizational costs from cyber-crimes.

This inaction is compounded by the increasing complexity of global supply chains and the speed and connectivity of operations required by companies to stay competitive. Furthermore, the growing skill of the attackers to find novel ways of accessing crucial data (Reuters, 2012), and the limited information and tools available to manage these threats, requires organizations to be more resilient to cyber-attacks that can cripple their supply chains.

Companies can prepare for potential attacks by applying appropriate supply chain risk-management tools and techniques both to reduce the likelihood of an intrusion and to deal with any disruption should an attack be successful. Every business that depends on a supply chain needs to build in cyber-resilience. But what exactly is cyber-resilience in the context of supply chains, and how can it be incorporated into current supply chain risk-management approaches?

Cyber-risk has been defined by the Institute for Risk Management (IRM, 2015) as "any risk of financial loss, disruption or damage to the reputation of an organization from some sort of failure of its information technology systems". The ISO 27005:2008 defines information security risk as "the potential that a given threat will exploit vulnerabilities of an asset or group of assets and thereby cause harm to the organization" (BSI, 2008). Both of these terms are being widely used in industry, and this article will consider these terms as equivalent.

We define supply chain cyber-resilience "as the capability of a supply chain to maintain its operational performance when faced with cyber-risk".

In light of the above challenges, the purpose of this article is to create an agenda for future research that could help supply chain and IT personnel to recognize and take a proactive team-based approach to supply chain cyber-resilience. More specifically, the aims of this study are to:

1. Explore current supply chain risk and resilience frameworks

2. Analyze these frameworks and determine whether they incorporate cyber-risk

3. Create a research agenda for cyber-risk and cyber-resilience.

The remainder of this article is structured as follows. First, the process used to find and review the key literature is explained. Next, the main findings of the literature review are discussed. Finally, a research agenda for supply chain cyber-resilience is proposed, including recommendations for both academia and industry.

Methodology

A systematic literature review was conducted, based on documented guidelines (Tranfield et al., 2003) through which a comprehensive, explicit, and reproducible method is followed. This method consists of ten steps that can be grouped into five main phases:

1. **Planning:** The planning phase focused on defining a review question to guide the search: "Do the current supply chain risk and resilience frameworks incorporate cyber-risk?"

2. **Searching:** The searching phase was guided by the identification of the relevant databases where the search was to be done, the keywords to be used during these searches, and the appropriate timeframe for the resulting documents to be included in the research. We searched for literature using the following databases: Scopus, Web of Science, ProQuest, and Google Scholar. The search keywords were determined from a knowledge domain analysis around the concept of cyber-resilience for the supply chain (see Figure 1). The three main knowledge domains to be scanned were identified as "supply chain management", "information technology management", and "risk (& resilience) management".

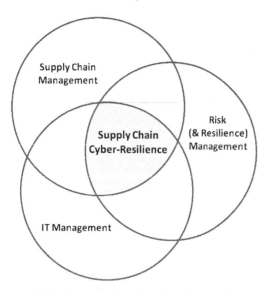

Figure 1. Main knowledge domains in supply chain cyber-risk management

3. **Screening:** After the initial, broad literature search was carried out, we conducted a preliminary analysis of the document titles and abstracts, if available. This step was followed by a more detailed analysis of the document abstracts, in the case of papers, and extended content in other cases. We applied explicit inclusion and exclusion criteria (e.g., document type, themes covered, research approaches) to identify a refined selection of documents for this analysis. Finally, the references of this refined set of articles were reviewed to identify relevant documents that might not have been identified through our initial

broad search. Our final list consisted of 213 documents (24 articles, 137 peer-reviewed journal papers, 51 reports by specialized agencies, and 1 thesis). The documents covered the areas of supply chain risk management (131 documents), supply chain cyber-risk management (SCCRM), and information technology risk management (44 documents), ranging from the years 1998 to 2015.

4. **Extracting and synthesizing:** The documents were analyzed and synthesized using a spreadsheet format that allowed us to categorize the documents according to methodological approaches, contexts, outcomes, etc.

5. **Reporting:** In the next section, we report on our findings from the literature review.

Findings

Some of the earliest evidence of supply chain resilience can be found in the work of Christopher and Peck (2004), which was derived from earlier research on supply chain agility as a way of counteracting for uncertainty in the demand (Christopher & Towill, 2001), This perspective emerged after the foot-and-mouth disease event in the United Kingdom and the 9/11 terrorist attacks in United States, both of which occurred in 2001. Christopher and Peck proposed a reference model for the characterization of resilience in the supply chain, and the main aspects contributing to supply chain resilience were identified as re-engineering, organizational culture, agility, and collaboration.

Sheffi and Rice (2005) presented a disruption model based a proposed disruption theory for production systems (Asbjornslett, 1999), where this model was represented as a transient decrease in process performance. The Sheffi and Rice model identified eight sequential phases describing a disruption event: preparation, disruptive event, first response, initial impact, time of full impact, preparation for recovery, recovery, and long-term impact. Based on this model, Sheffi and Rice propose an enterprise "vulnerability map" through which the different disruption event probabilities and consequences are compared and ranked for prioritization.

Sheffi and Rice (2005) also identified product demand as the main source of uncertainty in the supply chain and acknowledged the increase in global uncertainty due to increased customer expectations, more global competition, longer and more complex supply chains, greater product variety, and shorter product lifecycles.

They considered organizational resilience as a strategic initiative to reduce vulnerability and therefore reduce the likelihood of occurrence of a disruption. Finally, they identified three important factors for building resiliency in an organization: redundancy, flexibility, and cultural change.

A number of other resilience frameworks have been suggested in literature. Linkov and colleagues (2013) proposed a resilience matrix of four steps representing a process for the event management cycles of disruptions: i) plan/prepare, ii) absorb, iii) recover, and iv) adapt. Each of these steps are described for different domains within the organization (i.e., physical, information, cognitive, and social). These authors have further suggested how to measure resilience according to this matrix.

Based on the framework proposed by Christopher and Peck (2004) as well as an empirical research study to identify vulnerabilities and capabilities within organizations, Pettit, Fiskel, and Croxton (2010) proposed the supply chain resiliency assessment and management (SCRAM) framework. This framework identifies an active relationship between the capabilities and the vulnerabilities in an organization, and its resulting resilience. They argue that the level of resilience that a company has to aim for is a balance between developing too many vulnerabilities (due to a lack of investment in capabilities), which could result in disruptions with undesirable economic effects, and investing in too many capabilities, which would erode profitability. Hence, they highlight an economic tradeoff between investment (capabilities) and risk (vulnerabilities).

Blackhurst, Dunn, and Craighead (2011) proposed a global resiliency framework based on systems theory and the framework proposed by Sheffi and Rice (2005). They distinguish between "resilience enhancers" and "resilience reducers", which are organizational attributes that either increase or decrease the ability of a firm to recover quickly and efficiently from a disruptive event. They identified 13 resilience enhancers and seven resilience reducers, each within three categories. Their work derives these attributes from an industrial setting and therefore can serve as basis for further research in the empirical confirmation of these or other resilience attributes.

The World Economic Forum (WEF, 2013) presented a resilience framework as part of its Supply Chain Risk Initiative. This framework attempts to quantify the risk to an organization's physical and intangible assets through a combination of effects from the existing risks to the organization and its vulnerabilities. The World Economic Forum's (WEF, 2013) resilience report also provides four recommendations for organizations to build resilient supply chains: i) put in place strong policies for the creation and adoption of resilience standards; ii) develop agile and adaptable strategies in organizations; iii) use data-sharing platforms for risk identification and response; and iv) enter into partnerships that involve all stakeholders in the risk assessment process.

Cyber-risks within the supply chain resilience framework
Our literature review did not find any supply chain resilience framework that incorporated the phenomenon of cyber-risk or information risk explicitly. However, our analysis revealed that the most influential sources for the development of cyber-resilience policy are the insurance industry, governmental requirements, and international organizations such as the World Economic Forum.

In 2012, the World Economic Forum created an initiative called "Partnering for Cyber-Resilience", led by Elena Kvochko, as a response to the increasing importance of cybersecurity. With more than 100 organizations involved, this initiative has created a series of reports describing principles for cybersecurity, recognizing interdependence, leadership, integrated risk management, and uptake by partners in the supply chain, as crucial aspects for resilience building. Additionally Kvochko has recently published an initial framework for the measurement of cyber-threats, through the calculation of a cyber-risk value and by combining eight factors grouped in three categories: vulnerability, assets, and attacker profile (WEF, 2015).

At a government level, there are several initiatives in place concerning cyber-risk and cybersecurity. In 2003, the United States government published the "National Strategy to Secure Cyberspace" (White House, 2003), and as part of a wider strategy from the Department of Homeland Security as a response to the 9/11 terrorist attacks and in line with Presidential Directive 63, which provides a framework for the protection of critical infrastructure (White House, 1998). In 2005, Germany started the "National Plan for Information Infrastructure Protection", with its main objectives being prevention, preparedness, and sustainability of the information infrastructure through the setting of international standards (German Federal Ministry of the Interior, 2005). By 2015, all EU member states except Portugal had published national cybersecurity strategies, with Estonia having been the first in 2008 (ENISA, 2015; Keegan, 2014). In 2013, the United States government released Presidential Policy 21 and Executive Order 13636 to focus national attention on cyber-infrastructure resilience. In particular, Executive Order 13636 establishes a risk-based standard to protect critical infrastructure against cyber-threats. However, standards based on risk assessment do not necessarily create resilience (Linkov et al., 2013).

Conclusions and Recommendations

Our systematic literature review highlights that there is limited literature and no specific frameworks for cyber resilience in the supply chain, despite the increasing importance of the topic. The main supply chain resilience theories were proposed in the early 2000s, and the main advancements to those theories have been through the empirical identification of organizational attributes that increase or decrease resilience, as well as theoretical relationships between organizational vulnerabilities and capabilities as related to resilience. Additionally, we found that the existing supply chain resilience frameworks could be extended to consider cyber-risks through aspects such as cultural change (Sheffi & Rice, 2005) or collaboration and organizational culture (Christopher & Peck, 2004). Cyber resilience theory can also be advanced through the empirical quantification of the cyber-resilience of an organization, through case studies and stress testing of organizations with techniques such as non-invasive games (Gerencser et al., 2003).

A key contribution of this article is a definition for supply chain cyber-resilience: "the capability of a supply chain to maintain its operational performance when faced with cyber-risk". Furthermore, as a result of this study, we offer the following recommendations for academia with the goal of developing a future research agenda for supply chain cyber-resilience:

1. **Develop theory to demystify cyber-risk and cyber-resilience in supply chains:** Academics should conduct in-depth (systematic) literature reviews that confirm or expand on this study to devise methods of incorporating cyber-resilience with existing frameworks in supply chain resilience and indeed develop new models and frameworks. Finally, and fundamentally, they should align supply chain thinking and personnel with information technology issues and personnel to develop a team approach to supply chain cyber-resilience.

2. **Develop applicable tools and techniques:** There is a need for models (e.g., models of dynamic behaviour, machine-learning models for real-time monitoring of performance conditions) and practitioner workbooks (e.g., to evaluate the likelihood of detection or the probability of attack), to help practitioners better manage the causes and effects of cyber-risk to the supply chain.

3. **Generate case studies:** In-depth and longitudinal case studies within different industrial sectors are required to increase our understanding of the occurrence, detection, and reaction to cyber-attacks. Such case studies will enable researchers to validate theory and conceptual frameworks and models.

4. **Investigate the different types of cyber-attacks:** Studies should examine the attack goals (e.g., data theft, data modification, data falsification), the technical nature of attacks (e.g., tools, physical or digital barriers, verification procedures, data integrity), as well as human dimensions (e.g., cyber-attacker motivation, incentives).

5. **Propose strategic ways of managing cyber risks:** For example, academia may suggest portfolio investment to hedge risk by diversifying the business structure, where different areas counterbalance the effect of cyber-attacks. Furthermore, academia may suggest establishing appropriate key performance indicators or reviewing organizational culture and leadership, which should be empowered for proactive management of supply chain cyber-resilience.

For industry, we offer the following recommendations:

1. **The search for solutions to cyber-risks must be approached in terms of distributed accountability, instead of centralized authority:** The increasingly complex supply arrangements are creating conditions for "malevolent actors to recruit, coordinate and inflict harm across the whole network" (WEF, 2012). This challenge will require companies to adjust the current paradigm of centrally controlling risk management with routine evaluation processes (Deloitte, 2012).

2. **Re-arrange resources and develop contingency plans when necessary:** Organizations that thrive are those that can quickly recognize unusual operating conditions. It is no longer possible to prepare for every possible threat scenario. Instead, organizations

should prepare by encouraging team members to speak up when they detect an anomaly, having strategies in place to create customized contingency plans as necessary, and using automatic detection systems (e.g., machine learning) to identify real-time suspicious variations in performance indicators. There is a need for a new level of coordination in organizations for risk management and security response. In environments with high volatility, central controls are not sufficient and "structural integration is key to addressing uncertainties" (Boyson, 2014).

3. **Include recovery costs in the cost evaluation of cyber-attacks:** Recovery costs can surpass the direct organizational losses from cyber-attacks (Ponemon, 2014). Including recovery costs in the evaluations will highlight the real economic implications of delayed action.

4. **Create a cyber-crisis team within each organization:** Such teams should be empowered to work across organizational silos.

5. **Collaborate with academic institutions:** Academics can assist companies through training programs in cyber-resilience, by introducing new tools for the evaluation of cyber-resilience, or by providing methods for the real-time monitoring of conditions (e.g., through machine-learning methods) to detect potential threats.

6. **Promote a proactive culture:** Organizations should provide incentives for early-bird alerts on anomalous operating conditions, which promote flexibility and a proactive response in the face of an unforeseen threat.

About the Authors

Omera Khan is a Full Professor of Operations Management at the Technical University of Denmark. She works with leading organizations on a range of supply chain and logistics issues and is advisor to many universities developing courses in logistics, supply chains, and operations management. She has led and conducted research projects commissioned by government agencies, research councils, and companies in supply chain resilience, responsiveness, sustainability, and the impact of product design on the supply chain. Her latest area of research focuses on cyber-risk and resilience in the supply chain. Omera is an advisor to many organizations and provides specialist consultancy in supply chain risk management. She is a highly acclaimed presenter and is regularly invited as a keynote speaker at global conferences and corporate events. She has published her research in leading journals, contributed to several book chapters, and is lead author of *Handbook for Supply Chain Risk Management: Case Studies, Effective Practices and Emerging Trends*. She founded and was Chair of the Supply Chain Risk and Resilience Research Club and the Product Design and Supply Chain Special Interest Group. She has also been a visiting professor at a number of leading business schools.

Daniel A. Sepulveda Estay is a PhD researcher at the Technical University of Denmark, where he researches cyber-risk and security in the global supply chain. He has worked in the engineering and supply divisions of a number of multinational companies, both in strategic/leadership and operational roles for over 11 years, having partially led initiatives such as the implementation of lean manufacturing in Coca-Cola Company Latin America and supply rationalization in BHP Billiton´s copper projects division. Daniel has a BSc in Mechanical Engineering from the Federico Santa Maria Technical University in Valparaiso, Chile, an MSc degree in Industrial Engineering from the Pontifical Catholic University of Chile in Santiago, Chile, and an MSc degree in Management from the MIT Sloan School of Management, in Boston, United States.

References

Asbjornslett, B. E. 1999. Assess the Vulnerability of Your Production System. *Production Planning & Control*, 10(3): 219–229. http://dx.doi.org/10.1080/095372899233181

Bailey, T., Miglio, A. Del, & Richter, W. 2014. The Rising Strategic Risks of Cyberattacks. *McKinsey Quarterly*, 2 (2014): 17–22.

Blackhurst, J., Dunn, K. S., & Craighead, C. W. 2011. An Empirically Derived Framework of Global Supply Resiliency. *Journal of Business Logistics*, 32(4): 374–391. http://dx.doi.org/10.1111/j.0000-0000.2011.01032.x

Boyson, S. 2014. Cyber Supply Chain Risk Management: Revolutionizing the Strategic Control of Critical IT Systems. *Technovation*, 34(7): 342–353. http://dx.doi.org/10.1016/j.technovation.2014.02.001

BSI. 2008. *BS ISO/IEC 27001:2008 Information Technology – Security Techniques – Information Security Risk Management*. London: British Standards Institution.

Burnson, P. 2013. Supply Chain Cybersecurity: A Team Effort. *Supply Chain Management Review*, June (2013): 6–8.

Christopher, M., & Peck, H. 2004. Building the Resilient Supply Chain. *International Journal of Logistics Management*, 15(2): 1–14. http://dx.doi.org/10.1108/09574090410700275

Christopher, M., & Towill, D. 2001. An Integrated Model for the Design of Agile Supply Chains. *International Journal of Physical Distribution & Logistics Management*, 31(4): 235–246. http://dx.doi.org/10.1108/09600030110394914

Deloitte. 2012. *Aftershock: Adjusting to the New World of Risk Management*. London: Deloitte Development LLC.

Deloitte. 2013. *The Ripple Effect: How Manufacturing and Retail Executives View the Growing Challenge of Supply Chain Risk*. London: Deloitte Development LLC.

ENISA, 2015. National Cyber Security Strategies in the World. *European Union Agency for Network and Information Security*. Accessed April 1, 2015: http://www.enisa.europa.eu/activities/Resilience-and-CIIP/national-cyber-security-strategies-ncsss/national-cyber-security-strategies-in-the-world

Gerencser, M., Weinberg, J., & Vincent, D. 2003. *Port Security War Game: Implications for U.S. Supply Chains*. Booz & Company.

German Federal Ministry of the Interior. 2005. *National Plan for Information Infrastructure Protection*. Berlin: Bundesministerium des Innern.

Intel Security. 2014. *Net Losses: Estimating the Global Cost of Cybercrime*. Santa Clara, CA: Intel Security

IRM. 2015. Cyber Risk and Management. *Institute for Risk Management*. Accessed April 1, 2015: https://www.theirm.org/knowledge-and-resources/thought-leadership/cyber-risk/

Keegan, C. 2014. Cyber Security in the Supply Chain: A Perspective from the Insurance Industry. *Technovation*, 34(7): 380–381. http://dx.doi.org/10.1016/j.technovation.2014.02.002

Linkov, I., Eisenberg, D. A., Bates, M. E., Chang, D., Convertino, M., Allen, J. H., Flynn, S. E., & Seager, T. P. 2013. Measurable Resilience for Actionable Policy. *Environmental Science and Technology*, 47(18): 10108–10110. http://dx.doi.org/10.1021/es403443n

Pettit, T. J., Fiksel, J., & Croxton, K. L. 2010. Ensuring Supply Chain Resilience: Development of a Conceptual Framework. *Journal of Business Logistics*, 31(1): 1–21. http://dx.doi.org/10.1002/j.2158-1592.2010.tb00125.x

Ponemon. 2014. 2014 *Global Report on the Cost of Cyber Crime*. Traverse City, MI: Penemon Institute.

Reuters. 2012. *Cyber Crime - How Can Firms Tackle This Fast-Emerging Invisible Menace?* London: Thomson Reuters.

Sheffi, Y., & Rice, J. B. 2005. A Supply Chain View of the Resilient Enterprise. *MIT Sloan Management Review*, 47(1): 41–48.

Tranfield, D., Denyer, D., & Smart, P. 2003. Towards a Methodology for Developing Evidence-Informed Management Knowledge by Means of Systematic Review. *British Journal of Management*, 14(3): 207–222. http://dx.doi.org/10.1111/1467-8551.00375

WEF. 2012. *Risk and Responsibility in a Hyperconnected World - Pathways to Global Cyber Resilience*. Geneva, Switzerland: World Economic Forum.

WEF. 2013. *Building Resilience in Supply Chains*. Geneva, Switzerland: World Economic Forum.

WEF. 2015. *Partnering for Cyber Resilience: Towards the Quantification of Cyber Threats*. Geneva, Switzerland: World Economic Forum.

White House. 1998. *Presidential Decision Directive NSC-63 on Critical Infrastructure Protection*. Washington, DC: The White House.

White House, 2003. *The National Strategy to Secure Cyberspace*. Washington, DC: The White House.

Keywords: resilience, supply chain management, cyber-risk, cybersecurity, theoretical foundation

26

Cybersecurity and Cyber-Resilient Supply Chains

Hugh Boyes

" Our technological powers increase, but the side effects "
and potential hazards also escalate.

Alvin Toffler
Writer and futurist
in *Future Shock*

There has been a rapid growth in the use of communications and information technology, whether embedded in products, used to deliver services, or employed to enable integration and automation of increasingly global supply chains. Increased use of information technology introduces a number of cybersecurity risks affecting cyber-resilience of the supply chain, both in terms of the product or service delivered to a customer and supply chain operation. The situation is complicated by factors such as the global sourcing of technology components or software, ownership of the systems in a supply chain, different legal jurisdictions involved, and the extensive use of third parties to deliver critical functionality. This article examines the cyber-resilience issues related to the supply of products, services, and the supply chain infrastructure considering the nature of threats and vulnerabilities and the attributes of cybersecurity. In doing so, it applies a model for cybersecurity that is adapted from the Parkerian hexad to explore the security and trustworthiness facets of supply chain operations that may impact cyber-resilience.

Introduction

Over forty years ago in his book *Future Shock*, Alvin Toffler (1971) recognized that our rapid technological advances were accompanied by side effects and hazards. This is certainly true of supply chains in the 21st century, where information technology is often an integral part of both the supplied product or service, and the supply chain infrastructure.

To stay competitive in a global economy, deliver timely responses to changing customer demands, and meet increasing service expectations, organizations have adapted their supply chains by incorporating computer-based management systems (Christopher & Towill, 2002), automating many processes using cyber-physical systems, and reducing stocks through the deployment of just-in-time manufacturing and production-to-order systems. This widespread use of information technology and advances in connectivity have transformed many businesses and transferred supply chain information flows from paper or the telephone to digital transactions and databases (WEF, 2013). The improved communications flow has also delivered significant advances in the service offered by supply chains to their customers, enabling the tracking of goods through the logistics chain.

These innovations place significant demands on supply chains, with the role of information technology now critical to the delivery of responsive, cost-effective manufacturing and supply (Christopher & Peck, 2004; Khan & Stolte, 2014).

This article discusses how, in many information technology systems, insufficient attention has been paid to overall system resilience and security issues, creating significant cybersecurity and cyber-resilience vulnerabilities. It examines what is meant by cyber-resilience and cybersecurity, and outlines the attributes that affect the cyber-resilience of a system or system-of-systems. Although the underpinning work originates in the construction and built-environment sectors, this article demonstrates that it can be applied more widely.

What Do We Mean by Cyber-Resilience and Cybersecurity?

The World Economic Forum (WEF, 2012) defined cyber-resilience as "the ability of systems and organizations to withstand cyber events, measured by the combination of mean time to failure and mean time to recovery". The use of the term "cyber" is intended to encompass the "interdependent network of information technology infrastructures, and includes technology "tools" such as the Internet, telecommunications networks, computer systems, and embedded processors and controllers in critical industries". Although not defined by the WEF, it is assumed that a cyber-event is therefore any disturbance to this interdependent network that leads to loss of functionality, connectivity, performance, or capacity (i.e., a breach of the network's cybersecurity). Such events are all too common, with frequent publicity about yet another serious security breach on an IT system. Notable recent examples include the cyber-attacks on Sony and Target. The latter incident is of particular significance given that the attack originates in the company's supply chain, with the initial compromise of an HVAC supplier's systems (Krebs, 2014).

There is a common misconception, reinforced by media coverage of incidents, that cybersecurity is solely about technology. This is not the case: good cybersecurity is based on a holistic approach that encompasses people, process, physical, and technological aspects (Boyes, 2014a). A weakness in the treatment or implementation of one or more of these aspects will undermine the overall cybersecurity of a system or business process. For example, if an individual does not practice good cyber-hygiene or fails to follow established security processes – such as failing to protect sensitive physical storage media from theft or loss – then there is an increased risk of compromise.

The lack of attention to system security and resilience, referred to in the introduction, is illustrated by the Apple "goto fail" bug and the "Heartbleed" vulnerability (Boyes et al., 2014). In the case of the former, a simple coding error exposed all iOS users to a serious vulnerability in the Transport Layer Security (TLS) protocol, which is used by applications to secure Internet communications. In the latter, poorly written code, which had not been subject to adequate inspection or test, exposed users of OpenSSL to a serious vulnerability. The affected OpenSSL software had been deployed by many of the major industrial control systems (ICS) suppliers. In both cases, the cause of the security breach is poor software engineering and a failure to detect coding errors during integration and testing.

Figure 1 illustrates the categories of risk that need to be considered when assessing the cyber-resilience of a supply chain. The presence of nature may seem at odds in a discussion of cyber-resilience, however, it is important to recognize that natural events can have significant impact on communications and IT infrastructure. For example, solar storms can disrupt wireless communications, both on a global scale for satellite communications and on a local scale for mobile communications (3G and 4G). Natural causes, such as earthquakes, floods, and damage by animals may also damage or disrupt cable connections carrying telephony and Internet traffic, thus interfering with a supply chain.

To improve the cyber-resilience of a supply chain, it is essential to understand the various aspects that should be addressed in designing for cybersecurity. Much of the good practice currently available is based on the information assurance community's use of the "CIA triad": confidentiality, integrity, and availability. However, this approach does not adequately address the cyber-security of complex global information technology systems or the cyber-physical systems used in our supply chains. An alternative approach, which is better suited to these complex systems, is to start by considering the Parkerian hexad (Parker, 2002), which comprises confid-

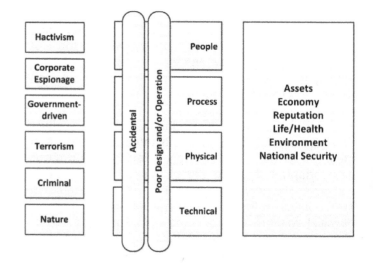

Figure 1. Threats and vulnerabilities that affect cyber-resilience

entiality, integrity, and availability, plus utility, authenticity, and possession. The rationale for this approach is that the hexad better encompasses the security considerations that apply to control systems and cyber-physical systems (Boyes, 2014b); however, it does not fully address the need for systems to be trustworthy.

The United Kingdom Government has supported the development of a publicly available specification for trustworthy software, where trustworthiness is based upon five facets: safety, reliability, availability, resilience, and security (BSI, 2014). It is therefore proposed that, in considering the cyber-resilience of the complex systems in the supply chain, we should augment the Parkerian hexad with two additional attributes, safety and resilience, as illustrated in Figure 2. Although the reliability of the supply chain is a by-product of addressing the other attributes, the model associates it with availability.

This model for cyber-security enables us to consider the supply chain from three perspectives:

1. The continuity of operations, including safety of personnel and assets (i.e., availability, safety, and resilience)

2. The control of access and system operations (i.e., confidentiality and possession)

3. The quality and validity of information, including the system's configuration (i.e., integrity, utility, and authenticity)

This model has been developed based on investigation of the security and resilience issues affecting cyber-physical systems (Boyes, 2014b) and has been extended to fully integrate the facets of trustworthiness (BSI, 2015).

The importance of the individual perspectives and their underpinning attributes will vary between supply chains, but serious vulnerabilities in any attribute or perspective are likely to result in significant loss of overall cyber-resilience. In the following sections, this model will be applied to explore the cyber-resilience of the supply of products, the supply of services, and the supply chain infrastructure.

Cyber-Resilience and the Supply of Physical Products or Assets

The scale and complexity of the supply chains for physical products or assets vary widely, but the generic end-to-end process may be represented as shown in Figure 3. From a cyber-resilience perspective, there are a number of areas that could be disrupted:

• the specification and design process for new, bespoke, or customized products

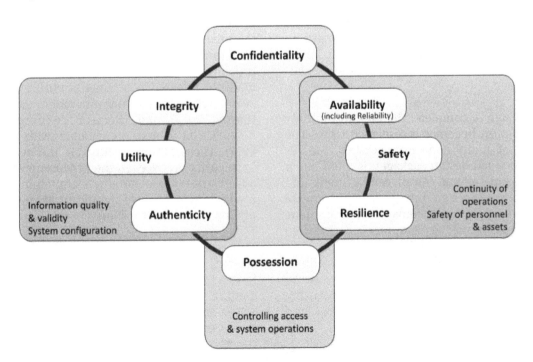

Figure 2. Cybersecurity attributes that affect cyber-resilience

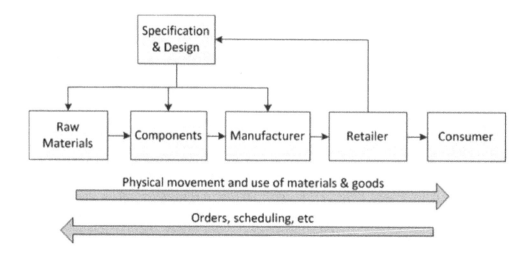

Figure 3. Generic supply chain for physical products or assets

- the flow of orders, scheduling ,and associated information

- the coordination and control of the movement of supplies and finished products through the supply chain

The nature of cyber-resilience issues will vary over a product's lifecycle. For example, during product specification and design, threats and vulnerabilities that affect the integrity or authenticity of information are particularly important. A manufacturer of high-availability pumps used in hazardous environments discovered this when an unauthorized change to tolerances of a critical mechanical component led to premature failures of the installed product and escalating warranty claims.

Once product design is complete, the long-term utility of design information becomes a resilience issue. The typical lifecycle of many software packages, for example, computer-aided design packages, is often much shorter than the operational life of capital items and major assets. The packages go through regular software revisions and their operating systems become obsolete. For manufacturers employing computer-aided design and computer-aided manufacturing (CADCAM) today, this may be a serious issue if they need to access original design information in say 10 or 20 years. This problem is already a reality for documents created using common word-processing packages in the 1980s and early 1990s.

In some cases, it is the metadata associated with a physical product that may be at risk. For example, the use of collaborative tracking and tracing by the Swedish fresh fish supply chain to track codfish catches from trawlers though the supply chain to the end consumer (Mirzabeiki, 2013). The raw fish is a perishable product that is handled by multiple organizations as it moves from sea to plate. There are ample opportunities for this tracking to fail due to human actions or the breakdown or failure of IT equipment.

There are also integrity and authenticity issues regarding digital information and software embedded in products. In particular, there are risks associated with the presence of counterfeit electronic products, assemblies, and software in supply chains. Examples of this problem include the discovery that Dell had shipped malware infected components during 2010 (Grainger, 2010), HP shipped malware-laden switches in 2011 (Rashid, 2012), and Microsoft discovered during 2012 new PCs in China preinstalled with malware (Kirk, 2012). These examples illustrate the need for good cybersecurity practices in the procurement, manufacture, and distribution of products containing software: failure to do so can cause significant disruption to the supply chain and its customers.

The recent cyber-attack on a German blast furnace (Zetter, 2015) illustrates how poor cybersecurity can have a major impact on the continuity of operations, including safety of personnel and assets (i.e., availability, safety, and resilience). In this case, there appears to have been a serious breach of the access controls on the plant's industrial control systems, allowing the attacker to cause the plant to malfunction and resulting in physical damage and operational disruption. Managing the control of access and system operations (i.e., confidentiality and possession) can be a complex task, particularly on large sites where there is wireless access to these systems. This challenge was illustrated by the Maroochy water treatment works incident, where a former contractor had unauthorized access to the plant controls (Abrams & Weiss, 2008). The cause of the sewage spillages was a mystery until a site engineer witnessed a valve being remotely changed.

From a cyber-resilience perspective, the above examples illustrate the importance of good cybersecurity in the supply of items containing electronic data or software and in the operation of cyber-physical systems. With fragmented supply chains spanning the globe, there is a need for constant vigilance and good situational awareness to counter emerging and existing threats that affect cyber-resilience.

Cyber-Resilience and the Supply of Services

The supply of services creates a number of additional challenges in terms of a supply chain's cyber-resilience. Depending on the nature of the service, a cyber-event may make it difficult for personnel and systems involved in service delivery to receive, process, and fulfill service requests. Typically, the cyber-resilience issues affecting the supply of services will predominantly relate to the operation of call centres, websites, payment systems, and where the service involves electronic delivery of content, for example playing a pay-per-view video, the fulfillment systems.

Often predominantly Internet-based, the service delivery infrastructure is vulnerable to a range of generic cybersecurity attacks, for example denial of service (DoS), distributed denial of service (DDoS), and the hacking of servers, routers, and switches. The techniques for dealing with DoS and DDoS attacks, and protecting infrastructure from hacking are understood, although often not applied. From a cyber-resilience perspective, organizations offering services need to invest in appropriate hardening and protection of all critical digital aspects of their supply chain.

It is important to recognize that, for service delivery supply chains, the threats and vulnerabilities in Figure 1 may affect only parts or all of the supply chain. This is particularly relevant where key components rely on outsourced or bought-in elements, over which the service operator may have minimal control. For example, where the service is ordered and paid for online prior to service delivery, to meet the payment card industry's security standards (PCI DSS), it is common practice for websites to employ payment gateways operated by third parties. These gateways have themselves been the target of cyber-attacks, denying the use of their service and therefore either preventing organizations receiving payment or seriously degrading the performance of the payment systems. To mitigate such events and maintain cyber-resilience, an organization would need to have business continuity plans in place that allow use of alternative payment engines or otherwise restore the performance of the payment process.

Organizations also need to put in place adequate capacity to handle peaks in demand. There have been a number of cyber-resilience incidents where a website has crashed or otherwise failed to handle peak traffic volumes. Examples include problems with national authorities websites on the deadline day for submission of personal tax returns, the collapse of ticketing systems for major events such as concerts and sporting events, and the launch of online sales events. These peaks of traffic are generally predictable and cyber-resilient systems should be able to satisfactorily handle surges in demand.

Cyber-Resilience and Supply Chain Infrastructure

Given the global nature of both trade and supply chains, there are three infrastructure elements that will have a significant impact on their cyber-resilience. These are the ports used to handle goods and raw materials, the navigation systems used by both cargo carry vessels and delivery vehicles, and the global data processing, storage, networking, and communication infrastructure. The latter elements are often referred to as "the cloud".

In October 2013, there were press reports about an operation in the port of Antwerp, where police discovered that a criminal gang had gained access to the port's logistics systems in order to smuggle drugs through the port (Bateman, 2013). This sophisticated cyber-attack, which it is believed had started two years earlier, allowed the gang to access the computer system used to manage the handling and release of shipping containers, enabling the gang to remove the drugs from the port without being detected. The sophistication of this attack mirrors other unreported incidents, where it is understood that valuable goods have been targeted and stolen. Breaches of security have serious implications for the integrity of supply chains, both with regard to the protection of goods or materials in transit, and to prevent substitution of counterfeit supplies.

The widespread use of global navigation satellite systems (GNSS) is taken for granted by most transport and fleet operators. The benefits are considerable from a logistics perspective, in particular, the ability to precisely locate and route aircraft, vessels, and road vehicles. Unfortunately, these navigation signals from satellites are vulnerable to jamming and interference, which can severely degrade navigation in affected areas. While the occasional presence of localized interference or jamming is generally an inconvenience, if a large solar storm were to occur, of a similar magnitude to the 1859 Carrington event (tinyurl.com/mhsmve), disruptions to satellite transmissions could have a serious impact on the cyber-resilience of many supply chains.

The use of cloud computing is increasing rapidly, but this is not without risk. At the end of January 2013, 2e2, an IT systems and cloud service provider in the United Kingdom went into liquidation (Robinson, 2013). The immediate effect was that 2e2 customers lost access to their hosted systems and data, and were faced with demands for payment from the liquidator if they wished to keep the data centres running or retain access to their data. To reduce IT costs, organizations are being encouraged to replace their own locally-based servers with cloud-based services. The cyber-resilience consequences of such actions need to be carefully assessed, particularly where the hosted services are mission critical.

A consequence of the increased adoption of cloud services, as well as the global nature of many supply chains, is the dependence on smooth functioning of the global communications and networking services. The nature of these services is complex, relying largely on undersea telecommunications cables that span the globe. These cables are vulnerable to both natural and human damage, the former due to geological incidents such as earthquakes. In May 2013, it was reported that the SEA-ME-WE4 cable had been cut near Alexandria in Egypt (Malik, 2013). This was a deliberate act, although it is more common for such cuts to be the result of cables snagging on fishing nets or anchors. The cut resulted in a dramatic slow down in communications traffic speeds in Africa, the Middle East, and part of India, by as much as 60% in some locations. This type of damage could have serious consequences if the link is carrying time-sensitive supply chain scheduling data or provided connectivity to business critical cloud-based services. From a cyber-resilience perspective, supply chain managers should consider the impact that any loss or degradation of global communications infrastructure may have on their operations.

Conclusion

This article has considered the cyber-resilience of supply chains that deliver both physical products and services. In both cases, there are key cybersecurity issues that need to be addressed if an acceptable level of cyber-resilience is to be achieved. It is important that cyber-resilience, like cybersecurity, is not considered to be a purely technical issue, as it is also affected by personnel, process, and physical aspects.

A model of cybersecurity based on the Parkerian hexad has been outlined, which addresses important aspects that determine whether a system or process is cybersecure. This model is particularly relevant to complex, time-critical and cyber-physical systems as it fully addresses continuity of operation, control of access and systems operations, and data quality and systems configuration. It is currently being documented for use in the construction industry supply chain to support deployment of security-minded building information modelling (BIM) in the United Kingdom. As illustrated in this article, it is applicable to other supply chains. When considering the elements in this model, it is essential that personnel, process, and physical aspects are addressed in addition to underlying technical issues.

When designing or modifying a supply chain, it is essential that the organizations involved consider the cyber-resilience implications of the global technology components they plan to use. Moving applications into the cloud and the remote storage of data can introduce significant cyber-resilience issues, particularly where time-critical processing or data access is required.

Supply chain managers should examine the vulnerabilities of the technologies involved, including the physical location of business-critical elements, the interdependence of components and business processes, and the skills required by personnel involved in supply chain operations. Achieving cyber-resilience will involve a holistic approach to security, given that purely technical solutions are unlikely to address the breadth of potential threats and vulnerabilities.

Recommended Reading

Code of Practice for Cyber Security in the Built Environment (Institution of Engineering and Technology, 2014; tinyurl.com/oyjkkk6).
This book provides a strategic approach to managing the cybersecurity of cyber-physical systems that is also of relevance to supply chains.

About the Author

Hugh Boyes is a Principal Fellow at WMG at the University of Warwick, United Kingdom, where he focuses on cyber-resilience and the cybersecurity of cyber-physical systems. He is a Chartered Engineer, a Fellow of the IET and holds the CISSP credential issued by (ISC)2. Hugh is also the Cyber Security Lead at the Institution of Engineering and Technology (IET), where he focuses on developing cybersecurity skills initiatives for engineering and technology communities. This work is particularly focused on the design and operation of physical-cyber systems (e.g., industrial control systems, building automation systems). He has written two guidance documents for the Institution of Engineering and Technology (IET) on cybersecurity in the built environment, and with Alex Luck, is the joint technical author of a BSI publicly available specification (PAS) on security-minded building information modeling, digital built environments, and smart asset management.

References

Abrams, M., & Weiss, J. 2008. *Malicious Control System Cyber Security Attack Case Study - Maroochy Water Services, Australia.* National Institute of Standards and Technology, Computer Security Division.

Bateman, T. 2013. Police Warning after Drug Traffickers' Cyber-Attack. *BBC News,* October 16, 2013. Accessed March 14, 2015: http://www.bbc.co.uk/news/world-europe-24539417

Boyes, H. A. 2014a. *Code of Practice for Cyber Security in the Built Environment.* London: Institution of Engineering and Technology.

Boyes, H. A. 2014b. Cyber Security Attributes for Critical Infrastructure Systems. *Cyber Security Review,* Summer 2014: 47–51.

Boyes, H. A., Norris, P., Bryant, I., & Watson, T. 2014. Trustworthy Software: Lessons from `goto fail' & Heartbleed bugs. In *Proceedings of the 9th IET International Conference on System Safety and Cyber Security:* 2.2.1. http://dx.doi.org/10.1049/cp.2014.0970

BSI. 2014. *PAS 754:2014 Software Trustworthiness – Governance and Management – Specification.* London: British Standards Institution.

BSI. 2015. *PAS 1192-5:2015 Specification for Security-Minded Building Information Modelling, Digital Built Environments and Smart Asset Management.* London: British Standards Institution.

Christopher, M., & Peck, H. 2004. Building the Resilient Supply Chain. *International Journal of Logistics Management,* 15(2): 1–13. http://dx.doi.org/10.1108/09574090410700275

Christopher, M., & Towill, D. 2002. Developing Market Specific Supply Chain Strategies. *International Journal of Logistics Management,* 13(1): 1–13. http://dx.doi.org/10.1108/09574090210806324

Grainger, M. 2010. Dell Shipped Malware Infected Components. *PCR,* July 22, 2010. Accessed March 14, 2015: http://www.pcr-online.biz/news/read/dell-shipped-malware-infected-components/021984

Khan, O., & Stolte, T. 2014. The Rising Threat of Cyber Risks in Supply Chains. *Effektivitet,* 4 (2014): 32–35.

Kirk, J. 2012. Microsoft Finds New PCs in China Preinstalled with Malware. *PCWorld,* September 14, 2012. Accessed March 14, 2015: http://www.pcworld.com/article/262308/

Krebs, B. 2014. Target Hackers Broke in Via HVAC Company. *Krebs on Security,* February 5, 2014. Accessed March 14, 2015: http://krebsonsecurity.com/2014/02/target-hackers-broke-in-via-hvac-company/

Malik, O. 2013. Underseas Cable Cut Near Egypt, Slows down Internet in Africa, Middle East, South Asia. *Gigaom,* March 27, 2014. Accessed March 14, 2015: http://gigaom.com/2013/03/27/undersea-cable-cut-near-egypt-slows-down-internet-in-africa-middle-east-south-asia/

Mirzabeiki, V. 2013. *Collaborative Tracking and Tracing – A Supply Chain Perspective.* Gothenburg, Sweden: Chalmers University of Technology.

Parker, D. B. 2002. Towards a New Framework for Information Security. In S. Bosworth & M. E. Kabay (Eds.). *Computer Security Handbook* (4th ed). Hoboken, NJ: John Wiley & Sons.

Rashid, F. Y. 2012. HP's Malware-Laden Switches Illustrate Supply Chain Risks. *PC Magazine,* April 12, 2012. Accessed March 14, 2015: http://securitywatch.pcmag.com/pc-hardware/296547-hp-s-malware-laden-switches-illustrate-supply-chain-risks

Robinson, D. 2013. 2e2 Collapses Amid Failure to Find Buyer. *Financial Times,* February 6, 2013. Accessed March 14, 2015: http://www.ft.com/cms/s/0/2332e418-7077-11e2-a2cf-00144feab49a.html

Toffler, A. 1971. *Future Shock.* New York, NY: Bantam Doubleday.

WEF. 2012. *Partnering for Cyber Resilience: Risk and Responsibility in a Hyperconnected World – Principles and Guidelines.* Geneva, Switzerland: World Economic Forum.

WEF. 2013. *Building Resilience in Supply Chains.* Geneva, Switzerland: World Economic Forum.

Zetter, K. 2015. A Cyberattack Has Caused Confirmed Physical Damage for the Second Time Ever. *Wired,* January 8, 2015. Accessed March 14, 2015: http://www.wired.com/2015/01/german-steel-mill-hack-destruction/

Keywords: cyber-resilience, cybersecurity, supply chain, risk management, threat management

Permissions

All chapters in this book were first published in TIMR, by Talent First Network (Carleton University); hereby published with permission under the Creative Commons Attribution License or equivalent. Every chapter published in this book has been scrutinized by our experts. Their significance has been extensively debated. The topics covered herein carry significant findings which will fuel the growth of the discipline. They may even be implemented as practical applications or may be referred to as a beginning point for another development.

The contributors of this book come from diverse backgrounds, making this book a truly international effort. This book will bring forth new frontiers with its revolutionizing research information and detailed analysis of the nascent developments around the world.

We would like to thank all the contributing authors for lending their expertise to make the book truly unique. They have played a crucial role in the development of this book. Without their invaluable contributions this book wouldn't have been possible. They have made vital efforts to compile up to date information on the varied aspects of this subject to make this book a valuable addition to the collection of many professionals and students.

This book was conceptualized with the vision of imparting up-to-date information and advanced data in this field. To ensure the same, a matchless editorial board was set up. Every individual on the board went through rigorous rounds of assessment to prove their worth. After which they invested a large part of their time researching and compiling the most relevant data for our readers.

The editorial board has been involved in producing this book since its inception. They have spent rigorous hours researching and exploring the diverse topics which have resulted in the successful publishing of this book. They have passed on their knowledge of decades through this book. To expedite this challenging task, the publisher supported the team at every step. A small team of assistant editors was also appointed to further simplify the editing procedure and attain best results for the readers.

Apart from the editorial board, the designing team has also invested a significant amount of their time in understanding the subject and creating the most relevant covers. They scrutinized every image to scout for the most suitable representation of the subject and create an appropriate cover for the book.

The publishing team has been an ardent support to the editorial, designing and production team. Their endless efforts to recruit the best for this project, has resulted in the accomplishment of this book. They are a veteran in the field of academics and their pool of knowledge is as vast as their experience in printing. Their expertise and guidance has proved useful at every step. Their uncompromising quality standards have made this book an exceptional effort. Their encouragement from time to time has been an inspiration for everyone.

The publisher and the editorial board hope that this book will prove to be a valuable piece of knowledge for researchers, students, practitioners and scholars across the globe.

List of Contributors

Mackenzie Adams
Technology Innovation Management (TIM) program at Carleton University in Ottawa, Canada

Maged Makramalla
Technology Innovation Management (TIM) program at Carleton University in Ottawa, Canada

Tony Bailetti
Sprott School of Business and the Department of Systems and Computer Engineering at Carleton University, Ottawa, Canada

Renaud Levesque
Core Systems at the Communications Security Establishment (CSE) in Ottawa, Canada

D'Arcy Walsh
Communications Security Establishment (CSE) in Ottawa, Canada

Nadeem Douba
Carleton University in Ottawa, Canada.

Bjorn Rutten
National Security and Public Safety with The Conference Board, Canada

David Scheidl
Global Politics program at Carleton University in Ottawa, Canada

Paul Soble
Communications Security Establishment (CSE) in Ottawa, Canada

D'Arcy Walsh
Communications Security Establishment (CSE) in Ottawa, Canada

Mohamed Amin
Technology Innovation Management program at Carleton University in Ottawa, Canada

Zaid Tariq
Technology Innovation Management at Carleton University in Ottawa, Canada

Derek Smith
Technology Innovation Management (TIM) program at Carleton University in Ottawa, Canada

Asrar Alshaikh
Technology Innovation Management (TIM) program at Carleton University in Ottawa, Canada

Rawan Bojan
Technology Innovation Management (TIM) program at Carleton University in Ottawa, Canada

Anish Kak
Technology Innovation Management (TIM) program at Carleton University in Ottawa, Canada

Mohammad Mehdi Gharaei Manesh
Technology Innovation Management (TIM) program at Carleton University in Ottawa, Canada

Walter Miron
Technology Innovation Management (TIM) program at Carleton University in Ottawa, Canada

Kevin Muita
Technology Innovation Management (TIM) program at Carleton University in Ottawa, Canada

Lars Jensen
London Business School and the Copenhagen Business School.

George Cybenko
Dartmouth College in New Hampshire, United States

Gopalakrishna Palem

Adrian Davis

Michael "Monty" Widenius

Linus Nyman
Hanken School of Economics in Helsinki, Finland

Luca Urciuoli
Industrial Engineering from Chalmers University of Technology in Gothenburg, Sweden

Michael Weiss
Department of Systems and Computer Engineering at Carleton University in Ottawa, Canada

Mika Westerlund
Carleton University's Sprott School of Business in Ottawa, Canada

Risto Rajala
Department of Industrial Engineering and Management at Aalto University in Helsinki, Finland

Anas Al Natsheh
Centre for Measurement and Information Systems (CEMIS-Oulu) in Oulu, Finland

Saheed A. Gbadegeshin
University of Oulu, Finland

Antti Rimpilainen
University of Oulu, Finland

Irna Imamovic-Tokalic
Kajaani University of Applied Sciences, Finland

Andrea Zambrano
Kajaani University of Applied Sciences, Finland

Tony Bailetti
Carleton University's Technology Innovation Management (TIM) program in Ottawa, Canada

Erik Zijdemans
Carleton University in Ottawa, Canada

Dan Craigen
Carleton University in Ottawa, Canada

David Grau
Threat Response, Intelligence, and Defensive Technologies at TD Bank Group

Charles Kennedy
Information Technology (Information Assurance) from the University of Maryland – University College

Dan Craigen
Carleton University in Ottawa, Canada

Nadia Diakun-Thibault
Department of Computer Science and Engineering at North Carolina State University in the United States

Randy Purse
Faculty of Education at the University of Ottawa, Canada

Juho Lindman
Hanken School of Economics in Helsinki, Finland

Linus Nyman
Hanken School of Economics in Helsinki, Finland

Mehdi Kadivar
Technology Innovation Management at Carleton University in Ottawa, Canada

Cheri F. McGuire
George Washington University and the University of California, Riverside

Jeff Greene
Boston University in the United States and the University of Maryland, also in the United States

Brent Maheux
Technology Innovation Management from Carleton University in Ottawa, Canada

Omera Khan
Technical University of Denmark

Daniel A. Sepulveda Estay
MIT Sloan School of Management, in Boston, United States.

Hugh Boyes
University of Warwick, United Kingdom

Printed in the USA
CPSIA information can be obtained
at www.ICGtesting.com
JSHW051444221024
72173JS00006B/1573

9 781682 850206